D1498973

THE PHENOMENON OF MAN REVISITED

Pierre Teilhard de Chardin, S.J.

The Phenomenon of Man Revisited

A Biological Viewpoint on Teilhard de Chardin

Edward O. Dodson

COLUMBIA UNIVERSITY PRESS
New York
1984

Library of Congress Cataloging in Publication Data

Dodson, Edward O. (Edward Ottway), 1916–
  The phenomenon of man revisited.

  Bibliography: p.
  Includes index.
  1. Teilhard de Chardin, Pierre.   Phénomène humain.
  2. Cosmology.   3. Evolution.   4. Philosophical
  anthropology.   I. Title.
  B2430.T373P59 1984   113   83-20959
  ISBN 0-231-05850-0 (alk. paper)

Columbia University Press
New York   Guildford, Surrey
Copyright © 1984 Columbia University Press
All rights reserved

Printed in the United States of America

Clothbound editions of Columbia University Press Books
are Smyth-sewn and printed on permanent and durable
acid-free paper

Contents

Preface

AS A HIGH SCHOOL STUDENT, I was profoundly interested in philosophy, and I read a wide variety of philosophers: Plato, Aristotle, Spinoza, Hegel, Schopenhauer, Nietzsche, and so many others. They all influenced my thinking, yet I never felt fully committed to any of them, although I particularly admired Spinoza, Plato, and Aristotle. As a college student, however, it was not philosophy to which I was attracted as a major. I had enjoyed the study of languages in high school, and I found Latin especially stimulating, not only because of its intrinsic interest and its illuminating effect upon the understanding of English and other modern languages but because I was privileged to study under two gifted teachers who themselves understood the importance of classical studies in the modern world and who were able to transmit to their students some of the excitement and importance inherent in true scholarship in any field. The study of Vergil under such a teacher is a germinal experience: in me, it germinated the desire to study Homer in the original, and so I studied Greek in college. Because I found my professor of Greek (the late Herbert Pierrepont Houghton) outstanding, I decided to major in Greek, although I had no intention of pursuing a career in that field. However, one effect was to heighten my interest in Greek philosophers.

Concurrently I studied biology. Actually, I qualified for majors in both Greek and zoology, and it is in the latter that I have my profession. While cultivating these not-too-closely related interests, my interest in philosophy lay fal-

low, awaiting the opportune moment. That moment came
on a spring evening in 1935, when a group of students were
engaged in a "bull session," one of those unplanned, un-
directed discussions which occasionally play a significant
role in the education of young men and women. In the heat
of an avid discussion, in which the principal participants
were Richard Blomfield, John Knoble, and myself, I succeeded in formulating a philosophy out of the materials
provided by my past reading, critical reflection, and my
then current studies in biology. The latter was, perhaps,
dominant, for the philosophy which I propounded during
that very long evening was an analogy of the whole reality
to an organism.

Let me outline that philosophy. In the physical world,
the microcosm of the atom, with its complex nucleus and
its electrons in orbit, finds a parallel in the solar system,
with the sun taking the place of the nucleus of the atom
and the planets in their orbits taking the place of the electrons. The solar system in turn is part of a galaxy of an
enormous number of stars, as well as a great mass of inter-
stellar gas. While a system of planets is specifically known
only for our sun, some data favor the possibility that some
other stars do have systems of planets. In view of the difficulties of either proving or disproving this, and in view
of the secure fact that at least one star *does* have a system
of planets, it seemed reasonable to accept this probability
at face value, and today many astronomers consider it more
likely than not that our galaxy and the universe include
many other stars with planetary systems not unlike our
own. The organization of the galaxy as a whole might be
compared with a complex molecular system. Finally, the
universe comprises uncounted galactic systems, a more
limited model for which defies the imagination. The whole
physical universe is not an eternal constant but an *evolving
system*. At the time, the dominant model of cosmic evolution was the primeval atom theory of Lemaître. According
to this theory, the original state of all of the matter of the

universe was that of an extremely compact mass of enormous density. Then some great force upset the equilibrium of this primeval atom, and in the ensuing explosion—the moment of creation—the atomic species which we know were born. The stuff of the expanding universe thus created initially had a certain coherence, like the material of a soap bubble, but then the bubble burst, and the galaxies which were its droplets went hurtling off into space, each an island universe dissociated from all of the others and receding from all of the others at an ever increasing speed.

Such a hierarchy of levels of being and an evolutionary relationship among them are even more readily apparent in the world of life. At the lowest level are the viruses, submicroscopic nucleoprotein bodies which share properties of both living and nonliving systems. Like the latter, they do not respire, they are crystallizable, and in the crystalline form they can be stored indefinitely without loss of their main characteristics, including infectivity. Like the former, they reproduce, they force the host to carry on chemical activities (metabolism) appropriate to the virus rather than to the host, and they have genes which can mutate just as do those of higher organisms. Whether they should be considered living or nonliving was hotly debated in 1935. Today, a then unsuspected degree of genetic complexity has been demonstrated in viruses, as a result of which there is now fairly general agreement that they are living organisms. That there was a possibility of such a debate, however, is itself highly significant: it signifies the probability that life arose from nonliving matter almost imperceptibly, passing through a stage comparable to a free-living virus (although all known viruses are parasitic).

At the next level are the bacteria and the blue-green algae (or blue-green bacteria), single-celled organisms of microscopic dimensions (and so much larger than the viruses). These include in their makeup nucleoproteins, which are the hereditary material controlling the reactions of life, and cytoplasm, the complex mixture of proteins and other materials in which the processes of life are carried out. Unlike higher organisms, however, the nucleoproteins are free in the cytoplasm: there is no morphologically identifiable nucleus. More advanced is a bewildering array of algae and protozoans (single-celled animals). In general, these grade from the size of bacteria up to the macroscopic. Many are strictly unicellular and microscopic, but in all groups there are lines of descent in which there is a tendency to form colonies of cells, and these may become increasingly complex and integrated until finally they blend into unequivocal multicellular organisms. This is particularly true of the algae. Among the protozoans, colonialism does not have as striking a culmination among extant forms, but less spectacular colonialism is widespread, and the inference is hard to avoid that these, together with the more highly developed colonial algae, give some intimation of the manner in which metazoans (many-celled animals, including all of the larger animals) must have arisen from protozoan ancestors in the remote past.

Further, even the distinction between plants and animals is by no means clear, for they grade into one another, particularly among those unicellular organisms which move by means of flagella (whiplike protoplasmic processes). In these, closely related species may show affinities to different kingdoms.

Metazoans probably arose from protozoan ancestors via some group comparable to the Mesozoa or Coelenterata of today. During the early ages of metazoan development, the most fundamental features of metazoan organization were achieved, and perhaps some clue to these stages can be seen in the more primitive metazoan groups of today and in the earliest stages of the embryos of higher animals. These fundamental features include establishment of the first tissues, then organs and organ systems, bilateral symmetry, a coelom or body cavity in which the major organs are contained, and the beginnings of cephalization, the concentration of sense organs and feeding functions at the anterior end of the organism to form a head.

Most of these basic steps in metazoan organization are at least discernible, and some are quite advanced, in the flatworms and an array of minor phyla at the same general level of organization. Higher phyla (the broadest groups of animals) have developed along two major lines of descent. One passes through a series of minor phyla to culminate in the Annelida (segmented worms, like the earthworms) and the Arthropoda (crustaceans, insects, and their allies) in one subline and in the Mollusca (chitons, clams, snails, octopi, and their allies) in another. The other major line of descent passes through a few minor phyla, the Echinodermata (sea stars and their allies), and culminates in the phylum Chordata, which includes two primitive subphyla, the great array of fishes, amphibians, reptiles, birds, and mammals, including man.

There is thus in the animal kingdom a great structural progression, beginning with the simplest microorganisms and culminating in man. Yet there has been a remarkable degree of functional conservatism. The basic metabolic pathways show a remarkable uniformity throughout the world of life. The synthesis of amino acids and proteins, those fundamental compounds of life, is much the same from virus to man. Much the same vitamins are required from bacteria to man. The differences are far less important than the common properties. In one area, however, really new functional properties have been developed during the evolutionary sequence, and this is the area of integration of the organism, unified control, and awareness. In almost all metazoans, nervous systems subserve these functions, although the last (awareness) is probably rigorously limited in all but the highest animals. Hormones, sometimes defined as chemical messengers which are distributed through the blood, also serve the first two functions, and their importance has been demonstrated to be very great. It is commonplace that the cells which comprise the bodies of higher organisms are "elementary organisms," each roughly comparable to a protozoan and each capable of carrying on the fundamental processes of life. Yet, through the agencies of the nervous system and the hormones, their separate functions are integrated into a unified whole, an *organism*, not a chaotic plurality of discordant parts. Awareness of self and of the environment is a function of the organism as a whole: while it operates through the cells, especially the nerve cells, it is extremely improbable that the cells individually have more than the first rudiments of awareness or consciousness, or that they are aware of their contributions to the whole, or even of the existence of the whole.

In a word, the suggestion which I made on that spring evening was simply this, that the progression of the physical world from atoms through molecules and systems of molecules to the solar system, the galaxy and systems of galaxies, and finally the universe, might be paralleled in the biological and psychological spheres by a progression from the unconscious beginnings of life through the various stages of dimly conscious invertebrates and lower vertebrates, to acutely conscious man, and then perhaps on beyond to a *biological macrocosm* in which the whole might have a life and a consciousness as far beyond ours as ours is beyond that of our component cells. In this system, the basic role of the individual is to contribute to the well-being of the whole of which it is a part. A sound morality clearly becomes one which promotes the well-being of this greater whole. Evil is dysgenic behavior in the context of the biological macrocosm. Great benefactors, including the great moral teachers, might be regarded as comparable to hormones, serving a stimulating or regulating influence upon the other members and thus making greater than ordinary contributions to the welfare of the whole. Similarly, crime and moral evil would correspond to disease or poisoning.

It was evident that, in suggesting the idea of the biological macrocosm, I had redefined God and that this was essentially a pantheistic definition. All three of us were practicing Christians, and we were aware of the inconsistency between a pantheistic god and the God of Christian revelation. Nonetheless, we believed that we had felt the pulse of truth that night, and we believed that this problem could be resolved. We believed that our insight should be shared, and so we sought an appointment the next afternoon with the president of our college (Dr. Donald J. Cowling, Carleton College, Northfield, Minnesota). We presented our idea to him and asked for support from the college so that we might work together on a manuscript to develop our idea for publication. Dr. Cowling told us that we were obviously at a rather preliminary stage in our education; that we had, however, expressed a grand idea rather well; that sometimes greatness depends in part upon what might be regarded as premature exploitation of an opportunity; that it is problematical whether Lincoln would have been a great man had he been more formally educated; that our philosophy was so close to his own that he would not want to see us do anything less than an excellent job on it; and that in conclusion he would arrange for us to board and room at the college for the summer in return for part-time work which would leave us adequate time for writing. In our plan, Richard Blomfield was to be especially concerned with the problems of harmony of our philosophy with Christianity and with its significance for practical morality. John Knoble was to be responsible for the excellence of the manuscript as an English composition. Finally, the basic idea and its development were to be my responsibility.

This was not to be. Our plans had scarcely been formulated when I chanced upon a newly published book, *The Philosophy of a Biologist,* by John Scott Haldane. I read it, and I recognized *our* book, stated with greater erudition and sophistication than we could have done, but still very much the same philosophy. So we let it lie fallow.

Meanwhile, unbeknown to us, Père Pierre Teilhard de Chardin, half a world away in China, was working on a related manuscript, the very important *Phénomène humain,* which he completed in 1940. As is well known, his superiors in the Society of Jesus were uncomfortable about his orthodoxy, and so his manuscript was circulated only privately until after his death in 1955. Soon afterward it was published, and it was rapidly established as one of the most important books of our time.

Upon reading *The Phenomenon of Man*, I again recognized something very closely related to the philosophy which I had expounded on that spring night so long ago. I saw it, however, from a viewpoint quite different both from that of the enthusiastic youth on the threshold of his education and from that of the distinguished priest-paleontologist who wrote on the basis of long years of fieldwork. I was quite naturally predisposed to admiring agreement with Teilhard, for I recognized in his book something very closely related to my own unwritten book. The relationship of his Omega point and biological macrocosm is clear. Like him, I have devoted my professional life to the study of evolution, I from the viewpoint of a geneticist, he from that of a paleontologist. Finally, like Père Teilhard, I am a Catholic, and I have always been interested in the essential harmony of faith and science. My great interest in Teilhard and *The Phenomenon of Man* scarcely needs further explanation.

With all of that, however, I found as I read *The Phenomenon of Man* that my agreement was subject to serious reservations. On one occasion, I participated in a panel discussion on the book under the auspices of the Faculty of Philosophy of the University of Ottawa. I took the position that, although Teilhard regarded his book as strictly scientific, I felt that neither his data nor his use of them were scientific in the usual sense. One of the philosophers who spoke (in a tone of approbation, although he regarded the book as science rather than philosophy) said indignantly that my comments were very similar to G. G. Simpson's harshly critical review of *The Phenomenon of Man*. I could only acknowledge that I found myself in agreement with Simpson at many points. We finally agreed that Teilhard had written a book which was not scientific in a strict sense but which could only have been written against the background of his scientific knowledge.

What, in general, were my reservations with regard to *The Phenomenon of Man*? Much may be indicated by two short sentences from book II: "I intend to develop a simplified but structural representation of life on earth; a vision so homogeneous and coherent that its truth is irresistible. I provide no minor details and no arguments, but only a perspective that the reader may see and accept—or not see" (1959:103). This statement reveals conviction, great conviction, which might well, I fear, override scientific judgment. Teilhard is as good as his word when he says "I provide no minor details," yet one of the essentials of scientific method is *inductive reasoning from observed data*, in other words, from "minor details." There is a place for deductive reasoning in science, but only after suitable generalizations have been securely established inductively. Because he reversed this, I feel that Teilhard erred when he considered his book to be purely scientific, in spite of the rich scientific background upon which he drew.

Second, I am disturbed by some of Teilhard's statements of biological "facts." As he wrote on the basis of a lifetime of experience in mammalian paleontology, it is hardly surprising that he was at his best when discussing the mammals. As he goes down the scale of the vertebrates, however, he becomes less reliable, and I feel that his discussion of the invertebrates is quite misleading. At best, this weakens his case; at worst, it damages his case badly.

Third, in contrast to almost all modern students of evolution, Teilhard placed great value on orthogenesis, the idea that evolution of the various groups follows a predetermined course to an inevitable end, and in Lamarckism, the idea that the environment *induces* those variations which are most adaptive to it. An enormous mass of experimental and observational data has failed to substantiate these ideas.

On the contrary, it is well established that the appearances of orthogenesis found in the fossil record depend upon *exclusion* of part of the data, actual or potential, and that hereditary variations are random in the sense that those variations occurring in any particular environment have only a low probability of being especially adaptive to that environment. Adaptation results from selective elimination of those variants which are less well fitted to their environment and conversely from the selective advantage of those with more fortunate variations.

Teilhard's espousal of these ideas may have resulted in part from the time when he matured as a scientist, for orthogenesis and Lamarckism were commonly favored by paleontologists of the day. Partly, it may have been a result of his long years in the collecting fields of China, where limited library facilities made it difficult to keep abreast of new studies on the genetics of evolution. It may, however, be partly an example of his strong convictions overriding his scientific judgment. Orthogenesis and Lamarckism seemed necessary to him because they seemed to support his major thesis, and I believe that it is urgently important that it be investigated whether Mendelian genetics and Darwinian evolution may not be more harmonious with his major thesis than he thought.

Fourth, one of the most essential aspects of sound scientific method is that conclusions must be testable by experiment and thus potentially disprovable. This is the property which has made modern science a self-correcting discipline and which has resulted in the extraordinary success of modern science. Granted that many scientists err against this principle from time to time and that its corrective effect is sometimes delayed for many years because of the influence of prominent scientists who are committed to erroneous ideas, still the universal conviction among scientists that experiment is the final arbiter is eventually asserted, and conclusions which cannot stand the test of experiment are rejected. Teilhard drew conclusion after conclusion which would seem to be beyond the possibility of experimental test. Such speculations may be necessary and important; they may even be correct; but they cannot be scientific, and their presentation in a book which is offered as pure science has undoubtedly prejudiced many scientists against Teilhard's thesis.

Finally, Teilhard's meaning is often very obscure. One can read and reread a paragraph without being sure of the intention of the author. Dobzhansky has pointed out a contributing factor of great importance. *Le Phénomène humain* is highly poetic, although the poetry has suffered badly in the English translation. Those who read poetry as though it were the usual prosaic scientific treatise are bound to misunderstand it rather badly. Teilhard's book needs a restatement which is simpler, more precise, and more prosaic. I hope that I may provide it in this book.

Yet all of the above is much too negative. Overshadowing everything else is Teilhard's superb insight. History bears witness that the conflict between the proponents of evolution and Christianity was once a cause célèbre. Many scholars have contributed to the resolution of that conflict, many papers have been published in the effort to show that the conflict was unnecessary, resulting from misunderstandings and mistakes on both sides, and in most quarters this issue is now considered to have been resolved. But Teilhard went much further than this: he developed the thesis that evolution and Christianity each suggest and complement the other. All Christian students of evolution must feel deeply indebted to him, and the present work is my effort to repay my debt to him.

Another aspect of *The Phenomenon of Man* and its author should be mentioned. Teilhard was that rare man whose life was completely unified: a scientist, a priest, and a poet—the three were completely unified in him and in his book, with none of the usual tendency to compartmentalize our personalities. This is certainly an admirable trait, but it has increased the difficulties of understanding his book. Because Teilhard thought of himself primarily as a scientist, he described his work as pure science.* Many a scientist has read it and dismissed it as philosophy or theology with a gloss of science. It must be understood as a unification of science, philosophy, and theology presented in a highly poetic blend.

Thus, as one who has shared with Teilhard a common professional study of evolution, a common philosophical extrapolation from that background, and a common religion, I read his great book with admiration and with partial agreement, but also with the reservations stated above. It is at once because of my admiration for Teilhard and because of the importance of these reservations that I have the temerity to write the present manuscript, which stands in a complex relationship to *The Phenomenon of Man:* in part, it is a revision or a restatement; in part, it is a critique; in part, it is an appreciation; and in part, it is an original, independent, but parallel work.

The present book then, will differ from *The Phenomenon of Man* in several important respects. First, I will present the biological data of evolution ("minor details") rather more extensively, together with the inductive arguments which lead to evolutionary generalizations. Second, in doing this, I shall aim for a broader, less fragmentary presentation of groups other than the mammals. Third, I shall reject orthogenesis and Lamarckism in favor of Mendelian genetics and Darwinian evolution. In fact, a major purpose of the present work is to investigate whether, as I think probable, it may not be possible to develop Teilhard's major thesis as effectively on a Darwinian–Mendelian basis as he did on an orthogenetic–Lamarckian basis. Fourth, like Teilhard, I shall have to speculate beyond the limits of ex-

*Cuénot has explained this on quite another basis. He says that *The Phenomenon of Man* is a phenomenology and that Teilhard described it as pure science in order to avoid confusion with the phenomenologies of Husserl and Sartre. I think, however, that Teilhard could have avoided such confusion rather more simply and hence that my explanation is more probable.

perimental science from time to time. When I do this, I hope that I shall make it clear that I have left science for speculation. In general, these sections will be much briefer and less detailed than Teilhard's. I shall try to restrict them to what seems to me to be absolutely essential. In so doing, I must concede that my book is not purely scientific, yet I will not claim that it is philosophy either, for surely I am more innocent of philosophic competence than was Teilhard, and it is an understatement to say that philosophers have not been unanimous in claiming him as one of their own. If there be an intermediate category of philosophically oriented science or scientifically oriented philosophy, then that is where the present work probably belongs.

Finally, the present work will differ from Teilhard's in one more important respect: it will lack the inspiration of genius which is so apparent in *The Phenomenon of Man*. I tender it with the humility which befits one who treads in the footsteps of a great man and with the apologies which befit one who may occasionally step upon the toes of the great man.

Acknowledgments

I WANT to thank M. Georges Bentchavtchavadze for the many excellent photographs in this book, Mr. Peter Fortey for the portrait of Teilhard, and Dr. Theresa Aniskowicz for her original drawings. The National Museums of Canada generously provided specimens. I am indebted to Professors Claude Cuénot, Theodosius Dobzhansky, Jean Piveteau, Alexander Wolsky, and Miss Mary Lukas for reading the entire manuscript and for their helpful suggestions and encouragement. Finally, I am indebted to the late Mlle Jeanne Mortier for the hospitality of the Fondation Teilhard de Chardin in Paris during the researches upon which this book is based.

THE PHENOMENON OF MAN REVISITED

CHAPTER ONE

The Phenomenon of Man

THE PHENOMENON OF MAN is Teilhard's effort to formulate a unified outlook upon all of the reality, a *Weltanschauung*, encompassing at once his experience as a working scientist (a paleontologist) and his profession as a priest. Basic to this unification is the belief that man in his totality, including not only physical but mental and spiritual attributes, is a phenomenon which is subject to study, like any other natural phenomenon. Such a study, however, must be made from an evolutionary point of view, for all of reality is a process of development (an evolution) in several great phases: first, the physicochemical phase, of which the physical universe, including the great array of chemical elements and compounds, stars, planets, and galaxies are the major results; second, the phase of biological evolution, which, starting from simple beginnings in the most complex products of physicochemical evolution, resulted in the origin of life and its diversification into three great kingdoms (according to one current system), something on the order of forty to fifty phyla (a phylum being the broadest subdivision of the kingdoms of life), and literally millions of species, or individual kinds of life; and third, a psychosocial phase, made possible by one of the most recent products of biological evolution, the human species. Each phase of evolution depends upon and includes the preceding phases, and so the phenomenon of man encompasses the whole of evolution and of nature.

Teilhard could only think of evolution in its three great phases as an ever continuing process, never as a completed and static fact. Accordingly, he preferred words which suggested process, transition, becoming: *cosmogenesis* rather than cosmology; *evolution* rather than creation; *hominization* rather than origin of man; and *noogenesis* for the continuing development of mind and all of its consequences.

Teilhard saw the grand sweep of evolution, from the origin of matter up through hominization and beyond, as fundamentally one continuous process of increasing complexity, but a process characterized by critical points on opposite sides of which a change of state occurs, just as H_2O is solid ice below 0°C, liquid water above that temperature, and gaseous steam above 100°C. He believed than any process, continued over a wide range, would include such critical points or thresholds. So impressed was he by the production of ever greater levels of complexity by evolution that he proposed a law of *complexification,* by which he meant simply that the production of ever greater levels of complexity is a necessary characteristic of evolution. The most important critical points are those which separate the three main phases of evolution. Thus, one such critical threshold lies between the most complex of nonliving molecules and the simplest of living organisms, while another separates the human species from the other primates.

A basic Teilhardian principle which is repeated throughout *The Phenomenon of Man* is that every evolutionary movement has its roots in the past, its present reality, and its projection into the future. Teilhard called this the principle of coherence or scientific symmetry. Paraphrased, it means that evolution is a continuum in which nothing arises *de novo.* We are acutely aware of our consciousness, and many aspects of the behavior of other mammals and birds are most readily interpreted in terms of a comparable consciousness. The consciousness of cold-blood vertebrates may be less acute, and among most of the invertebrates it is quite equivocal. Finally, the most primitive organisms, such as bacteria, show no signs of consciousness, although other evidences of life are clear. In the viruses, even life is debatable, while in the inorganic world we see no evidence of anything of the sort. Drawing on the principle of coherence, with everything having its roots in the past (i.e., in an earlier stage of evolution), Teilhard postulated that a forerunner of consciousness must be present not only in the simplest of organisms but even in the atomic particles of inanimate matter. This elementary basis of the properties of life he called the *within* of matter, and he considered it to be synonymous with consciousness or spontaneity. Perhaps *pre-life* would be clearer. Evidence of the within can be found only in organisms, and especially in the more evolved organisms. Its presence in all matter is an inference, and a controversial inference, from the principle of coherence. Of course, the within contrasts to the *without* of matter, which encompasses all of the ordinary physicochemical properties of matter.

It is commonplace to observe that evolution has run counter to the direction of entropy, the physical principle that in any reaction some energy is lost as heat. The result is that the amount of available energy is gradually reduced, and order is replaced by disorder. Physicists anticipate that, in a remote future, this will result in the death of heat, a uniformly cold, lifeless, and disordered universe. The contradiction between the ideas of entropy and of complexification is quite evident. Teilhard tried to resolve this problem by postulating two kinds of energy, which he called *tangential energy* and *radial energy*. Tangential energy is characteristic of the without of matter; it is the energy of ordinary experiments in physics and chemistry; and it is fully subject to the laws of thermodynamics, including the law of entropy. Radial energy is the energy of the within of matter; it increases with the increasing complexity of matter (that is, a given mass of protein has more radial energy than an equal mass of sodium chloride, and the same mass of living cells has more radial energy than does the protein); and it is at least potentially independent of entropy.

Because evolution is a process, Teilhard believed that it could not be understood or evaluated solely in terms of its origin but that its *direction* must also be taken into account. It was, and is, much debated whether evolution has an inherent direction. He believed that it did, with complexification playing a key role. Once the threshold of life was crossed, it began the diversification which resulted in the astonishing abundance and variety of life of the world today. Teilhard took account principally of the animal kingdom. He was impressed by the evolution of ever greater levels of complexity. This resulted in two principal climaxes to animal evolution, one in the insects, the other in the vertebrates, and most especially in the mammals and man. In both, complexification (to use Teilhard's word) is shown especially in the organization of the nervous system, but this system has evolved along radically different lines in the two groups. In the insects, the nervous system has specialized for automatic, instinctive responses to the ordinary problems of insect life. In the vertebrates, the nervous system has specialized for processing information to permit variable responses. In both, the elaboration of the nervous system is diagnostic for high levels of radial energy, and Teilhard regarded the progressive elaboration of nervous systems as the clearest indication that evolution does have a direction. In the case of the insects, however, the type of specialization forms a dead end, while the vertebrate type of nervous organization is open-ended, permitting much further complexification, with an attendant increase in radial energy.

Indeed, in the order Primates the rising level of radial energy approached and then crossed a major critical threshold: on one side of that threshold was typical mammalian life, highly conscious, knowing much, but, in spite of flashes suggestive of the highest human faculties, incapable of reflection or of abstract thought; on the other side of that critical threshold was—and is—man, a typical mammal and primate in most respects, yet not only knowing, but knowing that he knows, capable of reflection and abstraction, capable of compassion, capable of a new kind of evolution, psychosocial evolution, which is no longer dependent upon the slow, genetic mechanisms of biological evolution. Thus, the crossing of this critical threshold in the increase of radial energy produced a change of state resulting in a new type of life: life dominated by thought, human life.

The evolution of mind and all of its consequences Teilhard referred to as *noogenesis,* and this is now the dominant phase of evolution. The term is synonymous with psychosocial evolution, and largely so with hominization. He also used the term *noosphere* to include the total systems of thought of the thinking animals—human beings—and he sometimes described this as a membrane of thought enveloping the world. The lithosphere (the rocky substrate of the earth), the hydrosphere (or waters), and the atmosphere all existed before the origin of life. Life developed mainly at the interface of the atmosphere with the other two layers. As life became abundant and ecologically diversified, it formed a complex over the earth which Teilhard (and many others) liked to call the biosphere. Hence the term *noosphere* suggests that a web of thought, or of thinking creatures, over the earth constitutes yet another terrestrial layer. *Noogenesis* is a word which encompasses the evolution of that layer, past, present, and future.

There is yet another significant difference between the human species and all others. Evolution has generally been divergent. A successful species occupies a large territory and breaks up into a series of subspecies. Some of these may become good and distinct species, and further evolution of these may result in new genera or even higher groups. Such divergence is typical throughout the world of life—except for the human species, which has spread over the entire earth while yet remaining one single species. In fact, we have become more closely knit as tribal organization has been replaced by nations, and nations have been supplemented by federations, commonwealths, treaty organizations of many types, and, most inclusive today, the United Nations. To describe this fact, Teilhard asserted that *convergence* had replaced divergence as the dominant trend in human evolution, and he attributed this to the cohesive effects of noogenesis. The effects of convergence include the formation of societies, religions, institutions, governments—the whole gamut of psychosocial phenomena. Here, too, complexification is accompanied by an increase of radial energy, the highest manifestation of which is love.

But what of the future? Will we continue much the same sort of noogenesis indefinitely, elaborating more complex types of human organization and generating ever higher levels of radial energy? Teilhard thought not. He thought that yet another critical threshold was predictable as rising levels of radial energy push upward what Julian Huxley has picturesquely called the "psychosocial temperature." Continued convergence and very intense radial energy will result, on the other side of that final critical threshold, in the substantial unification of mankind to form a hyperpersonal biological macrocosm. Yet within this biological macrocosm, the individual personalities will be preserved and perfected, just as the cells, tissues, and organs of the body are preserved and differentiated within the individual. Convergence, however, must be toward a focal point, and he called that the point Omega, implying that it is the final goal of the phenomenon of man, in contrast to the alpha of our atomic starting point. The intense radial energy of the biological macrocosm, the hyperperson, may then be freed from its material envelope and permanently united with Omega, which is Christ, outside time and space.

Is such a triumphant climax a certainty, or is it possible that evolution and the phenomenon of man will end in an anticlimax of some sort? Teilhard considered a number of potential causes of failure, but then he concluded that man, who has become conscious of his evolution, must take control of it and must not permit it to fail. Will all of mankind participate in the biological macrocosm and its union with Omega, or might there be a convergence of evil as well as of good? Teilhard described the alternative possibilities, but he did not decide between them. He only noted that the second alternative accords better with traditional eschatology than does the first.

Such a successful outcome of evolution requires the development of certain conditions in the noosphere. These include the development of global unity, while retaining profound respect for individual and cultural differences; love, which is the highest manifestation of radial energy and which promotes goodwill and cooperation; personal integration and harmony between persons; and knowledge, especially knowledge of man, which, in the Teilhardian sense, encompasses all knowledge. The entire synthesis is based upon Teilhard's conviction of the supreme importance of personality.

Such was the *Weltanschauung* of Pierre Teilhard de Chardin, a vision which encompasses within a single comprehensive synthesis his profession as a scientist and his vocation as a priest. While I have presented it very tersely, I hope that I have done so accurately and clearly. In the succeeding chapters, I will expand upon and analyze each facet of the Teilhardian synthesis.

Teilhard was by no means the first to make evolution the cornerstone of a *Weltanschauung*. Some of the more important evolutionary syntheses were published by Herbert Spencer (1862), Henri Bergson (1907), C. Lloyd Morgan (1923), Jan Christiaan Smuts (1926), and John Scott Haldane (1935). Of these, it is certain that Teilhard studied Bergson's most important book, *L'Evolution créatrice,* prior to his ordination as a priest in 1912. It was a factor in developing his interest in evolution, but his own ideas developed along very different lines from those of Bergson. Teilhard does not seem to have been familiar with the others, although he did share some ideas with them. Because the present work is concerned with Teilhard and *The Phenomenon of Man,* rather than with evolutionary syntheses generally, only the briefest sketch of these forerunners will be given.

Herbert Spencer was an English social philosopher whose interest in evolution antedated the publication of *The Origin of Species* by many years. In fact, it is probable that Spencer introduced the word *evolution* (which Darwin seldom used) into the biological vocabulary. While he was often regarded as the philosopher of Darwinism, he formulated his ideas before the publication of *The Origin of Species* and under the influence of Lamarck, although he subsequently incorporated the idea of natural selection. Over a period of many years, starting in 1862, he published a ten-volume work, *A System of Synthetic Philsosphy,* of which volume 1, *First Principles,* is much the most important. In this, he developed the thesis that all of reality is understandable as an evolving system. He defined knowledge as the ordering of separate phenomena in relation to some previously known and more general phenomenon. Accordingly, he divided reality into knowable and unknowable spheres. The ultimate and most general phenomena must remain unknowable because there is nothing more general to which one can relate them. Thus, not only religion but such fundamentals of science as force and time are unknowable. Within the knowable, few things are so general as evolution, and it is this which gives unity to the sciences, from chemistry through biology to sociology and psychology. Indeed, Spencer's sociology is one of the principal sources of what has been called social Darwinism. Because laissez-faire economics approaches the model of natural selection in biology, it is most likely to result in a successful and happy humanity. Spencer defined the good as what is best fitted to survive in free competition, and he then advocated free competition as the best means of attaining that good!

Henri Bergson was the most influential philosopher in Europe during the first half of the twentieth century. His most important book, *L'Evolution créatrice*, was published in 1907 (in English, *Creative Evolution*, 1911). In it, he abandoned the old search for eternally fixed essences and espoused duration and movement as the essential qualities of reality. Life, to him, was a continual process of becoming, a thoroughly evolutionary idea. While he accepted the idea of final causes, these were not predetermined and immutable; rather, the evolving organism could change its goals as it progressed. Evolution for Bergson was indeed creative, not simply an unfolding of something which was there from the start, like the development of a seed. The driving force of evolution (and of all life) was an undefined *élan vital*, or vital force. While the study of *L'Evolution créatrice* undoubtedly augmented Teilhard's interest in evolution, Bergson's approach was highly metaphysical, whereas Teilhard had minimal inclination toward metaphysics. The two shared little beyond agreement in placing evolution at the center of their syntheses.

C. Lloyd Morgan was an English biologist and psychologist, one of the founders of comparative psychology. His major book, *Emergent Evolution*, was published in 1923 at the height of what has been called the agnostic reaction against Darwinism. The anatomical-embryological studies which had formed the backbone of nineteenth-century Darwinism were now *vieux jeux*. The assimilation of genetics into evolutionary studies had scarcely begun, and there was widespread pessimism about the possibility of gaining any understanding of the causal factors in evolution. Facile mechanism had failed, and irrational vitalism violated the convictions of the scientific mind. Against this background, some biologists enthusiastically hailed emergent evolution as a third alternative.

Morgan's basic idea was that, in the sequence of natural events, new combinations of materials may give rise to genuinely new attributes which could not have been predicted from the combining materials. A much belabored example is that of the combination of two gases, hydrogen and oxygen, to form water, which is utterly unpredictable from the properties of the constituent gases. The properties of water may be said to *emerge* from the combination as something truly new and unpredictable. Good biological examples are afforded by the origin of life from complex molecular systems, the origin of mind, and the origin of reflective thought. In each case, the new property has emerged, unpredictably, from new combinations of materials. Whereas mechanistic studies have emphasized the physicochemical or anatomical forerunners, Morgan emphasized the emergent properties, without denigrating the former. He specifically rejected any kind of *élan* or other nonmaterial factor in evolution, regarding the principle of emergence as an adequate explanation for the origin of novelty in the world of life. Had Teilhard been familiar with *Emergent Evolution,* it seems quite probable that he would have interpreted emergence in terms of complexification and critical thresholds. The relationship of the concepts is evident.

By profession, Jan Christiaan Smuts was neither a biologist nor a philosopher. He had a highly distinguished career as a soldier and stateman. Nonetheless, he was well informed biologically, and his biological philosophy was presented in *Holism and Evolution* (1926). This is a system of emergent evolution, but it goes much further than Morgan's. Surveying much the same array of data as did Teilhard, he saw a tendency at every level, from the atomic to the human, for nature to organize into coherent systems, which he called *wholes.* Further, he found that the concepts of matter, life, and mind approached each other and partially overlapped. This suggested to him that a single principle was expressed at all three levels. This tendency to form wholes at progressively more complex levels of organization he called *holism,* and he regarded holism as the ultimate principle of the universe. Holism, then, is the great driving principle of the universe, compelling it toward integration of wholes at ever more complex levels of organization, starting with inorganic nature, ascending through the various levels of life, and culminating in the mental, artistic, and spiritual life of man. As he himself summarized it, "Holism in all its endless forms is the principle which works up the raw material of unorganized energy units of the world, utilizes, assimilates, and organizes them, endows them with specific structure and character and individuality, and finally with personality, and creates beauty and truth and value from them" (1926:107). Holism, then, includes all of Teilhard's complexification, but it also includes part, but not all, of the attributes of the point Omega. Teilhard arrived at the conclusion that point Omega and Christ were one, and it has been observed that the complex of creative ideas which Smuts called holism others call God.

John Scott Haldane was a British physiologist who, at the end of a long and distinguished career, published *The Philosophy of a Biologist*. Haldane's approach differs radically from all of the others in that evolution, while assumed as a fact, is not the primary basis for his reasoning. His method was the examination of science in relation to philosophy. Beginning with physical science, he found that it necessarily leads to an incomplete picture of reality. Because only physicochemical facts go into its reasoning, only physicochemical conclusions can be expected, even if reality includes other factors. The incompleteness of physical science is complemented by biology, so that biology gives a truer insight into reality than does physical science. Biology is also incomplete, however, for it neglects the personality factors which are the domain of psychology. Of all of the sciences, then, psychology best approximates reality, but it too is incomplete, for the universality of the personal principles of goodness, truth, and beauty requires that the real universe be a universe of personality and that our individual personalities (which are studied in psychology) exist in relationship to a universal personality, which is God.

God is thus the fundamental fact of reality, and the various natural sciences are imperfect revelations of His nature. In Haldane's synthesis, the interactions of individual personalities result in the formation of a biological macrocosm, a hyperpersonality comparable to that discussed above. It is not always clear whether he regarded God as equivalent or transcendent to the biological macrocosm. Thus, although Haldane's reasoning was totally different from Teilhard's, he arrived at a similar conclusion, and at much the same conclusion at which I had arrived, via the evolutionary pathway, just before reading Haldane's book.

CHAPTER TWO

Preliminary Considerations

EVOLUTION PROCEEDS on three broad levels, each of which is dependent upon and includes the preceding levels. The first is physicochemical evolution, including the problem of the origin of the physical universe, the origin of the chemical elements and of their compounds, and the origin and development of stars, solar systems, nebulae, and galaxies, all of the grand framework of the physical universe. The second level is that of biological evolution, including the origin of life, its diversification into the three kingdoms Mychota (viruses, bacteria, and blue-green algae), Plantae (including fungi, a vast array of algae, mosses and their allies, and the higher plants which collectively make the world green), and Animalia (including the unicellular Protozoa, the sponges, and the vast array of more complex animals). Biological evolution proceeds primarily on the basis of genetic (hereditary) mutations and natural selection of those mutations which best adapt the organism to its conditions of life. It utilizes and includes the physicochemical laws and properties which are the results of the first order of evolution, but it adds much more. Finally, there is the psychosocial evolution of man. Man is a product of biological evolution, and his biological evolution continues, but superimposed upon this is the evolution of the mind and of the social behavior and institutions which are among the results of the mind of man. The latter is very much more rapid than biological evolution, upon which it is dependent and with which it interplays.

The historical development of knowledge of these three levels of evolution has been extremely disparate and largely uncoordinated. Physics and chemistry—especially the former—have been studied since remote antiquity, but success in developing systematic sciences in these fields was extremely limited until the Renaissance, and it was only in the nineteenth century that they matured as well-developed sciences. Nineteenth-century physics and chemistry, however, were in no sense evolutionary sciences. The materials of the universe and the laws and principles which govern their relationships were conceived as eternal constants. The discovery of radioactivity by Henri Becquerel in 1896 provided the first suggestion that this viewpoint might not be correct, but it was many years before the idea of evolution, of development, in the physical universe became widely accepted.

Biology, too, participated in the great upsurge of knowledge in Renaissance and post-Renaissance times. The great explorations included among their results the discovery of large numbers of new kinds of plants and animals. One result was the development of the science of taxonomy, the naming and classification of plants and animals, by Carolus Linnaeus (1707–1778). Linnaeus undertook the description of the entire world of life in his *Systema Naturae*. (The tenth edition, 1758, is the standard, for in it he perfected the method of nomenclature which is still in use.) It was a magnificent work, but one of its effects was to make impossible another work with the same objective, for it stimulated much further biological exploration and description, and the number of known kinds of plants and animals increased at a stunning rate. *Das Tierreich* is a massive German work, in many volumes, which attempts to describe all known species of animals. It was begun in 1896, and by 1929 it comprised about seventy very large volumes, yet the editor, R. Hesse, estimated that, at the then current rate of production, it would require 750 years to complete the work *if no new species were discovered in the meantime,* but of course many new species are discovered every year.

Simultaneously, other biological sciences burgeoned. Among the first was anatomy, beginning with Vesalius (1514–1564). Some very tentative studies in physiology were made much earlier, but physiology became a systematic science only with Claude Bernard (1813–1878), while ecology emerged from the less precise study of natural history only after the middle of the nineteenth century. One result of this explosive development of biology in post-Renaissance times was a chaotic mass of data which was not organized on any broad, basic principle. The later success of Darwinian evolution can be attributed in part to the fact that it provided such a theoretical framework upon which the disparate facts of biology could be organized.

Biology, too, in its origins was an essentially static science. "There are just so many species," wrote Linnaeus, "as in the beginning the Infinite Being created" (1758). Nonetheless, since remote antiquity, scholars had noticed that organisms seemed almost to blend from one level of complexity to another, and the suggestion was inherent that the less advanced may have given rise to the more advanced. With the rising volume of biological knowledge in the eighteenth century, various biologists, such as the Comte de Buffon (1707–1788) and Geoffroy St. Hilaire (1772–1844), considered the possibility of evolution quite seriously, but in the absence of a good working theory to explain evolution they were unable to achieve conviction that the observed variety of life was the result of evolution. Jean Baptiste Lamarck (1744–1829) overcame this difficulty by the development of a theory based upon direct induction by the environment of appropriate variations and upon inheritance of these acquired characteristics. He first published his theory in 1809, and he devoted the rest of his life to its defense. Biologists generally, however, remained unconvinced. Many reasons contributed to this skepticism, but two may be mentioned. First, the development of geology as a science was still largely in the future, and it was generally believed that the earth was only a few thousand years old. It seemed futile to appeal to a theory (evolution) which would require much longer periods of time to produce its results. And second, the simplest aspects of heredity were still largely unknown, yet Lamarckism required a specific theory of heredity, a theory which was not supported by the rise (much later) of the science of genetics.

Half a century later, in 1859, Charles Darwin published *The Origin of Species*. In it, Darwin presented a closely reasoned argument for natural selection as the working principle of evolution, and he presented a great mass of evidence that evolution actually had occurred, evidence drawn from such diverse sciences as domestication, comparative anatomy, comparative embryology, comparative physiology, and paleontology. He accepted the Lamarckian theory of the inheritance of acquired characters, but the cornerstone of his theory was natural selection, the differential survival of those variants best suited to their conditions of life and the differential mortality of the less well adapted.

Darwin's argument will be developed more fully below. Let it suffice to say here that he convinced biologists generally so thoroughly that most of the biology of the latter half of the nineteenth century was carried out under the inspiration of Darwinian evolution and that evolution has since become as basic to biology as the laws of thermodynamics are to physics.

In the immediate post-Darwinian era, social Darwinism enjoyed considerable prestige under the leadership of such men as Herbert Spencer. It was short-lived prestige, however, and for very good reasons. Its advocates attempted an overly facile transfer of strictly biological interpretations, based on animals lacking the complex mental and social attributes of man, to the problems of human behavior and societies. It was used to justify such things as war, class oppression, and economic aggression, all of which were justified as favoring survival of the fittest. Quite properly, a reaction against social Darwinism set in, but the reaction tended to reject the whole idea of psychosocial evolution as well as the abuses of it which provoked the reaction.

This antievolutionary reaction among social scientists has perhaps not been entirely resolved yet. Nonetheless, psychologists, sociologists, social anthropologists, and others who work in this general area have long realized that their studies deal with a developmental process, a historical process which changes with time, and such a process is by definition evolution. However, now that they have again become evolutionists, they still reject the canons of social Darwinism: they now realize that they are dealing with a third order of evolution, based upon and including the preceding orders but adding new laws and potentialities of its own.

Thus, students of the three great orders of evolution have successively arrived at their respective positions from originally static backgrounds. As static sciences, there was no reason to expect important relationships among them. But once the fact of evolution at each level had become apparent, it required only the insight of genius to synthesize all into one comprehensive view of reality based upon evolution from the origin of matter to the highest powers of man and beyond. It was Pierre Teilhard de Chardin who achieved that great synthesis. "Is evolution a theory, a system, or a hypothesis?" wrote Teilhard, "It is much more: it is a general condition to which all theories, all hypotheses, all systems must bow and which they must satisfy henceforward if they are to be thinkable and true. Evolution is a light illuminating all facts, a curve that all lines must follow" (p. 218).*

As a lifelong student of evolution, I can only admire the elegance of that statement and the profound insight which is crystallized in it. In the succeeding chapters, I will try to develop the basis for Teilhard's beautiful statement.

---

*Unless otherwise indicated, all quotations are from *The Phenomenon of Man,* American edition, Harper & Row, Publishers, Inc.

CHAPTER THREE

The Stuff
of the Universe

DURING THE PAST three hundred years or less, chemists have identified the building blocks of the universe, an array of kinds of atoms ranging from hydrogen, the lightest of elements, to uranium, the heaviest. In recent years, a few "transuranic" elements have been discovered, principally by the methods of atomic physics, including bombardment of materials in a cyclotron. Thus, about a hundred elements are now known. A few of these are familiar to almost everyone, such as the gases hydrogen, oxygen, and nitrogen; many metals, such as iron, silver, gold, chromium, and tin; and nonmetallic solids such as carbon and sulfur. Many others are less common and less familiar, but they are well known to physicists and chemists. For all of the diversity of these elements, Teilhard saw in them three properties shared by all, "the three faces of Matter" (p. 40): plurality, unity, and energy.

ELEMENTARY MATTER

Plurality is suggested by the enormous variety of forms under which we see matter and by the particulate character of most of them, from stars through raindrops, snowflakes, stones, and sand to the finest dust. Such familiar properties as color and texture are associated with these aggregates of molecules, but these properties lose their meaning when one goes down to the atomic level. Plurality is especially striking at the atomic level, for the numbers of atoms in even a very small fragment of matter, such as a speck of dust, are astronomically large.

But it goes much further than this. The atom itself, once conceived as an indivisible unit, is in turn made up of smaller elementary particles. These are principally protons (positively charged), electrons (negatively charged), and neutrons (uncharged), but physicists have identified an extensive array of additional elementary particles, mostly by bombardment of the atomic nucleus. These elementary particles are not distributed randomly in an atom, but rather protons, neutrons, and the various recently discovered particles form the nucleus of the atom, a compact central mass; while the electrons encircle the nucleus in well-defined orbits.

Plurality is, indeed, a general property of matter.

Nonetheless, there is also fundamental unity in matter. It is all constructed of the same particles—protons, electrons, and all of the rest. They are organized in a specific way, with the hydrogen molecule as the basic unit. A hydrogen molecule consists of one proton with a single electron orbiting about it. Larger molecules can be thought of as combinations of hydrogen molecules, with many protons in the nucleus and an equal number of electrons in orbit. This is an oversimplification for several reasons. First, under usual terrestrial conditions, at any rate, hydrogen atoms do not merge to form larger atoms. Second, this statement ignores the role of other elementary particles. And finally, it ignores the fact that the electrons do not all follow the same orbits and that the successive orbits are associated with different energy levels.

The mass of the atom can be measured. Expressed as multiples of the mass of the hydrogen atom, this mass is called the atomic weight, and this is one of the fundamental properties of an element. It was originally thought that atomic weights should, in principle, be whole numbers, integral multiples of the mass of hydrogen, which is by definition 1.0. In fact fractional numbers are always obtained, and these were at first attributed to experimental error. It now appears, however, that fractional numbers result not only from experimental error but also from two other factors: first, the influence of other elementary particles in the atom; and second, the existence of the same element as two or more isotopes, physicochemical identities with different atomic weights, so that an average of several isotopes is measured.

Unity also results from the interrelationships of atoms. They influence each other. In the first place, there is a gravitational attraction between any particle of matter and all others in the universe—a weak attraction, especially at great distances, but nonetheless a real one, and collectively one of the major factors determining the characteristics of the universe. Second, the atoms interact at close range to form first molecules of a single atomic species and then compounds of two or more atomic species. Finally, matter collectively is held together in the array of compounds, structures, planets, stars, and galaxies which comprise the universe.

Teilhard was so impressed by the influence of one atom upon another that he wrote that "each . . . can only be defined by virtue of its influence on all around it . . . its realm is coextensive, at least potentially, with that of every other atom" (p. 41). One may stop short of that sweeping conclusion yet still agree that unity based upon mutual influence of atom upon atom is a true property of matter.

The last of the three faces of matter is energy. Energy exchanges are familiar from everyday experience. All of our activities involve energy exchanges. Whenever atoms unite to form compounds, or whenever compounds decompose to yield their constituent atoms, energy exchanges occur. In recent times, the energy of radioactivity, of atomic fission, and of hydrogen fusion have become familiar. We now know that hydrogen fusion in the sun is the source of the enormous amount of radiant energy with which the sun floods the earth and which is the driving power for the evolution of life on earth.

Finally, Einstein demonstrated that matter and energy are interchangeable: one can be converted into the other. Energy thus appears as the most elementary stuff of the universe.

TOTAL MATTER

The properties of matter discussed above can be seen in any fragment of matter, but the universe exists not as so many fragments but as a whole. Teilhard called it "the only real indivisible," and he saw this as "a *system*, a *totum* and a *quantum*: a system by its plurality, a totum by its unity, and a quantum by its energy" (p. 43).

The systematic character of nature is at once intuitively obvious and the basis of all scientific study. Elementary particles form atoms, and atoms form compounds according to orderly laws which constitute much of the science of chemistry. On a much larger scale, the myriad compounds which comprise the earth undergo successive transformations which are studied in the science of geology. And on the grandest scale, the planets, the solar system, and the galaxies of which they form parts all show interrelationships and follow laws which are the basis for the science of astronomy. There is system in nature.

When Teilhard said that the universe is a totum, he meant that no part of it is adequately representative of the whole. A small sample of cloth is adequately representative of the whole bolt because the weave is repeated identically throughout, as is the pattern of colors. He found no such repeated pattern in the universe: molecules have properties which are not apparent from their constituent atoms. Thus, the gases hydrogen and oxygen combine to form liquid water. A planetary system may be compared with an atom in a rough way, but they are radically different in their properties. The solar system is not a gigantic atom. Finally, going to the galaxies and systems of galaxies, they again have no counterpart at lower levels, and so Teilhard concluded that "the mesh of the universe is the universe itself" (p. 45). There is just one point in this sequence where the argument may not be conclusive. Astronomers sometimes refer to galaxies as "island universes," and it may be that each one is, at least in principle, enough like the others to be considered as a repeating unit.

Because Teilhard thought of the universe as an indivisible whole, he was driven to think of the energy of the universe as all one, indivisible whole, a quantum, as already suggested in the discussion of the unity of matter. Once again, I must suggest that perhaps the conclusion goes beyond scientific necessity, perhaps beyond scientific feasibility. For in principle, every scientific conclusion should be testable by experiment and so potentially disprovable. This is not to say that Teilhard's conclusion is necessarily wrong. Truths are not necessarily always provable by scientific means. Gödel's theorem is perhaps applicable here (and at many points in the present study). This was described as follows by D. M. MacKay:

In 1931, K. Gödel in Vienna established a theorem which has been described as the most decisive result in modern mathematical logic. Broadly speaking, Gödel showed (*Monatshefte für Mathematik und Physik,* vol. 38) that any proof of the self-consistency of a logical deductive system—comprising definitions, axioms, and all the theorems derived from them—would itself involve a specific contradiction within the system. That is to say, undecidable statements exist; within a given logical system certain assertions (which may even be known to be true) can be neither proved nor disproved. In particular, such a logical system can never be self-validating, in the sense that any discussion of its internal consistency must appeal to a higher context beyond the system itself (Wolstenholme 1963:181).

Of course, Gödel was concerned only with mathematical logic, and it is not self-evident that his conclusions are transferable to other fields. It seems probable, however, that less rigorous disciplines are more, rather than less, troubled by such undecidable statements.

Teilhard may be forgiven, then, if he has not done the impossible. If his conception of the universal quantum of energy may be beyond the possibility of experimental test, nonetheless it is related to the law of the conservation of energy, as will appear below.

THE EVOLUTION OF MATTER

"Physics was born . . . under the double sign of fixity and geometry. Its ideal . . . was . . . a mathematical explanation of a . . . system of stable elements in a closed equilibrium" (p. 46). The progress of physics, however, forced a developmental, evolutionary viewpoint to the fore. The discussion of total matter was based upon classical, static physics. We now turn to evolutionary physics.

Scientists have called the study of the origin of the universe cosmology, but Teilhard preferred to call it *cosmogenesis*, because it suggests continuing development. Many theories have been proposed, but they all represent variants of four, which may be called the *condensation, explosion, steady state,* and *cyclical* theories. According to the condensation theory, primitive matter was diffused through limitless space, when suddenly it condensed, as salts crystallize out of a saturated solution, as a result of which the chemical elements, the stars, and galaxies were formed. This theory is an old one which now lacks support, largely because it seems to contradict the observation that the various galaxies are *receding* from one another at an ever increasing rate.

The steady state theory of Hoyle has enjoyed great prestige in recent years. This theory proposes that there are in the universe centers in which matter is constantly being created, while it is being destroyed elsewhere. As long as creation and destruction are in balance, the net condition of the universe remains more or less constant. The cyclical theory has also found its supporters. This theory proposes that the universe goes through alternate cycles of expansion and contraction, each several billion years in duration. Each expanding phase is equivalent to a new creation, each contracting phase to destruction of the preceding creation. The major difficulty with this theory is that we can only observe the one expansion phase now in progress. All of the rest is inferred from inadequate data.

The explosion theory is the one most generally accepted today. As developed by Lemaître (beginning in 1927), the theory proposes that all of the matter of the universe originally comprised an extremely compact mass of enormous density. Then, at the moment of creation, this primeval atom exploded, producing all of the elementary particles, which became organized into "the harmonic series of simple bodies, strung out from hydrogen to uranium on the notes of the atomic scale" (p. 48). The force of the explosion continued in the production of stellar masses, nebulae, and galaxies, and that it has not yet spent its forces is shown by the continuing recession of the galaxies from one another.

Once the chemical elements were formed, they began to react. The number of compounds possible is very large. Classical chemistry recognized ninety-two elements, but several more have been discovered in recent years (table 3.1). For ease of calculation, let us arbitrarily say that there are one hundred elements. Then, if each element were capable of forming a simple binary compound, like NaCl (common table salt), with all of the others (a false assumption—no element can react with all of the others), the number of such compounds would be $100^2 = 10^4 = 10,000$. While not all of these binary compounds exist, their number is large. But more complex compounds may also be formed.

The potential number of compounds with three atoms each would be $100^3 = 10^5 = 100,000$. But much more complex molecules exist, and their potential numbers increase exponentially with the complexity of the molecules. Of course, a large proportion of these potential compounds may never be formed. The point is that the enormous release of energy by the primitive explosion began at once to be expressed in random reactions among the nascent elements, producing ever greater numbers of ever more complex compounds, until finally there resulted the very complex compounds in which we recognize life. In all of this array of compounds, only the one series of atoms, made up of a few kinds of elementary particles, occurs. This tendency to form ever more complex compounds is an example of what Teilhard called "the law of complexification" (p. 48). He also pointed out that these reactions are not evenly distributed through the universe, rather they are concentrated near the stars, where enormous amounts of energy are released.

Several sorts of evidence favor the explosion theory. Calculations based upon disintegration of radioactive elements, the red shift (Doppler effect) of distant stars and galaxies, and backward projection of the dispersal of the galaxies all indicate a zero point some five to ten billion years ago.

Whatever theory of cosmogenesis may be correct, Teilhard regarded them as equivalent in the sense that they place us in a developing corpuscular environment from which there is no escape, although we may transcend it via the interior life (see chapters 11 and 12).

In all of the transformations of matter, the laws of thermodynamics prevail. Two of these, the law of conservation of energy and the law of entropy, may be discussed briefly. The law of conservation of energy states that the total amount of energy in a system remains constant. If one structure is built up, another must be torn down to provide the energy for construction. That is why the evolution of the more complex states of matter occurs in the vicinity of

Table 3.1. Periodic Table of the Elements, Simplified

Period 1	Period 2	Period 3	Period 4
1 Hydrogen	3 Lithium	11 Sodium	19 Potassium
	4 Beryllium	12 Magnesium	20 Calcium
			21 Scandium
			22 Titanium
			23 Vanadium
			24 Chromium
			25 Manganese
			26 Iron
			27 Cobalt
			28 Nickel
			29 Copper
			30 Zinc
	5 Boron	13 Aluminum	31 Gallium
	6 Carbon	14 Silicon	32 Germanium
	7 Nitrogen	15 Phosphorus	33 Arsenic
	8 Oxygen	16 Sulfur	34 Selenium
	9 Fluorine	17 Chlorine	35 Bromine
2 Helium	10 Neon	18 Argon	36 Krypton

the stars, where enormous amounts of nuclear energy are being released. It is the flood of radiant energy from the sun which drives the evolution of matter and life on earth.

Every synthesis, however, exacts a price, for no reaction is completely efficient: part of the energy input is always lost as heat. To put it another way, concentrations of energy, as in complex compounds, are relatively improbable, while simpler compounds and more diffuse distribu-

Period 5	Period 6	Period 7
37 Rubidium	55 Cesium	87 Francium
38 Strontium	56 Barium	88 Radium
39 Yttrium	57 Lanthanum	89 Actinium
	58 Cerium	90 Thorium
	59 Praseodymium	91 Protactinium
	60 Neodymium	92 Uranium
	61 Promethium	93 Neptunium
	62 Samarium	94 Plutonium
	63 Europium	95 Americium
	64 Gadolinium	96 Curium
	65 Terbium	97 Berkelium
	66 Dysprosium	98 Californium
	67 Holmium	99 Einsteinium
	68 Erbium	100 Fermium
	69 Thulium	101 Mendelevium
	70 Ytterbium	102 Nobelium
	71 Lutetium	103 Lawrencium
40 Zirconium	72 Hafnium	
41 Niobium	73 Tantalum	
42 Molybdenum	74 Tungsten	
43 Technetium	75 Rhenium	
44 Ruthenium	76 Osmium	
45 Rhodium	77 Iridium	
46 Palladium	78 Platinum	
47 Silver	79 Gold	
48 Cadmium	80 Mercury	
49 Indium	81 Thallium	
50 Tin	82 Lead	
51 Antimony	83 Bismuth	
52 Tellurium	84 Polonium	
53 Iodine	85 Astatine	
54 Xenon	86 Radon	

tion of energy are more probable. Hence, while more complex compounds are being built up, and with them greater concentrations of energy, more and more of the total amount of energy becomes diffused, and organization yields to the more probable disorganization. This is the law of entropy. Based upon it physicists have predicted that the final state of the universe will be one of maximum entropy, which is minimum concentration of energy—the death of heat.

THE WITHIN OF THINGS

We now come to the heart of Teilhard's analysis, and at the same time to the part which is most difficult to defend on purely scientific grounds, for it would seem to be beyond the possibility of experimental test. This is that, in addition to the external properties of matter, there is also a *within* in which exist the potentialities of life. "The *within, consciousness*, and *spontaneity*," wrote Teilhard, "three expressions for the same thing" (p. 57). He preferred *within*, but *consciousness, life*, or *pre-life* might be clearer.

Teilhard's reasoning is essentially that scientific symmetry (which he called coherence) requires that life (or pre-life) characterize every material particle. In other sciences, properties which are decisive at one level may be inconsequential at another. Thus, moderate velocities have no apparent influence on matter, but extreme velocities may increase its mass many fold. Stability is usually one of the most striking properties of the elements, one which defied centuries of efforts by alchemists to transmute base elements into precious metals. Yet radioactivity demonstrates atomic decay. Over short periods of time, the mountains and the stars are proverbially changeless, but over long periods the earth's crust is continually changing, and "the heavens sweep us along in a cyclone of stars" (p. 54). Nonetheless, Teilhard pointed out that none of these properties is confined to that portion of the spectrum of physical phenomena in which it is most obvious. "*Every* mass is modified by its velocity. *Every* body radiates. *Every* movement is veiled in immobility when sufficiently slowed down" (p. 55).

Similarly, consciousness (and all that goes with it) is intuitively recognized in ourselves. And higher animals have so much in common with man that it is difficult to avoid the inference that they, too, have consciousness like our own, if perhaps less acute. Among lower invertebrates, consciousness is equivocal, and the bacteria show no indications of consciousness, yet other manifestations of life are undeniable. Thus, from the highest to the lowest forms of life, there is a gradual decrease in the ease of identification of consciousness, although other manifestations of life remain clear. In the viruses, life itself is equivocal, and in the inorganic world it escapes detection. By comparison with the physical properties cited above, which characterize all matter but are readily identified only in special cases, Teilhard proposed that life or pre-life (the *within*), too, must characterize all matter, however dimly and however difficult to identify, except by the requirements of scientific symmetry. Only thus can a coherent conception of all reality be achieved.

Reasoning again largely from symmetry with the physical properties (*without*) of matter, he attributes certain characteristics to the pre-life (*within*) of matter. It is corpuscular. As one traces it back in time (to an earlier stage of evolution), it tends to disappear. And it is manifested most clearly in those bodies which are physically most complex. It is self-evident that psychic activity requires energy, and he pondered the question of the relationship between physical and psychic energy. He concluded that all energy is basically psychic (misprinted as *physical* in the first English editions) but that it has two components, a *tangential* component, which comprises the ordinary forces of physics, and a *radial* component, which is psychic energy in the more usual sense. The latter is prominent only in organisms, and in man it is the predominant form of energy. For the present, I shall not discuss detailed relationships between the two, partly because I do not believe that it is necessary to do so and partly because in this regard Teilhard's views are particularly difficult to test by the usual scientific means, or so it seems to me.

One might ask, Why the terms *tangential* and *radial* energy? The question is not easily answered, but I believe that it is primarily a question of Teilhard's viewpoint. The very designation of the physical properties of matter as the *without* and the personal properties as the *within* tends to locate the latter at the center of its material system. Teilhard sometimes referred to a person, in whom the within predominates, as a center. As the energy of life, of personality, connects one such center to another (most completely in love, but also in other interpersonal relations), the suggestion is that this energy is directed along the radii from one center to another. The ordinary physical interactions, however, do not involve the centers, and so these forces may be said to be tangential. These terms do not seem to be essential, and they are somewhat obscure. *Physical* (tangential) and *psychic* (radial) energy would probably be clearer, and their meanings are more obvious.

Let me point out, however, that there is no dualism here. Indeed, the avoidance of dualism was one of Teilhard's major objectives, for he could not reconcile dualism with his scientific conscience. The objective content of the statements that all energy is psychic and that all energy is physical is the same: both mean that there is basically only one kind of energy and that its properties are those which may be determined by experiment and by logical analysis. But the two statements represent very different attitudes. The latter tends to interpret the higher forms of matter (life) in terms of the lower, while the former—Teilhard's viewpoint—tends to interpret the lower forms of matter in terms of the highest.

As I have stated my belief that the reasoning which led Teilhard to the concept of the within or pre-life of matter is not scientific (although it may be true), it is only fair to say that other scientists have thought along similar lines. J. S. Haldane developed a similar thesis in his book of 1935, and Teilhard (p. 57) quotes J. B. S. Haldane in much the same vein. Another related theory is that of Joseph Wood Krutch (a highly knowledgeable amateur biologist as well as a distinguished man of letters). In a book published in 1957, Krutch pointed out that the atom seems to have some properties of freedom, of choice, as well as strictly deter-

minate properties. Thus, we know that a specific proportion of the atoms of a radioactive material will break down
in a given period of time, but we have no clue as to why a
specific atom breaks down while its neighbors remain in-
tact. Similarly, in many chemical reactions, a portion, let
us say 35 percent, of the molecules react, while the remaining 65 percent fail to react. Again, there is no clue as to the
difference between the molecules which do and do not react.
Krutch suggested that life might have originated by the development of such powers of choice, which remained secondary in inorganic matter.

Finally, I should like to recount a story about the vi-
rologist Wendell Stanley. In 1940, Stanley gave the Hitch-
cock Lectures at the University of California at Berkeley.
He was introduced by Karl Meyer, an inspired and inspir-
ing bacteriologist, who gave a rousing introduction based
upon the legend of St. George and the dragon. The dragon
which had laid waste the fields of biology was the idea of
spontaneous generation. Originally, when spontaneous
generation of such large animals as rats, snakes, and flies
was commonly accepted, St. George in the persons of Spal-
lanzani and Redi came forth to slay the dragon. As soon as
life on a smaller scale was discovered, bacterial life, the
dragon was restored to life and again laid waste to biology,
until St. George came forth in the person of Pasteur, once
again to vanquish the dragon. But Pasteur had no sooner
passed on than viruses were discovered, and once again
the dragon of spontaneous generation reared its fearsome
head. Fortunately, however, St. George was once again
present in the person of Wendell Stanley, the speaker of
the evening. St. George then strode to the podium—and
lay down with the dragon. I cannot quote him verbatim,
but I was privileged to be there on that memorable occasion, and I remember the substance of his remarks well.
He pointed out that the characteristics which we associate
with life are highly developed in the highest organisms;
that they are less clear in many microorganisms, especially

bacteria; that we do not recognize life in chemical compounds generally; but that the viruses were at once intermediate in their characteristics between very complex compounds and simple bacteria; and that it was hotly controversial among virologists whether they should be regarded as living or nonliving. He concluded that life was a property of all matter but that we were able to recognize it only when it reached a certain minimum level of complexity. Or, to put it another way, life was concentrated in typical organisms but too diffuse for ready recognition in typical inorganic chemicals. Viruses were intermediate, and their status was therefore controversial.

Thus, Teilhard's ideas on the within may not be testable in the usual scientific manner, but he was in excellent scientific company in this regard. Perhaps most scientists make some excursions beyond the strict limits of science, and they do not always realize that they have done it.

THE EARTH IN ITS EARLY STAGES

We have discussed matter in general, and now we come to the earth in particular. There are several theories of the origin of the earth. According to one, the primitive sun was surrounded by a swirling nebula. As it slowly cooled, eddies within it tended to condense, and these formed the planets, including the earth. Another theory envisions great sparks being hurled from the surface of the sun, sparks which cooled and condensed to form the planets. Under either theory, the earth was established at an intermediate distance from the sun, close enough to be bathed in warmth and energy, distant enough to permit formation and maintenance of complex compounds. Of course, in the incandescent heat of the sun itself (and of other stars), matter can only exist in its simplest, uncombined forms.

By whatever method, the early earth soon formed a

metallic core of very high density, the barysphere, over which was formed the lithosphere, or coat of rock. When the earth cooled sufficiently, this was partially bathed by a layer of water, the hydrosphere. The entire earth was surrounded by an envelope of gas, the relatively dense atmosphere near the surface of the earth and the rarified stratosphere at greater heights, blending into the void of space.

Teilhard pointed out that the great mass of the earth is made up of materials which crystallize—that is, like atoms fit into a latticework of geometrical regularity, without forming new compounds. The familiar crystals of table salt are a good example, but snowflakes (figure 3.1) provide an example which is both more beautiful and more varied. As Teilhard put it so poetically, "Considered in the mass, the earth is veiled in geometry as far back as we can see. It crystallizes" (p. 69). On the surface of the earth, however, and especially at the interface between lithosphere, hydrosphere, and atmosphere, there are small amounts of carbonates, nitrates, hydrates, and other compounds which did not crystallize, rather they polymerized—that is, they joined together in a true chemical union to form new and much larger, much more complex molecules, organic molecules which are ordinarily associated with life and which in the primitive earth were the carriers of the potentiality of life. Their polymerization was powered by the enormous amounts of solar energy bathing the earth. Today, there is good evidence that this is true, but most of the work which established this was still in the future when Teilhard wrote. It should be added that he used the term *polymerization* in a somewhat broader sense than is usual among chemists, who generally restrict it to reactions joining rather similar compounds, as the joining of amino acids to form proteins, or of sugars to form starches.

In summary, Teilhard wrote, "We are back at the refrain which runs all the way through this book . . . nothing could ever burst forth as final across the different thresholds successively traversed by evolution . . . which

Figure 3.1. Snow crystals.

has not already existed in an obscure and primordial way" (p. 71). To paraphrase, because life is an important feature of the earth now, we must look for pre-life on the early earth.

Pre-life characterizes all matter, and of course the early earth was no exception. "Consciousness is that much more perfected according as it lines a richer and better organized material edifice," wrote Teilhard (p. 60). Now, the polymerized molecules which he believed to have characterized the early earth (and for which there is now much evidence) were by far the most highly organized form which matter had taken up to that time. It was here, then, that life was to appear.

CHAPTER FOUR

The Origin of Life

TEILHARD COMPLETED the manuscript for *The Phenomenon of Man* in 1940, and it is probable that he wrote the chapter on the origin of life much earlier. At that time, the overwhelming majority of scientists believed that the problem of the origin of life was, and probably always would be, beyond the reach of scientific study. It is most remarkable, therefore, that Teilhard treated the origin of life as a continuation of the evolution of the polymerized molecules discussed in chapter 3. Even as Teilhard wrote, the Russian biochemist A. I. Oparin was preparing a book (1968) on the origin of life. In it, he developed a plausible hypothesis of biochemical evolution, utilizing only established chemical and biochemical data. Much later, this resulted in experimental verification of key aspects of his hypothesis. Of course, the result was the establishment of the possibility, not the actual occurrence, of biochemical evolution, but it also changed the problem of the origin of life from one of apparent hopelessness to one of active experimentation and optimism. And all of this has developed along lines which Teilhard predicted. Apparently, Teilhard was not familiar with Oparin's work, but I cannot but feel that he would have been delighted with it.

TEILHARD ON THE ORIGIN OF LIFE

Let us begin by summarizing Teilhard's chapter.
In spite of having said that pre-life had existed all

along, it is proper to speak of the origin of life because, as matter became more highly organized, a change of state occurred, and pre-life passed into life. Such changes of state are well known in all branches of science. A curve changes direction, a solid melts, a liquid becomes a gas, or a cell divides. Such critical points have great importance, and Teilhard believed that the transition from a polymerized complex (pre-life) to the simplest living cell represented such a change of state, resulting from passing a critical level of complexity. At the time Teilhard wrote, it was controversial whether viruses were living or not. Teilhard treats them as macromolecular complexes which, along with other large organic molecules, must have accumulated in large amounts in the primitive seas over long reaches of time as a result of biochemical evolution in the early stages of the earth. He estimated that this must have required a period of time at least as long as from the beginning of the Cambrian to the present—a span of some 600 million years. This has proven to be a very conservative estimate.

At some point, this evolving complex crossed a threshold of complexity to achieve cellular structure—Teilhard called it the "cellular revolution . . a new type of material for a new stage of the universe" (p. 87). A typical cell is a bit of protoplasm limited by a membrane and containing a nucleus. The nucleus contains chromosomes, nucleoprotein bodies which carry genes and thus the hereditary and functional controls of the cell, nucleoli, and nuclear sap. The cytoplasm is even more complex. In Teilhard's time, it appeared to consist of colloidal proteins of very high molecular weights with fine rods, the mitochondria, Golgi apparatus, and centrosomes. Today, it appears even more complex, for the electron microscope has revealed complex structures within the mitochondria and Golgi apparatus, and the apparently homogeneous ground substance of the cytoplasm now appears as a complex array of membranes (endoplasmic reticulum) with attached ribosomes which function in the synthesis of proteins. Even more now than when he wrote it, the cell (figure 4.1) deserves Teilhard's

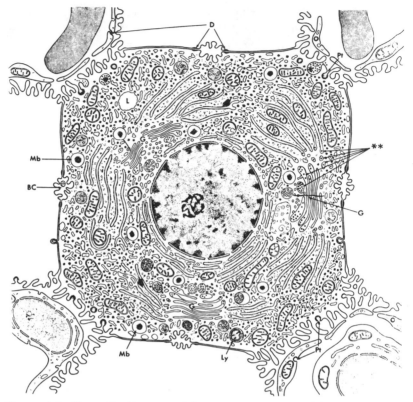

Figure 4.1. The cell, diagram of fine structure revealed by electron microscopy. Reprinted by permission of Lea and Febiger, publishers, from K. R. Porter and M. A. Bonneville, *Fine Structure of Cells and Tissues*, 4th ed., 1973.

description as "a triumph of multiplicity organically contained within a minimum of space" (p. 87).

Teilhard suggested that the first cells must have been extremely small and numerous. Further, he proposed that they probably could not have survived without an interrelationship, so that they formed a living film, a sort of diffuse or incipient superorganism, the biosphere. This idea was presented as an intuition without evidence. It may be mentioned, however, that it is often difficult to grow cultures of microorganisms (or of metazoan cells) unless the cells are present in a certain minimum concentration when the culture is started.

Further, Teilhard concluded that life as we know it, vast and varied as it is, includes only a part of what might have been. Thus, asymmetrical compounds (most bio-chemicals) are generally optically active, that is, they will rotate a beam of polarized light if the beam is passed through a solution of the chemical. Rotation may be either to the left or to the right. In principle, levo- and dextroro-tatory forms should be equally probable, but in fact a par-ticular type of compound is always of the same optical type in living organisms. Again, enzymes and vitamins are much the same in all organisms, but the range of substances which might have similar activity is much greater. Thus, there has been a selection: all of life represents only a part of what might have been.

It is demonstrable, then, that even the simplest living cell is at a level of complexity which is orders of magnitude greater than that of even the most complex of nonliving molecules. It includes all of the complexities of proteins, carbohydrates, fats, and other compounds, as well as new complexities of structural and functional interrelationships of these in the cell. In accordance with the principle that consciousness is more highly developed according to the level of complexity of the material in which it is included, one would expect, then, that consciousness, too, would be orders of magnitude more highly developed in the cell than in the most complex of polymers. In fact, this is what is found: life, with some suggestions of something akin to consciousness, is first unequivocally identifiable in simple cells, while in the most complex of polymers it is only sug-gested (whether to Teilhard or to Stanley) by intuition or by the application of the principle of symmetry, both of which would appear to be beyond the possibility of exper-imental test.

CONTEMPORARY SCIENCE AND THE ORIGIN OF LIFE

To most scientists, the origin of life appeared to be beyond the possibility of scientific study until the late 1930s. Then in 1938, A. I. Oparin published a book which changed this, for in it he showed that known data point to a plausible hypothesis of the origin of life. He estimated the probable chemical composition of the primitive earth by spectroscopic analysis of the sun and of stars in early stages of their physical evolution. All of the elements which occur in organisms were present, but only in inorganic compounds. Free nitrogen, hydrogen, and oxygen, so prominent in the atmosphere today, may have been present at the very beginning, but they were probably soon lost to outer space because the earth's gravity was not strong enough to hold these light gases at the high temperatures then prevailing. Thus, these elements were left only in compounds, and there was a *reducing* atmosphere, in contrast to the familiar oxidizing atmosphere of today. Large quantities of hydrogen and oxygen were probably united as water, but for long ages this was probably present mainly as superheated steam, which would rise toward the cold stratosphere, condense, and plunge toward the earth as rain, only to be converted to steam again before striking the earth. As the earth gradually cooled, rain fell to its surface, warm pools formed, and these merged to form warm, lifeless seas. The whole earth was then a great crucible for random chemical reactions.

Oparin showed that, the elementary composition of the earth's crust being what it is, long continued reaction under what amounted to reflux conditions would almost certainly result in formation of methane (CH_4, the smallest of organic molecules) and other small hydrocarbons, as well as their bromides and chlorides. Methane is present in the atmospheres of some of the cooler stars, and more complex hydrocarbons have been found in meteorites. Metallic nitrides would also be formed, and these would react with steam to form ammonium hydroxide and ammonia. From these primary materials, he theorized that, on the basis of their known reactions, a host of secondary reactions should lead to alcohols, aldehydes, ketones, carbohydrates, glycerine, fats, and even amino acids, the building blocks of proteins, and thus exceedingly important compounds.

Other known reactions are also capable of producing organic compounds (the compounds of carbon) in the absence of life. Ultraviolet irradiation of formic acid (the simplest organic acid) yields large organic molecules, including amino acids. The action of cosmic rays upon carbon dioxide and water vapor yields organic acids. And the discharge of lightning in an atmosphere of methane, hydrogen, ammonia, and water vapor yields a rich mixture of organic compounds, including some amino acids.

Granted that some of these reactions might be vanishingly slow, still with literally billions of years of reaction time, much should have been accomplished. The primitive seas gradually became a thin soup with an enormous quantity of dissolved organic matter in great variety. Some of the compounds would form colloids, and colloids of opposite charge would then mutually precipitate each other to form complex systems of coacervates, which resemble cytoplasm in appearance. Coacervate particles would tend to bind water at the surface and thus form a membrane and with it a sort of elementary individuality. It remained only for an autocatalytic molecule to form in such a coacervate, and one would have an elementary organism capable of growing and reproducing at the expense of the organic materials which had been stockpiled in the primitive seas.

Catalytic molecules are those which tend to increase, or catalyze, the rates of specific reactions, and enzymes are organic catalysts. Enzymes are very much more efficient than their inorganic counterparts. In the progress of the varied reactions described above, it would be surprising if some compounds with enzymatic activity were not formed. Most enzymes catalyze the reactions of substances which are unrelated to the enzyme itself. For example, lipase will split fats to give glycerine and fatty acids, or, under suitable conditions, it will catalyze the synthesis of fats from glycerine and fatty acids. But there are catalysts known which cause production of more of the catalyst itself. The duplication of the chromosomes is perhaps the best biological example. Such an enzyme is said to be autocatalytic (in the chromosomes, of course, it is the nucleic acid which behaves autocatalytically). A complex including an autocatalytic substance, then, would be a *self-reproducing* unit which would be expected to increase in abundance in the primordial seas at the expense of those materials which lacked this property. Current opinion favors a simple nucleic acid as the autocatalytic unit, but this was not included in Oparin's original hypothesis, and S. W. Fox has pointed out that the universality of nucleic acid in modern organisms does not exclude the possibility that less efficient autocatalytic systems may have characterized the earliest life.

If one adds mutability, that is, the capacity to undergo changes which can be reproduced without destroying the autocatalytic action of the molecule, he would have something like a free-living virus. It is plausible that these may have been an essential step in the transition of life. A virus such as described above might be closely analogous to a free-living gene, and indeed actual viruses have been described as "escaped genes." Until recently, it was hotly debated whether viruses were living. Like inorganic systems, they do not respire, and they can be crystallized without loss of infectivity. If a virus suspension is ultracentrifuged, it gives a sharp boundary, a characteristic of pure substances as opposed to mixtures. Further, viruses can be broken into nucleic acid and protein fractions, both of which are inactive, then recombined to reconstitute the fully infective virus. Thus, they appear to have a degree of homogeneity which is unknown among undoubted organisms. On the other hand, they subvert the metabolism of the host, and the products of this metabolism cause disease symptoms in the host. They reproduce, and they are capable of mutation. These are all characteristics of living organisms. It was mentioned above that viruses have been described as escaped genes. The genetic study of viruses has tipped the balance of opinion among virologists in favor of viruses as true organisms, for it has been proven that a virus contains a whole *system* of genes, a measure of complexity which is not conceivable except in a living organism.

A virus consists of a core of nucleic acid surrounded by a protein sheath. Mutation and growth in the primordial viruses might have resulted in the accumulation of more protein and other metabolites to form a sort of cytoplasm limited by a membrane—a cellular structure. The viruses would thus blend into bacteria. But there is a problem here. Viruses differ from bacteria not only by smaller size but more especially because viruses lack ribosomes and the whole machinery of intermediary metabolism, which all bacteria and higher organisms possess. How can this gulf be bridged? N. H. Horowitz has suggested a very plausible solution. The earliest organisms found all of their requirements dissolved in the water in which they lived, but as the organisms became more abundant, some of the less common nutrients must have become scarce. Let us suppose that an organism needs substance A, which is abundant, as are B and C, from which A can be synthesized if the appropriate enzyme is present. As long as A is abundant, presence or absence of the enzyme has no importance for the organism, and its presence would not be favored by selection. But when A becomes scarce, those organisms which have mutated to produce the enzyme will survive and multiply, while the others will fail, and the enzyme will become part of the normal equipment of the organism. But B, which is synthesizable from D and E, might also become scarce, and mutations for production of a second enzyme would then be favored. Such a process might continue until the organism had the ability to synthesize all of its requirements from the elements, as has indeed happened in the case of the green plants.

In this way, the metabolic apparatus of the cell could have been built up one step at a time. In general, only those lines which developed enzyme systems for the synthesis of food and for energy-producing reactions (respiration) could survive the depletion of the primitive stockpile of organic compounds. Some, however, survived by becoming parasitic on the more progressive organisms. Those which became parasitic before taking the first step in this process would be the viruses as we know them, while those which became parasitic at some later point in their evolution would be parasitic bacteria, or parasitic members of one of the higher groups. Their differentiation, however, takes us beyond the problem of the origin of life and well into that of biological evolution.

The first steps in Oparin's sequence have yielded to experimental attack. S. L. Miller and others have shown that, if a dilute mixture of the most common elements is sealed in a flask with a reducing atmosphere, then refluxed and subjected to electrical sparks for a prolonged period, the array of organic compounds predicted by Oparin actually is formed, including amino acids. Further, the study of viruses and primitive bacteria gives much information about the earliest stages of life, and again the data are consistent with Oparin's hypothesis. Thus it may be safely concluded that Oparin's pathway for the origin of life is a serious possibility. Further, ancient rocks have been analyzed, and traces of organic compounds have been found in rocks much older than the oldest known fossils. In one case at least, these rocks are nearly four billion years old! It is possible, of course, that these compounds are decomposition products from organisms the fossils of which have been completely destroyed, but it is at least as probable that these compounds are remnants of the prebiotic stockpile of organic compounds postulated by Oparin. Unfortunately, the step from proof of possibility—even of probability—to proof of actual historical occurrence is a long one, and one which may not be possible.

The description of the modern, scientific study of the origin of life differs from Teilhard's prediction principally in the wealth of detailed data, but in general outline, in evolutionary perspective, and in his confidence that the problem is concerned with the inherent potentialities of matter, they are identical. Or rather, this is true with respect to what Teilhard called the *without* of things, the external aspect of matter which is the usual concern of science.

But what of the *within*, the consciousness or preconsciousness, the psychic aspect of life? Because the simplest of living cells is more complex by whole orders of magnitude than the most complex of polymers, Teilhard proposed that the within, the consciousness of cells, must also be orders of magnitude more highly developed. He found his intuition verified by the fact that it is at the level of the simplest cells that the first rudiments of awareness, of consciousness, are commonly recognized, that life is unequivocally present. Is this judgment verified by the modern study of the origin of life? The theories and experiments of Oparin, Miller, Urey, and others on the origin of life are concerned exclusively with external aspects of matter, and it is difficult to find in them any implications, either positive or negative, for the within. Further, it is difficult to see how an experiment could be designed to test Teilhard's proposition.

Does this mean that Teilhard was wrong? Not at all, but it may mean that he has gone beyond the limitations of scientific method. As J. S. Haldane noted long ago, science uses only physicochemical data, and hence only physicochemical conclusions (the *without* or *exterior* in Teilhardian terms) can be expected, without prejudice to the possibility that truth may include much that is not physicochemical. Further, it is quite probable that Gödel's theorem applies here, so that, even if Teilhard were correct in regarding his theories of the within as scientifically necessary, it might not be possible to obtain rigorous proof. Finally, when scientists as brilliant and diverse as the Haldanes (J. S. and J. B. S.) and Wendell Stanley arrive at conclusions so similar to Teilhard's, it seems necessary to conclude that, if the theory of the within, the preconsciousness, of matter and of its intensification is not established by scientific methods and data, it must nonetheless be compatible with them, and it may very well be true.

In conclusion, then, the transition from nonliving matter to life was accomplished by means of biochemical evolution which blended into biological evolution. Teilhard proposed that all matter has, in addition to its without, the characteristics of which are the ordinary objects of a scientific study, a *within*, pre-life, or preconsciousness, which increases proportionately to the complexity of the matter of which it is an attribute. Because of the great gap in level of complexity between the most complex of polymers and the simplest of living cells, there is also a great increase in the psychic energy of these cells, and the rudiments of consciousness, of life as we know it, appear at the cell level. This proposition is not scientific in the sense that it does not appear to be amenable to experimental test, nonetheless, it does not appear to be inconsistent with scientific data either, and closely related ideas have appealed to first-rate scientists of quite different philosophical backgrounds. It is fair to say, then, that there is a good probability that Teilhard's proposal is correct in essence, even though some of the details (as he himself recognized) may require correction.

CHAPTER FIVE

Introduction to Organic Evolution

TEILHARD PROPOSED that all of nature—the physico-chemical world, the great array of plants and animals, and man, with all of his complex psychosocial attributes—could be understood only from an evolutionary point of view. Surely, a biologist's commentary upon this proposal should include an introduction to organic evolution, and this will be the purpose of the next four chapters. The present chapter will be devoted to the basis for Darwin's theory and to a sampling of the evidence which convinced biologists of the fact of evolution. Chapter 6 will discuss causal factors in evolution, chapter 7 will survey the historical course of evolution, and chapter 8 will review the history of the Primates and man.

Charles Darwin defined evolution as "descent with modification," closely related species resembling one another because of hereditary differences accumulated since the time of their last common ancestor. This was an ancient idea which was discussed by some of the Greek philosophers, yet it was never seriously considered by many competent biologists until 1859, when Darwin published *The Origin of Species*. Yet, within a short time of the publication of the *Origin*, most biologists were convinced. Why did Darwin succeed where so many brilliant predecessors had failed?

Darwin (figure 5.1) himself answered this question in the autobiography he wrote for his children:

I like this Photograph very much better than any other which has been taken of me.

Ch. Darwin

Figure 5.1. Photograph of Charles Robert Darwin by Margaret Julia Cameron. Under this photograph, Darwin wrote, "I like this photograph very much better than any other which has been taken of me." Reprinted courtesy of Professor R. D. Keynes and the Physiological Laboratory of Cambridge University.

The success of the *Origin* may, I think, be attributed in large part to my having long before written two condensed sketches, and to my having finally abstracted a much larger manuscript, which was itself an abstract. By this means I was enabled to select the more striking facts and conclusions. I had also, during many years followed a golden rule, namely, that whenever a published fact, a new observation or thought came across me, which was opposed to my general results, to make a memorandum of it without fail and at once; for I had found by experience that such facts and thoughts were far more apt to escape from the memory than more favourable ones. Owing to this habit, very few objections were raised against my views that I had not at least noticed and attempted to answer. (De Beer 1974:73)

I would like to present an alternative, or supplementary, explanation: Darwin succeeded because he was the first to develop a reasonable theory of how evolution could work, and he was the first to marshall a cogent array of data in support of the proposition that evolution actually had occurred.

DARWIN'S THEORY

Darwin's reasonable theory can be summarized in five points: (1) the prodigality of nature; (2) the constancy of adult populations; (3) hence, a necessary struggle for survival; (4) variation; and, hence, (5) natural selection, or the survival of the fittest. Let us discuss these points in order.

By prodigality of nature is meant the tendency of all species to reproduce in excess of the numbers which can possibly survive. A few examples will make this clear. The guinea pig, with a maximum of six young in a litter and a gestation period of seven weeks, has been a proverbial example of prodigal fertility since the publication of a short story, "Pigs Is Pigs", early in this century; nonetheless, these little rodents are slow breeders compared with many other animals. A bullfrog, for example, may spawn as many as 20,000 eggs in a season, while a codfish may spawn as many as 10 million. Even the latter, however, is unimpressive when compared with the ocean sunfish, *Mola mola*, which may spawn 300 million eggs anually! If all of these eggs were to develop, hatch, survive to maturity, and breed at the same rate, with complete survival in every generation, it would take only ten generations for the number of sunfish to exceed the estimated number of elementary particles in the visible universe (10^{79})!

The above examples were selected for high reproductive rates, yet even slow rates lead to similar results. Darwin cited the elephant as possibly the most slowly reproducing of all animals. Elephants may have a life span as long as one hundred years, with active breeding from about age thirty to ninety. They bear one young at a time, and the period of gestation is twenty months. During her long breeding life, a female probably never bears fewer than six young. Nonetheless, Darwin calculated that, if a single pair of elephants were to breed at this minimal rate, with complete survival of all the young, and if this were repeated in every succeeding generation, then the living descendants of that one pair after 750 years would number no less than 19 million! Expressing this in another way, let us make the very modest assumption that there were only 1,000 breeding pairs of elephants in the world in the year 1250, but that they and all of their descendants had reproduced ever since at the minimal rate, with complete survival of all young for the full, natural life span. We could then look forward to the year 2000 in anticipation of an elephant population of no less than 19 billion! And no room for anything else!

The prodigality of nature, which these facts illustrate, is a simple result of the fact that reproduction is a geometric process rather than an arithmetic one: that is, reproduction from generation to generation corresponds to the multiplication series 2, 4, 8, 16, 32, 64, 128, . . . rather than to the addition series 2, 4, 6, 8, 10, 12, 14, . . .

Nonetheless, the world has been swamped with neither sunfish, nor elephants, nor any other organism. Darwin observed that in any region the numbers of adults of the various species tend to remain fairly constant. This no longer appears to be true to the extent that Darwin believed. The science of ecology did not exist in his time, and techniques for the census of wild populations were still far in the future. All natural populations fluctuate over a more or less wide range. Most field biologists studying some particular species have found it so common at times that collections could be made with minimal effort, while in another season it may be so rare that collections can be made only with great difficulty. Some species show extreme fluctuations of population. Thus, the arctic hare periodically builds up to a very dense population in which "shock disease" spreads rapidly. Most of the population is decimated, and there follow several "no rabbit" years, from which the population recovers slowly at first, then explosively, until the whole cycle is repeated. The records of the Hudson's Bay Company show that these cycles have averaged 9.7 years over the past 200 years. Lemmings show similar cycles of 3 or 4 years' duration.

Most species, however, are at least partially stabilized by "population-stats" of various sorts. Territoriality of birds (and of many mammals, too) is such a mechanism. As the spring migrants arrive at the breeding grounds, the males occupy and claim a certain minimal territory, which they then defend against invasion by others of the same species (except the first female to arrive!). Other birds of the same kind do not contest the right of the first pair and their young to exclusive use of their territory. They are thus assured of an adequate food supply, and because many birds are unable to secure territories which supply the necessary breeding cover, this restricts the growth of the population. The unsuccessful birds, however, are ever ready to move in if a territory should be vacated (by the death of a territory holder, for example). V. C. Wynne-Edwards studied such population-stats deeply, and he concluded that a considerable variety of such mechanisms are important in maintaining some equilibrium between the abundance of species and their means of life.

In spite of population cycles and population-stats, the actual growth of populations always falls so far short of its potential that Darwin's argument retains its full logical force: in the presence of a great reproductive excess, a limited population is possible only if the great majority of young fail to survive to maturity and hence do not reproduce.

This brings us to the third point, that there must be a severe struggle for the means of survival, a struggle in which the great majority of contestants lose. One study of wild rodents, for example, showed that only 1 to 6 percent of those born each year survived as long as one year. And as low as this range may seem, it obviously must be very high compared with the survival rate of the ocean sunfish. Hence there must be keen competition for the means of survival.

The operation of these first three principles alone would control the numbers of living things, but it would not result in any change in their characteristics. However, variation is a universal rule of life. There is a range of variation in all species, both in trivial traits and in essential ones. One sees this in any large group of people, for they vary in so many and in such detailed traits that the individuality of each is recognizable with ease. In wild species, the range of variability may be less obvious, yet it is there. For example, a collection of field mice in a museum may seem quite uniform at a glance, but if one measures such things as total length, length of tail, length of hind foot, height of the ear above the crown, etc., the same array of variability emerges. "As alike as peas in a pod" is proverbial, but it is not factual. The peas in a pod differ obviously in size; they may differ in details of shape and color; some will germinate while others are inviable; and biochemical examination would reveal differences in concentration of particular enzymes, vitamins, and other substances. Variation, then, is a universal rule of life.

In highly competitive organisms, some of these variations must confer an advantage or a disadvantage in the struggle for the means of survival. Thus, deer with more acute senses or with greater endurance in running will have a better chance of escaping predators, while those which are less alert or slower are more likely to be taken. Thus, there is a *natural selection* whereby organisms which are less well fitted to their conditions of life tend to be eliminated, while those which are better fitted are more likely to survive and to leave progeny. The result can only be the gradual modification of species in the direction of greater adaptedness.

This argument was beautifully summarized by Darwin in the *Origin:*

> How is it that varieties, which I have called incipient species, become ultimately converted into good and distinct species, which in most cases obviously differ from each other far more than do the varieties in the same species? How do those groups of species, which constitute what are called distinct genera and which differ from each other more than do the species of the same genus, arise? All these results . . . follow from the struggle for life. Owing to this struggle, variations, however slight and from whatever cause proceeding, if they be in any degree profitable to the individuals of a species, in their infinitely complex relations to other organic beings and to their physical conditions of life, will tend to the preservation of such individuals, and will generally be inherited by the offspring. The offspring, also, will thus have a better chance of surviving, for, of the many individuals of any species which are periodically born, but a small number can survive. I have called this principle, by which each slight variation, if useful, is preserved, by the term natural selection. But the expression often used by Mr. Spencer, of the Survival of the Fittest, is more accurate, and is sometimes equally convenient. We have seen that man

by selection can certainly produce great results, and can adapt organic beings to his own uses, through the accumulation of slight but useful variations, given him by the hand of Nature. But Natural Selection . . . is a power incessantly ready for action, and is as immeasurably superior to man's feeble efforts as the works of Nature are to those of Art." (1936:51–52)

DARWIN'S EVIDENCE

Evidence for evolution is drawn from seven fields: biogeography, taxonomy or the classification of organisms, comparative anatomy and embryology, comparative physiology and biochemistry, paleontology or the study of fossil remains of past life, and genetics. A few detailed examples will be discussed to represent a vast array of data.

It was biogeography that first suggested the possibility of evolution to Darwin. As a young man, he served as naturalist aboard H.M.S. *Beagle* during a voyage around the world from 27 December 1831 to 2 October 1836. The *Beagle* sailed westward across the Atlantic, then south along the coast of South America, around the Horn, and then north to Peru. At every stop along the way, Darwin went ashore to collect flora, fauna, and geological samples. As they went south along the east coast of South America, he was struck by the progressive replacement of closely allied species one by another. But his most decisive observations came when the *Beagle* turned westward from Peru to the Galapagos Islands, an archipelago about six hundred miles off the coast of Peru. South America is a typical continent, with highly varied geological features: rugged mountains and fertile valleys, broad plains, arid lands, and swamps. It supports life in rich variety. The Galapagos Islands, by contrast, are just bits of volcanic rock thrust up out of the sea, sunscorched, and scoured by the trade winds, a most inhospitable environment. On the basis of the theory that the life of each land was created especially for it, the flora and fauna of South America and of the Galapagos would have been as different as any on earth, yet Darwin said that his collections in the islands soon struck him with their American character. The plants and animals seemed to be simply a limited sample of the South American flora and fauna, modified to adapt them to their new home.

Even within the archipelago, there was much to suggest modification of species. Thus land birds, although they may occasionally make long flights over water, are commonly stopped by a large body of water. Finches are widely distributed in the islands, but Darwin found a different species on every island, even though some of these species are rather similar. Almost all of these birds are endemics, that is, each species has a very limited distribution, commonly being found on only one island. Typical marine birds, on the other hand, are wide ranging. Of the eleven species of marine birds found in the Galapagos, however, only two are endemic.

As Darwin considered these observations, the thought occurred to him that species might not be immutable; but rather, having originated at one place, they then spread as far as they can, undergoing modification as they go, to adapt to the prevailing conditions of life; and he wrote to his friend, J. D. Hooker, that "it is like confessing a murder."

Another aspect of biogeography was the special province of Alfred Russel Wallace, a British biologist who, in 1858, sent Darwin an essay in which he proposed the same theory of the origin of species by means of natural selection which Darwin had been mulling over for twenty years. He thereby goaded Darwin into much earlier publication than would otherwise have been the case, and he also secured his place as codiscoverer. Wallace was much impressed by biogeographical studies which showed that each of the major regions of the world is characterized by a distinctive and self-consistent flora and fauna. In general, these biogeographical regions correspond to the great continental land masses, which are separated by deep and ancient

Figure 5.2. Biogeographical regions of the world. Reprinted courtesy of Willard Grant Press, from Dodson and Dodson, *Evolution: Process and Product*, 3d ed., 1984.

oceans, or by barriers of mountains or deserts. Six such biogeographical regions are generally recognized (figure 5.2): the Palearctic region, which includes Europe, Africa north of the Sahara Desert, and Asia north of the Himalayan Mountains and their eastward extension, the Ming Ling; the Nearctic region, which comprises North America southward to the southern edge of the Mexican Plateau (because of migration across the Bering Strait, these regions are faunistically less distinct than the others, and so they are often considered as a single great region, the Holarctic); the Ethiopian region, comprising African south of the Sahara Desert; the Oriental region, comprising Asia south of the Himalayan Mountains and the Ming Ling; the Neotropical region, comprising South America and Central America south of the Mexican Plateau; and the Australian region, comprising Australia and the associated islands (as in every case).

Within each of these regions, there is a characteristic flora and fauna, so that a biologically aware person might feel almost as though he were entering a different world when passing from one region to another. Thus, only in the Americas can one find opossums, although a far richer marsupial fauna characterizes Australia; tarsiers are found only in the Oriental region; there are rich cat faunas in both Oriental and Ethiopian regions, however the species are usually distinct; and the Ethiopian region includes a very rich fauna of herbivores. On the whole, the differences among the faunas of the several regions are so well marked that a zoologically informed person should be able to identify the source of a balanced collection from any of these regions.

That this should be so is readily understandable on Darwin's hypothesis: the biogeographical regions are separated by imposing barriers of great antiquity, so that migration from one region to another has been much restricted; thus, relatively few original forms evolving to abundance in each region should lead to self-consistent and rather distinct floras and faunas. Nonetheless, it must be admitted that much the same result might have followed from creation of each flora and fauna in its present locale. More persuasive is the exclusion of animals from regions to which they are well suited. Some species have highly discontinuous distributions. The alligator, for example, is found only in the Mississippi Valley of southeastern North America and in the Yangtze Valley of southeastern Asia. This distribution, which is paralleled by that of many kinds of animals and plants, seems strange at first, but it is readily understandable in Darwinian terms. Both of these areas of distribution, although so widely separated, are within the Holarctic region. During the Mesozoic era (the age of reptiles), there was a mild climate far to the north, and the continents were broadly connected across the Bering Strait region. Alligators flourished throughout this great expanse, as their fossil remains show. Then, during the Cenozoic era (the age of mammals), the great mountains of western North America were thrust up; the land level fell across the north Pacific, thus forming the Bering Strait; the climate became zonal and severe in the north; and as a result, the alligators became extinct over most of their former range, leaving only two small pockets of survival half the world apart.

Thus, the present distribution of alligators is a simple consequence of known historical events, according to Darwinian theory. Suppose, however, that alligators had been separately created in these two widely separated places. Why not alligators in the Ganges or the Nile, both of which are eminently well suited to them? While the Mississippi and Yangtze valleys are both Holarctic, the Ganges and Nile valleys are Oriental and Ethiopian, respectively. Thus, exclusion of alligators from these eminently suitable rivers is a simple consequence of the Holarctic origin of these reptiles. Such discontinuities within a biogeographic region are common, while similar discontinuities between regions are rare. Thus facts which flow harmoniously from the ev-

olutionary hypothesis are at least anomalous, if not inexplicable, under any other.

Historically, comparative anatomy has played a major
role in establishing the fact of evolution and in determining relationships among plants and animals. The key fact
is that, within any major group, a given structure appears
to be based upon a prototype which is simply varied from
subgroup to subgroup to adapt to its specific requirements,
much as a composer varies a theme in the composition of
a sonata. Figure 5.3 shows the forelimbs of four tetrapods

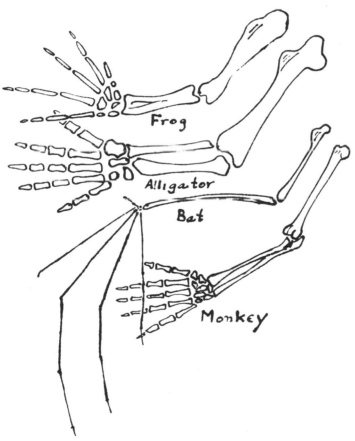

Figure 5.3. Limbs of tetrapods.

(four-legged, generally land-going vertebrates) represent-
ing three classes: a frog, an alligator, a bat, and a monkey.
In each of these, the limb is used in a very different way,
yet all are constructed upon a single plan: a long bone, the
humerus, joins the shoulder proximally and articulates with
two parallel bones, the ulna and radius, distally at the elbow; in some, the radius can rotate around the ulna, but
in the bat, the radius is reduced to a mere splint; next,
there is a cluster of small bones, the carpals or wrist bones;
and finally, the limb terminates in the metacarpals and
phalanges which form the hand. The similarities of the
limbs are so great that a person who has learned the bones
of one animal of this series can easily recognize the corresponding parts in any of the others. Adaptations to the
specific mode of life have been achieved largely by changes
of proportions among the parts. Thus, the alligator limbs
are massive, while those of the bat are much elongated and
very delicate. As important as these differences are, they
are far less striking than are the common characteristics.

Much the same sort of differentiation within unity can
be seen on a lower level among the orders of a class. Figure
5.4 shows the distal parts of the forelimbs of several different adaptive types of mammals: a tenrec (a very primitive
insectivore from Madagascar), a bat, a mole, a rhinoceros,
and a deer. The tenrec (A) has a very primitive mammalian
limb, while all of the others are specialized: the bat (B) for
flight; the mole (C) for digging, by the broad, foreshortened, shovellike form of the limb; the horse (D) for
running over hard terrain, by elongation of the limb and
the reduction and fusion of parts into a single long and
strong axis capped by a hoof rather than by a claw; the
rhinoceros (E) for bearing great weight, by the relative
shortening and thickening of parts, which are very closely
bound together; and the deer (F) by less extreme adaptations for running.

Again, all of the facts of comparative anatomy follow

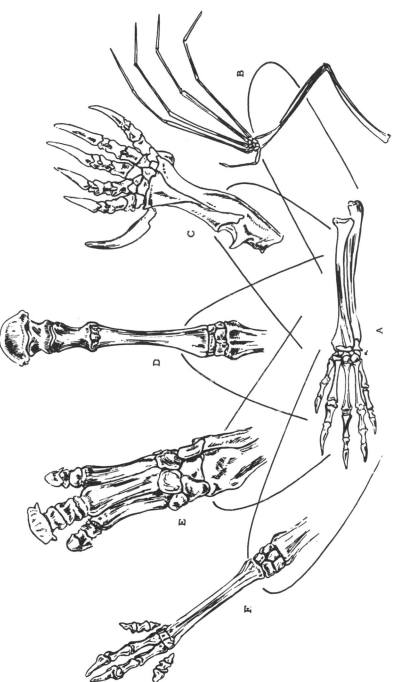

Figure 5.4. Adaptive radiation. Reprinted courtesy of Willard Grant Press, from Dodson and Dodson, *Evolution: Process and Product*, 3d ed., 1984.

necessarily from the evolutionary hypothesis of descent with modification, but they are unnecessary and anomalous under any other hypothesis.

Taxonomy also gives testimony to the fact of evolution. When Linnaeus laid the foundations of the taxonomic system, he did so under the conviction of fixity: "There are just so many species as in the beginning the Infinite Being created." However, he found it necessary to erect a hierarchy of categories in which each higher one includes those below it in the series. The most basic of these is the *species*, a single kind of organism, as a robin, a red squirrel, or a sugar maple. The many species are not all equally alike or unlike, however, but rather there are clusters of quite similar species, each species cluster being a genus. The scientific name of an organism consists of the generic name plus the specific name, as *Turdus migratorius*, the American robin, and *Acer saccharum*, the sugar maple. Linnaeus found that the genera, too, formed groups of similar ones, which he called orders. Finally, he grouped the similar orders into classes, the diverse members of which share only very fundamental characteristics. For example, the many orders of birds comprise the class Aves.

Linnaeus grouped the classes into the kingdoms Plantae and Animalia, but he found no need for intermediate categories. Modern taxonomists, however, universally use the family between genus and order, and they group classes into phyla. Every organism, then, belongs to a species, a genus, a family, an order, a class, a phylum, and a kingdom, the first being relatively small and homogeneous, the last being very broadly inclusive and heterogeneous, including as its most distant members some which seem to share little more than the essential characteristics of life. The intermediate categories become ever more inclusive in the order stated. By way of example, the complete classification of two organisms, the robin and man, follows:

Phylum Chordata	Chordata
Class Aves	Mammalia
Order Passeriformes	Primates
Family Turdidae	Hominidae
Genus *Turdus*	*Homo*
Species *migratorius*	*sapiens*

That it is possible to arrange all organisms in such a hierarchic fashion is an extraordinary fact which demands explanation. Linnaeus explained it by the archetypal theory, according to which the Creator worked from a limited series of plans, or archetypes, which were themselves classifiable as major and minor archetypes corresponding to the various taxonomic levels. The evolutionary explanation is simply that the various taxonomic categories correspond to degrees of blood relationship. Thus, members of a species differ only in minor characters, and their common ancestry is quite recent, while different species of a genus are a little less closely related, their common ancestors being a little further back, and so on up the series. Distant members of a phylum share only very fundamental characteristics, their common ancestor being in the remote past.

Thus, the very existence of the taxonomic hierarchy suggests evolution, but two more specific aspects of taxonomy will be discussed. First, when taxonomists tried to represent their conclusions by diagrams such as maps or ladders, they always failed, but they succeeded when they tried a taxonomic *tree.* Pre-Darwinian taxonomists did not understand why this should be so, yet they knew it as a matter of experience. That the parts of a real tree are related in branching fashion because of growth from the seed with branching and differentiation is a matter of observation, and the inference is strong that the taxonomic tree also owes its form to growth and differentiation from common ancestors, that is, to evolution.

A second aspect of taxonomy concerns those primitive, relatively unspecialized species which occur in most groups, perhaps as living species, perhaps only as fossils. These often share characters with species on branches of the phyletic tree other than their own. In other words, species near the branching points of the taxonomic tree show resemblances to both branches. This is exactly as expected under the evolutionary hypothesis, but it is unnecessary under any other.

Comparative biochemistry was unknown to Darwin, but it is now one of the most active areas of evolutionary science. A rapidly growing array of data may be exemplified by some data on the comparative biochemistry of DNA (deoxyribonucleic acid). The DNA molecule is central to modern biochemistry, for in it is encoded the hereditary information which tells the living cell how to make proteins, especially enzymes, and through these how to regulate the processes of life. The DNA molecule consists of a double helix of pentose (5-carbon sugar) and phosphate, joined together by organic bases, either adenine and thymine, or cytosine and guanine. Because these may be oriented in either direction, four types of bonds are possible: A-T, T-A, C-G, and G-C (figure 5.5). The sequence of the four kinds of bonds in the enormous DNA macromolecule determines the information content of the gene (the unit of heredity and biological control). The DNA complement of a single human cell is estimated to contain several billion base pairs.

A very interesting comparison of the DNAs of the various animals was published by Hoyer, McCarthy, and Bolton. They extracted DNA from a test species (for example, mouse, man, or fish). The two pentose-phosphate chains were separated by heating, then trapped in a gel so that they could not rejoin on cooling. Another animal had been given radioactive phosphorus to mark its DNA. This was similarly extracted and the strands separated by heating, but now the separated strands were sheared into small fragments, capable of diffusing through the gel (figure 5.6). Blocks of gel with the trapped, single strands of DNA from

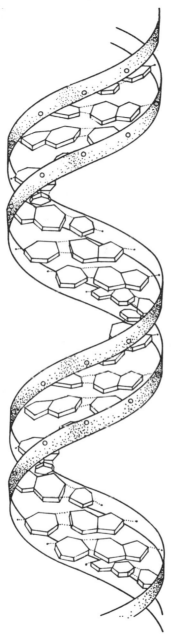

Figure 5.5. DNA, stereochemical diagram. Reprinted courtesy of Willard Grant Press, from Dodson and Dodson, *Evolution: Process and Product*, 3d ed., 1984.

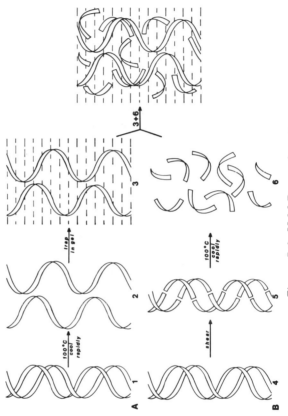

Figure 5.6. H-M-B experiment.

the test species (A) were then incubated with a solution containing the sheared fragments of DNA from the second species (B). If species A and B have any genes in common, then B fragments diffusing through the gel may meet and react with the complementary portions of the trapped strands, thus reestablishing double strands. As the B fragments were radioactively marked, the amount of radioactivity remaining in the gel blocks, after washing to remove uncombined fragments, should be proportional to the degree of genetic relationship of species A and B.

The results are summarized in table 5.1. When both samples of DNA are taken from the same species (A tested against A), only about 20–25 percent of the radioactivity is recovered, hence results between different species must be expressed as a fraction of this. Complete recovery does not occur because fragment may rejoin fragment, and complementary strands may, by chance, fail to meet even when present and uncombined. Measured in this way, members of the same order show about 20 percent relationship, while

Table 5.1. Radioactivity Recovered from Reaction of Mouse DNA and DNA of Other Species

Species B	Radioactivity Recovered (%)	Relationship of B to A (%)
Mouse	22	100
Rat	14	62
Hamster	12	53
Guinea pig	3	12
Rabbit	3	12
Human	5	21
Cow	4	16
Salmon	1.5	5
Bacterium	0.4	0
Agar lacking DNA	0.4	0

SOURCE: data of Hoyer, McCarthy, and Bolton, A molecular approach in the systematics of higher organisms, *Science* (1964) 144:959–967.

Note: Mouse DNA (species A) was trapped in agar, then allowed to react with fragments of DNA marked with radioactive phosphorous (P^{32}) from a second species (B).

members of the same phylum show around 5 percent relationship. More distant relationships fail to give positive results. It is noteworthy that even such distantly related vertebrates as fish and mammal do show a significant amount of common genetic material. The authors suggest that this may represent the genetic basis for the most fundamental vertebrate characters.

The proportionality of common segments of DNA between two species to their degree of relationship as determined by classical methods is again as easily explained by descent with modification as it is unnecessary and anomalous under any other theory.

Further examples and additional fields of evidence will not be sampled now. All concur in *suggesting* evolution with varying degrees of cogency, but most can be explained on other bases, albeit with some damage to the law of parsimony. The strongest evidence for evolution is the concurrence of so many independent probabilities. That such different disciplines as biochemistry and comparative anatomy, genetics and biogeography should all point toward the same conclusion is very difficult to attribute to coincidence. This reasoning is very much strengthened by Teilhard's proposition that all of nature, from the origin of matter through the future of man, is most consistent and coherent when considered from an evolutionary viewpoint.

Evolution, then, is one of the fundamental facts of nature.

CHAPTER SIX

Processes of Evolution

PRACTICALLY ALL of the processes of life have some bearing upon evolution, and in that sense, the entire content of biology is the subject of this chapter. In the interests of realism, priority will be given to four processes, or groups of processes, of primary importance for evolution. These are Mendelian genetics, the science of heredity; mutation, the change of genetic units or genes, clearly a special phase of genetics; natural selection; and, finally, the structure of populations.

GENETICS

The most elementary facts of Mendelian genetics will be summarized very tersely, but fuller explanations are readily available in genetics texts (see references, especially Beadle and Beadle 1966). The gene was mentioned in chapter 5 as a sequence of base pairs in the DNA molecule, in which is encoded hereditary instructions which tell the cell how to perform the vital processes. The gene was discovered over a century ago by a Silesian monk, Gregor Mendel (figure 6.1). Mendel demonstrated that these units were passed from generation to generation with mathematical regularity by the processes of sexual reproduction. His experiments proved that every organism carries a *pair* of genes for each hereditary trait, one gene of the pair being derived from each parent; that neither member of an unlike pair is

Figure 6.1. Mendel statue.

modified by their temporary association in a hybrid; that the two members of a pair separate clean into sister cells when sex cells, eggs or sperm, are formed; that eggs and sperm combine at random in fertilization; and finally, when two or more pairs of genes are followed at once, each behaves independently of the other. Collectively, these principles determine the classical Mendelian ratios.

Let us discuss an example. Pure breeding four o'clocks are available with either red or white flowers. When these two varieties are crossed, all of the hybrid plants (the F_1 generation) have pink flowers. When these were self-fertilized in an actual experiment, they yielded a progeny of 564 plants, of which 132 had red flowers, 291 pink, and 141 white. This was interpreted as one-fourth red, one-half pink, and one-fourth white, with random deviations. These data are summarized at the lefthand side of table 6.1.

Mendel's explanation is more readily apparent if the data are expressed in symbols (table 6.1, center). Let R symbolize the gene for red flowers and r that for white flowers. The original parental varieties—RR and rr—are pure-breeding because both genes of the pair are alike (homozygous). Each produces sex cells with just one of these genes. They combine to form the hybrid, Rr, and the unlike genes work together to produce *pink* flowers. When these hybrid plants produce sex cells, the genes R and r separate into sister cells, so that no "pink-determining" sex cells occur, only reds and whites. These now combine according to the laws of chance, so that the ratio of $1\ RR : 2\ Rr : 1\ rr$ results.

Notice that, in the parental generation, all of the plants were either red-flowering or white-flowering, and 50 per-

Table 6.1. A Simple Mendelian Cross in Four O'Clocks

P	red x white	RR x rr	plants red or white, genes 50% R and 50% r
F_1	pink	Rr	all plants pink, genes 50% R and 50% r
F_2	132 red : 291 pink : 141 white	$1\ RR : 2\ Rr : 1\ rr$	plants red, pink, or white, genes 50% R and 50% r

Note: R is the gene for red flowers; r, for white; P is the parental generation of pure-breeding plants; F_1 and F_2, the successive generations of progeny.

cent of the genes were R and 50 percent r. In the F_1, all of the plants were pink, but still 50 percent of the genes were R and 50 percent r. In the F_2, all three colors appear in the progeny, but the proportions of the genes remain unchanged:

$$1\,RR\ :\ 2\,R:r\ :\ 1\,rr$$
$$50\%\qquad :\qquad 50\%$$

This is a special case, for natural populations are unlikely to duplicate the ideal proportions of an experiment. In nature, one form of the gene (allele) may be very common and the other correspondingly rare; or their frequencies may be about equal; or any intermediate may occur. Regardless of the actual gene frequencies, however, the Mendelian behavior of the genes tends to keep their frequencies constant. This is a conservative factor in evolution, which is summarized as the Hardy-Weinberg law.

A common complication is the principle of dominance. In the above example, the two genes of the hybrid pair contributed equally to the character of the plant. In many cases, however, one of the alleles seems to be expressed to the exclusion of the other. Thus, in the peas which Mendel studied, tt determines dwarf growth habit, while either TT or Tt determines tall. As a result, the usual F_2 ratio of 1 TT: 2 Tt : 1 tt gives three tall plants to one dwarf, the famous 3:1 ratio.

Actual organisms, of course, have not single, isolated pairs of genes but thousands of pairs. Each pair is individually controlled by the Hardy-Weinberg law. Because of the mechanism of sexual reproduction, however, these genes are recombined in a multitude of ways. If a cross is made between organisms differing in two pairs of genes, each segregates as though the other were not there. This is shown by the fact that the F_2 ratio is 9 dominant for both traits, to 3 dominant for the first but recesssive for the second, to 3 recessive for the first but dominant for the second, to 1 recessive for both traits. This is simply the algebraic expansion of the expression $(3+1)^2$. For a trihybrid, the expression is $(3+1)^3 = 27+9+9+9+3+3+3+1$. The complexity of segregation increases rapidly as the number of pairs of unlike genes increases. The variability which is based upon such recombination is immense, and it provides an important part of the substrate of natural selection.

An important restriction on the freedom of recombination is the fact that the genes are not all independent: rather, they are part of the chromosomes. These are microscopic bodies in the cell nucleus which show perfectly regular behavior in cell division and in sexual reproduction, paralleling that of the genes in every detail. Genes typically number in the thousands, while chromosomes are few: four pairs in the fruit fly, ten in maize, twenty in the mouse, twenty-three in man. Hence, there must be many genes in each chromosome. This provides a damper on the rate of recombination of genes, because all of the genes of one chromosome will tend to be inherited as a block. It is only a damper, however, for exchanges between members of a pair of chromosomes do occur with some difficulty. It is called crossing over, while the association of genes in a chromosome is called linkage.

Mendelian genetics thus tends to keep the proportions of genes constant, but it continually reshuffles them into different combinations and thus provides a rich store of variability to be tested by natural selection.

Quantitative inheritance, or the inheritance of those traits which must be defined by measurement, has especial importance for evolution. Examples include size, proportions of parts, rate of production of an enzyme, and concentration of a protein. The genes which influence these traits are inherited in the usual way, but swarms of pairs of genes collaborate to determine each character. The effect of each gene is small, so that variation in a heterozygous population appears to be continuous. Dominance is often lacking, so there may be a simple additive effect of the genes present. Because of these characteristics, quantitative inheritance must be studied by statistical methods. Quantitative inheritance is particularly important for evolution because differences between related species are often based largely upon quantitative traits.

MUTATION

Mutation is the major source of evolutionary variability. Mutation may be defined as a sudden change in a gene, which is then inherited with the same regularity as was the original gene. Evolution deals with two classes of mutations, point mutations and chromosomal mutations. Point mutations are those which are not accompanied by any visible change in the chromosomes, and they were formerly defined as chemical changes in a single gene. It is now known that they are changes in the base sequence of the DNA of a limited part of the chromosome. Chromosomal mutations may involve changes in the architecture of the chromosomes or changes in the number of chromosomes. The former may be visible under the microscope if they are sufficiently large.

Changes of chromosome number are of several types, but one of these, polyploidy, is of especial interest. In polyploidy, whole sets of chromosomes are duplicated. This has been a major factor in plant evolution, and it is by no means unknown among animals, although it is less common. Much the most common type of polyploidy is tetraploidy, in which four basic chromosome sets are present. They may all be derived from the same source, but more commonly they are allotetraploids, derived by hybridization of two closely related species to form a sterile hybrid, which is then made fertile by doubling all of the chromosomes. For example, the hemp nettle, *Galeopsis tetrahit*, has sixteen pairs of chromosomes. Because other members of the genus have only eight pairs, A. Müntzing suspected that G. *tetrahit* might be a natural tetraploid. On the basis of their morphology, he thought that it was most probably derived from two of the eight-chromosome species, G. *pubescens* and G. *speciosa*. When he crossed the two species, a sterile hybrid was obtained, but they did produce a few viable gametes. Out of many trials, a single F_2 plant was obtained, and this proved to be a triploid, with two sets of chromosomes from the *speciosa* parent and only one from *pubescens*. This hybrid was then crossed to pure G. *pubescens*, and again a single viable offspring was obtained. This plant was tetraploid, with two sets of chromosomes from each of the parent species. It resembled natural G. *tetrahit* and was fully fertile in crosses with the latter but sterile in crosses to both of the parent species. It is therefore fair to say that Müntzing duplicated the feat of nature in synthesizing this species. This is a case of directly demonstrated evolution, and as such it has especial importance.

Mutations occur at measurable rates, varying from several percent of gametes to one in several million gametes. Rates vary from species to species, and even from gene to gene within a species, but a good overall average is one mutation per gene per 100,000 gametes. Some mutations, like white eyes in the fruit fly, are very common, while others are so rare that they are known only from a single occurrence. Yet all mutations are random in the sense that the great majority of mutations are harmful in the conditions under which they occur. Clearly, the environment does not induce mutations which are adaptive to that environment. Adaptation results from selection of the rare fortunate mutation from a vast array.

Biologists who have not thought through the consequences of the ordinary mutation rates sometimes doubt that so slow a phenomenon could provide a basis for the enormous range of diversity which is the result of evolution. Let us therefore consider a detailed example. A typical vertebrate such as a codfish may have on the order of

20,000 genes. Each of these has its own probability of mutation, but their average is on the order of 1/100,000 gametes per gene. As their separate probabilities may be *added* to get the probability that some gene—any gene—will mutate, the overall probability is one in five that any particular gamete will carry some new mutation. Now a codfish spawns in excess of 10 million eggs, so about 2 million of these may be expected to carry one or more newly mutated genes. Now, let us add the plausible but gratuitous assumption that only 1 mutation in 10,000 is potentially valuable to the species. This would still mean that in the spawn of a single codfish there would be as many as 200 eggs in which mutation had produced alleles of value to the species in its evolution—that is, in its continual adaptation to the changing conditions of life. It *is* plausible, then, that even so slow a process as mutation may produce enough hereditary variability to meet the requirements of evolution.

In the above example, the principal variables are the number of genes, the average mutation rate per gene, and the rate of reproduction. The number of genes is perhaps near maximal, but the other two may be either higher or lower. The example was selected as a favorable one for present purposes, but even a much less favorable one would still support the argument that the actual mutation rates are sufficient to provide the variability needed for evolution.

NATURAL SELECTION

Dandelions, *Taraxacum officinale*, from the Crimea, Leningrad, and Archangel were grown in experimental plots at Leningrad. Thus, the plants were adapted to temperate, subarctic, and arctic climates, respectively. They were planted in mixed plots at Leningrad at densities of every three centimeters or every eighteen centimeters. At the lower density, about 60 percent of the Crimean plants survived, but at the higher density (and hence more intense competition and selection) its survival rate plummeted to 1 percent. At the higher density, the Archangel strain did better than did the Leningrad strain (70 percent as against 11 percent), but at low density (which is more typical of natural growing conditions), there was a small but significant margin in favor of the local variety (96 percent as against 88 percent). These data show that differences between populations of the same species do result in differential survival when a mixed population is exposed to identical conditions. Second, they show that selection need not be an all-or-none phenomenon, but that it may work by the statistical transformation of populations.

An interesting group of cases in wild populations revolves around the introduction of insecticides—a severe selective force from the viewpoint of the insects. To combat the scale insects which attack citrus trees a tent is placed over the tree and fumigated with hydrocyanic acid. But in each of three species of scale insects, cyanide-resistant varieties have arisen and have rapidly replaced the original, cyanide-sensitive strains. A similar case has occurred with respect to DDT poisoning. When DDT first came into general use in 1945, it gave promise of being an almost perfect insecticide for the control of household pests, such as flies. Soon, however, DDT-resistant strains began to appear. Under the strong selective force of DDT campaigns, these resistant strains soon became well established, and in many localities they have largely replaced the sensitive flies.

The bridge between generations is, of course, sexual reproduction, and all agencies of natural selection act, directly or indirectly, by restricting access to the bridge or by narrowing the bridge itself. Reproductive efficiency is the test of the selective advantage of a species. It is important to add, however, that the actual number of young produced is less important than the number which survive to maturity to repeat the cycle.

Natural selection, then, is now an established fact of nature, demonstrated by experiment and by statistical study of natural populations. It is, as Darwin said, "a power incessantly ready for action, and is as immeasurably superior to man's feeble efforts as the works of nature are to those of Art."

POPULATION STRUCTURE

Finally, population structure is also a major factor in evolution. A typical species is distributed over a wide area, embracing quite different conditions. Thus, the deer mouse, *Peromyscus maniculatus,* ranges over most of the United States and considerable parts of Canada and Mexico. In this enormous area, some populations live on mountains and others on prairies. Some live on the shores of the Great Lakes, and others on the deserts of the Southwest. Some must adapt to the rigors of the Canadian winter, while others never know frost. It is obvious that the characteristics which adapt the species to such different habitats must be quite unlike. Hence natural selection will favor different alleles in different regions, and so recognizable geographic races, the subspecies, are formed.

Even the subspecies, however, may be widely distributed and very abundant. Each is, however, restricted by its ecological requirements to limited areas within its total range. The result is a checkerboard of moderate-sized mouse communities, ranging up to a few thousand mice. These are the real breeding populations, within which there is free exchange of genes. A considerable but more limited exchange occurs between neighboring local populations of a subspecies because of occasional migration of individuals. Finally, wherever subspecies meet, there is a certain amount of interbreeding, so that a slow exchange of genes occurs. This type of population structure is typical of wild species, and the mathematical studies of S. Wright show that this is also the optimal type of population structure for the effectiveness of natural selection.

This process has been tested and verified experimentally. The supposition that the same processes, continued over long reaches of time, would produce the more profound differentiation of species, genera, and even the highest categories is most attractive, but it is unproven, and some students of evolution have proposed various mechanisms by which it might be accelerated. The most disputed of these is R. B. Goldschmidt's suggestion of *systemic mutations*, which would have their primary effects on early embryonic processes, thus leading to profound modification of the adult. He believed that one or a few such mutations might form a new species rapidly. This would then be put to the test of natural selection at once, and, if successful, it would then be modified and diversified by the slower process already described. Again, Wright has suggested that, if selection pressure and predominant direction of mutation should happen to coincide, it might result in quite rapid evolution. Also, major steps in evolution may be aided by strong selection pressures. For example, when Devonian fishes first came out on dry land and gave rise to the Amphibia, they were rather poorly adapted to life on land, yet they were less well adapted to life in water than were their less progressive cousins. An enormous selective pressure must have favored either completion of the transition or return to the water. Again, when related species compete in the same area, they often become more strongly divergent than are the same species in areas where they occur separately. It is evident that selection favors differentiation because it places them in different ecological niches, thus reducing competition and so permitting survival of a greater number of individuals in the same area. W. L. Brown, Jr., and E. O. Wilson have studied this phenomenon extensively, and they call it character displacement. Some or all of these accelerating mechanisms probably supplement the more universal evolutionary processes discussed above.

A special aspect of selection in relation to population size deserves mention. The basic processes of heredity are chance processes, and therefore they are subject to sampling errors. A father with a normal Y chromosome may have only daughters. In a large population, such sampling errors in one part tend to cancel those in another part, but in very small populations, sampling errors may be decisive. A valuable gene may be irretrievable lost simply because it is discarded in a polar body or because it is carried by some of that vast majority of sperm which do not fertilize eggs. A harmful gene may become abundant, even being fixed at 100 percent, by similar accidents of sampling. Because such changes are independent of natural selection, permanently small populations tend to be rather badly adapted.

More important, however, typical populations are sometimes subject to severe fluctuations. Field biologists are all familiar with the bad year, when normally abundant species can be found only with great difficulty. A rather dramatic example is that of the arctic hare, which was discussed in chapter 5. Such minimal populations result from adverse forces which may be so severe as to be unselective, and hence chance will play a larger than normal role in determining the genetic makeup of these bottleneck populations. And because the larger population of future years will necessarily be derived from this, such bottleneck populations comprise one of the hazards of evolution.

In summary, mutation is the primary source of evolutionary variability, and this produces an array of alleles which is continually reshuffled into a great assortment of genotypes by the mechanism of sexual reproduction. These are then tested by natural selection, with the result that organisms with more advantageous genotypes tend to survive and leave offspring a little more often than do those with less advantageous genotypes. With the great numbers of individuals and the long reaches of time concerned, even a very small selective advantage may be significant. Natural species commonly total immense numbers, but these do not ordinarily comprise one great breeding population. Rather, they are broken up into a series of geographically replacing subspecies, each of which is more or less isolated from the others, although they generally interbreed where their ranges overlap. Within a subspecies, the ecological requirements of the organisms generally break it up into more or less separated local populations of a few hundred to a few thousand individuals. These are the actual breeding populations. Such a hierarchic population structure has been shown to enhance the effectiveness of natural selection.

CHAPTER SEVEN

The Deployment of the Living World

IN CHAPTER FOUR we reviewed the problem of the origin of life and saw the establishment of the viruses and bacteria. As the primitive stockpile of organic compounds dwindled, one of the most critical problems facing all organisms was that of a source of energy: how to obtain and metabolize energy-rich compounds. Living bacteria draw upon several different chemical sources of energy, including oxidation of compounds of nitrogen, sulfur, and iron. Fossil deposits show that these reactions were exploited in very remote times. Much the most important of the energy-fixing reactions, however, is photosynthesis with the release of oxygen, a reaction which developed in the blue-green bacteria (often called blue-green algae). The chlorophyll of these organisms is the same as that of plants. The energy of sunlight is used for the synthesis of sugar, with chlorophyll as a catalyst, and energy is stored at more than three times the rate of the best of the chemotrophic reactions mentioned above.

The great development of the higher forms of life is based in part upon the prodigious stores of energy-rich compounds which have thus been made available to organisms. In the earliest organisms (and in those of their descendants which have remained at the same level), this energy was released by anaerobic oxidative reactions. The development of more efficient aerobic metabolism was also made possible by the blue-green bacteria, for the photosynthetic reaction releases six molecules of oxygen for every molecule of sugar synthesized. It will be recalled that the primitive earth had a reducing atmosphere, but once the blue-green bacteria appeared, the change to an oxidizing atmosphere was underway. Fossils of these blue-greens are known which are more than two billion years old, and they may well be more than three billion years old. The accumulation of oxygen was extremely slow, and it probably required most of the history of the earth to accumulate enough to permit the development of organisms with intensive aerobic metabolism. These suddenly appear in the fossil record in profusion at the beginning of the Cambrian period, some 600 million years ago. Until recently, it was thought that these were the product of a billion years or more of slow diversification into the many invertebrate types and that earlier fossils were unknown because there were few hard parts which would be readily fossilized and because there had been much destruction of such fossils as were formed. It now appears more likely that it was only in late pre-Cambrian time that the oxygen content of the atmosphere became high enough to support complex organisms with intensive aerobic metabolism. Once that condition was met, however, they evolved with almost explosive rapidity.

Like many of the bacteria of today, the earliest organisms were anaerobic, and the addition of oxygen to the atmosphere must have been toxic to them, as it is to anaerobic bacteria today. Some survived by growing in habitats which were protected from air, but others developed reactions to bind the oxygen, thus detoxifying it. From here, it was but a short step to the more efficient aerobic metabolism.

All of the organisms discussed thus far—viruses and bacteria, including blue-greens—share certain primitive traits in which they contrast to all higher organisms. Thus, the chromosome of these organisms is mainly DNA, with little protein associated, whereas the chromosomes of all higher organisms consist of DNA complexed with much protein. In all of the higher organisms, the chromosomes are contained in a nucleus which is separated from the cytoplasm by a membrane, but in these primitive organisms there is no distinct nucleus. For this reason, they are called *procaryotes* (prenuclear organisms), while the higher organisms are called *eucaryotes* (true nuclear organisms). Eucaryote cells divide by a complex process called mitosis, while procaryotes divide in a much simpler way. Further, even among the simplest of eucaryotes, sexual reproduction is common, but it does not occur among the procaryotes. There are also cytoplasmic differences between the procaryotes and the eucaryotes. The former have no endoplasmic reticulum, and their ribosomes are free in the cytoplasm, whereas the latter have a complex endoplasmic reticulum (visible only with the electron microscope) to which their ribosomes are generally bound. Further, eucaryotes have a series of organelles (subcellular structures of special function) which are lacking in all procaryotes. First, there are mitochondria, granular or elongate bodies of complex structure which contain DNA and serve as centers of aerobic metabolism. Second, there is a whole series of structures—cilia and flagella (hairlike motile processes) with basal granules, the centrioles, which serve as centers for mitotic division, and the centromeres by which the chromosomes are moved—which have a cylindrical structure with nine pairs of filaments around the circumference and two in the center. These nine-plus-two organelles also have their own DNA. Third, in the blue-green bacteria, the chlorophyll is diffused through the cytoplasm, but in all photosynthetic eucaryotes (plants), it is contained in discrete bodies, the plastids or chloroplasts. Again, these have their own DNA. Finally, there are significant biochemical differences between procaryotes and eucaryotes, differences which will not be summarized here but which may be found in Cohen's review (1970).

All in all, the gulf between the procaryotes and the eucaryotes is an extraordinarily broad one. Before these divisive features were well understood, it was common to assign the procaryotes to the plant kingdom. It now appears, however, that the distinction between procaryote and eucaryote is more profound than that between plant and animal. Accordingly, it is necessary to place them in a kingdom apart, the kingdom Mychota or Monera (see Dodson 1971 and 1979, Margulis 1967 and 1971, and Whittaker 1970 for detailed discussions of this problem).

There would seem to be no source other than the procaryotes from which the eucaryotes might have been derived, but how might the great chasm which separates them have been bridged? The most plausible theory is one proposed by Margulis, who has suggested that the eucaryote cell is in fact a symbiotic association of a series of originally independent procaryotes. The starting point would be a relatively large, amoeboid procaryote which lived by ingesting other procaryotes. It first ingested some aerobic procaryotes which were not digested but continued to live symbiotically within the host cell, a phenomenon for which there are many known examples. These symbiotic aerobes then conferred upon the host cell the advantages of aerobic respiration, and they became integrated into the host cell as mitochondria. Next, this neo-aerobic procaryote ingested flagellate procaryotes with the nine-plus-two structure, and these were integrated first as flagella or cilia, then later by loss of parts as other nine-plus-two organelles. It was now possible to evolve typical nuclear structure, mitotic division, and sexual reproduction. Such a cell was really a primitive eucaryote, essentially a protozoan, or one-celled animal. Some of these ingested blue-green bacteria, which became integrated as plastids, and thus they became green plants. The three great kingdoms of organisms—Mychota, Animalia, and Plantae—were then all present. This basic division of the world of life into three great kingdoms is discussed in the references cited above, especially Dodson (1971).

As the present work is concerned primarily with man, the plant kingdom will be followed no further, but the main outlines of the animal kingdom should be sketched. At the outset, I would like to quote the late Libbie H. Hyman, one of the most learned of zoologists: "The exact steps in the evolution of the various grades of invertebrate structure are not and presumably never can be known. Statements about them are inferred from anatomical and embryological evidence and in no case should be regarded as established facts" (1940:255).

The Protozoa—single-cell animals—soon diversified into many types which fanned out into a variety of species, genera, families, orders, and classes. Today, one would even add phyla to the series, for the Society of Protozoologists as of 1980 has considered the Protozoa to be a subkingdom comprising no fewer than seven phyla. These exploit a variety of free-living and parasitic ecological niches. This tendency of successful groups to fan out into all available adaptive niches is called *adaptive radiation,* and it is one of the most universal of evolutionary phenomena. Teilhard liked to refer to the stem groups from which such radiations arose as *peduncles,* and to their deployment into many subtypes, their adaptive radiations, as *verticils.* In Darwinian terms, adaptive radiation occurs because a wide variety of mutations is constantly occurring in all species. Most of these are undesirable mutations whose prospective fate is elimination by natural selection. The occasional hopeful mutation is maintained and is constantly reshuffled with the genes already existing into a broad spectrum of variability, testing all facets of its habitat. Whenever a type is formed which succeeds in an area previously closed to the group, it expands and becomes established. Thus, the verticils expand.

The classes of Protozoa are based upon their locomotor organelles. (The new classification is disregarded here because it is too complex for meaningful presentation in a brief and nontechnical introduction.) Only two classes will be mentioned here, as it is these which have been most seriously discussed as probable sources of the Metazoa, the multicellular animals. The class Mastigophora comprises protozoans which swim by means of a flagellum, a long, hairlike process which whips about in the water to propel the animal. A significant feature of many of these flagellates is their tendency to form colonies of many individuals. The larger colonies may show some division of labor, and it is highly suggestive that Metazoa may have arisen by integration of such colonies.

Members of the class Ciliata swim by the coordinated beat of large numbers of short, hairlike processes, the cilia. These are the most complex of protozoans, having organelles which simulate whole organ systems of metazoans. Further, a typical ciliate has *two* nuclei, a micronucleus, which is the true genetic nucleus, and a macronucleus, which controls metabolic functions. It has been suggested that metazoans arose from ciliates by the multiplication of nuclei and subdivision of the body cells.

THE LOWER METAZOA

The simplest sponges are closely similar to some colonial flagellates, and it is almost certain that they were derived from flagellates. Nor have they progressed much beyond them, for sponges are at the *cellular* level of construction in the sense that each cell has a degree of autonomy not found in other Metazoa. The cells are organized neither into tissues nor into organs. As there is no nervous system, coordination within the sponge is minimal. Finally, they have given rise to no further groups, so sponges seem to be an evolutionary blind alley.

Several groups at the base of the animal kingdom are organized at the tissue level of construction—that is, cells are organized into coordinated tissues, but there are no or-

gans. The most important of these is the phylum Coelenterata (figure 7.1), comprising hydroids, jellyfishes, ane-
mones, corals, and their allies. This may not be the group
from which the Metazoa arose—there is no assurance that
that stem group is still extant—but almost certainly the
higher Metazoa passed through a stage of development
which was closely comparable to present coelenterates,
consisting of only two cell layers, an outer ectoderm and an
inner entoderm (gastrula-type construction). It is possible
that a very minor group at this grade of construction, the

Figure 7.1. Representative coelenterates. A, a jellyfish; B, a colonial hy-
droid; C, a hydromedusa; D, an anemone; and E, a coral.

Mesozoa (figure 7.2), are little-changed descendants of the common ancestor of all of the higher Metazoa. They are closely similar to coelenterate larvae.

The next advance was the formation of the third cell layer, the mesoderm, and of organs. The organ level of construction is represented by all animals above the coelenter-

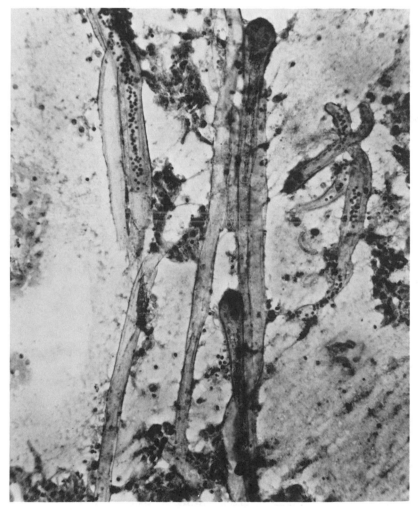

Figure 7.2. Mesozoans.

ates, and all of these are basically bilaterally symmetrical, again in contrast to the coelenterates, which are radially symmetrical. The most primitive of extant phyla at this level of construction is the phylum Platyhelminthes, the flatworms. They are morphologically very simple in most respects, and they have often been discussed as though they were but little changed from a remote ancestor which gave rise to all of the higher phyla. The flatworms (figure 7.3)

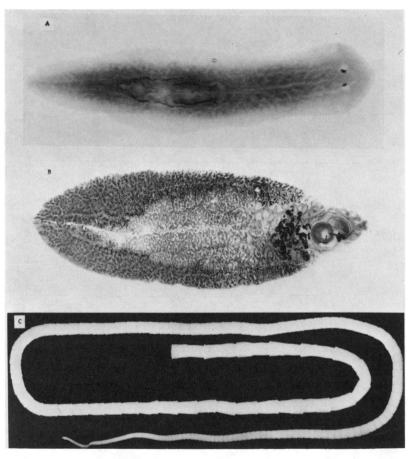

Figure 7.3. Representative platyhelminths. A, planaria; B, a liver fluke; and C, a tapeworm.

do, indeed, include the most primitive of extant bilaterally symmetrical metazoans, yet there are some objections to this viewpoint. Flatworms as we know them have a very long history, and they have produced some highly specialized forms, such as the tapeworms. In all of them, the reproductive system has become extraordinarily complex. Several more phyla at the same grade of construction demonstrate that a considerable variety is possible at this level, but only one of these, the Nematoda (figure 7.4), has achieved any great importance in the world of life. It seems probable that, in remote pre-Cambrian time, there may have been a phylum of still more primitive worms from which the phylum Platyhelminthes *and* the lines leading to the higher phyla were derived. Quite possibly, that unknown phylum may have been closely allied to the Mesozoa. The history of the Metazoa is summarized in table 7.1.

How these primitive metazoans were derived from protozoans is an unsolved problem. Hyman, a lifelong student of the flatworms, leaned toward a flagellate-coelenterate hypothesis; while J. Hadzi, a lifelong student of the coelenterates, was strongly committed to a ciliate-flatworm theory. It is at least plausible that each was right in excluding the group he knew best. The Mesozoa are an extraordinarily simple group whose structure approximates that of coelenterate larvae. It may well be that they are but little changed descendants of a remote pre-Cambrian group which gave rise to coelenterates, to flatworms, and to the more progressive groups.

COELOMATES

The next major advance was the formation of a coelom, or body cavity within the mesoderm, in which the major organs are contained. This is characteristic of all of the higher phyla, although in the adults of some groups the

Table 7.1. The Geological Timetable

Era	Period	Epoch	Duration in millions of years	Millions of years from beginning to present	Comments
Cenozoic (Age of Mammals)	Quaternary (Age of Man)	Recent	0.011	0.011	Man the dominant animal
		Pleistocene (Glacial Age)	2–3	2–3	Australopithecines, H. ere tus, then H. sapiens
	Tertiary (Age of Lower Mammals)	Pliocene	3	5	Primates evolving; apes brachiating; dryopithecin abundant and widespread early australopithecines
		Miocene	17	22	Mammals at peak; rich an thropoid fauna, especially dryopithecines, prebrachi tors, Oreopithecus
		Oligocene	12	34	First anthropoids, includi all 3 hominoid families; forerunners of many mod ern genera of mammals; e tinction of archaic mamm
		Eocene	24	58	Placental mammals diver- sify; lemurs and tarsiers i the fossil record
		Paleocene	5	63	Archaic mammals diversi early primates or primate like mammals present
Mesozoic (Age of Reptiles; Secondary)	Cretaceous		72	135	Dinosaurs at peak, then b come extinct; first modern birds; archaic mammals
	Jurassic		45	180	First birds; dinosaurs larg and varied; insectivorous mammals; first flowering plants
	Triassic		49	230	First dinosaurs; primitive mammals; gymnosperms the dominant plants

Era	Period	Epoch	Duration in millions of years	Millions of years from beginning to present	Comments
eozoic ge of chaic e)	Permian		50	280	Mammallike reptiles evolve; modern insects; much extinction
	Pennsylvanian (Upper Carboniferous)		25	305	Reptiles arise; insects common; forests of seed ferns and gymnosperms
	Mississippian (Lower Carboniferous)		40	345	Amphibians spreading and diversifying; sharks abundant; sea lilies at peak
	Devonian		60	405	First amphibians; sharks the dominant fishes; forests of primitive land plants
	Silurian		20	425	Fish diversifying; first insects; first fossils of land plants
	Ordovician		75	500	First fishes; corals and trilobites abundant; molluscs diversifying
	Cambrian		100	600	Most phyla of invertebrates appear in fossil record; trilobites and brachiopods prominent; plants limited to marine algae
cambrian*			3,900	4,500	No life at first; then fossil bacteria and blue-green algae appear; late in Precambrian, a variety of marine invertebrates appear

URCE: Simplified from Dodson and Dodson, *Evolution: Process and Product,* 3d ed. (Boston: llard Grant Press, 1984).

*For present purposes, it is not worthwhile to subdivide the Precambrian, yet it includes out 86 percent of all terrestrial time up to the present.

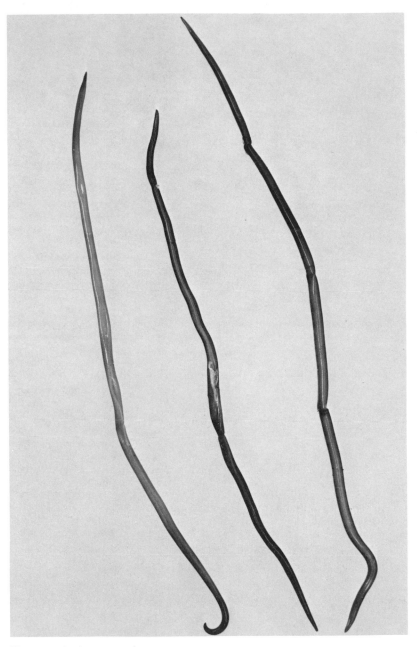

Figure 7.4. A nematode.

coelom has regressed. There are two major lines of descent among the higher phyla, characterized by different methods of formation of the coelom as well as by a series of other embryological differences. One of these lines includes an array of minor groups, then culminates in three of the major phyla of the animal kingdom, the Mollusca (figure 7.5), the Annelida (figure 7.6), and the Arthropoda

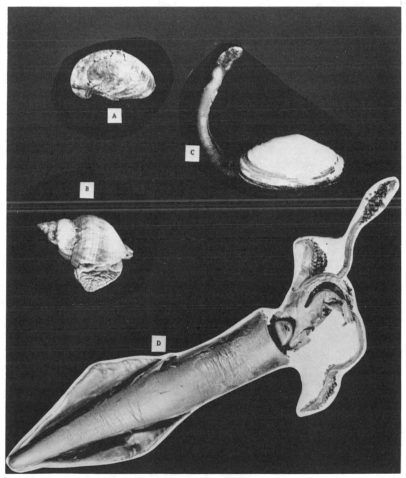

Figure 7.5. Representative molluscs. A, a slipper shell; B, a marine snail; C, a clam; and D, a squid.

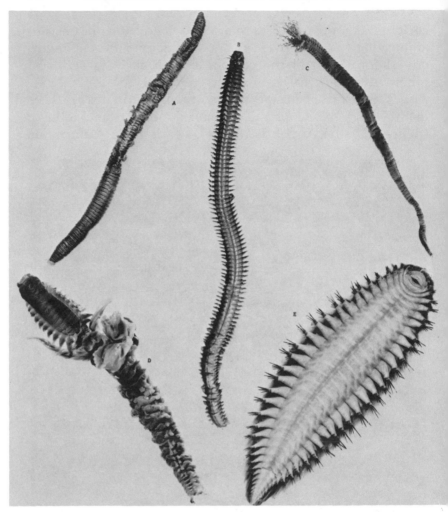

Figure 7.6. Representative annelids. A, *Arenicola;* B, *Nereis;* C, *Amphitrite;* D, *Chaetopterus;* and E, *Aphrodite.*

(figure 7.7). An impressive set of embryological traits unites this diverse assemblage. In all of them, cleavage is spiral, that is, the early divisions of the egg alternate in such a way that the cells overlap like bricks in a building. Further, cleavage is determinate, meaning that each cell of the early embryo has a fixed fate, so that removal of a specified

Figure 7.7. Representative arthropods. A, a horseshoe crab; B, a centipede; C, a beetle; D, a barnacle; E, a fiddler crab; and F, a spider.

cell results in a larva deficient in certain structures. Mesoderm, the middle embryonic layer from which many important structures are formed, is formed from stem cells the growth of which fills the space between the ectoderm and the entoderm, and the coelom is formed by the splitting of this layer. The blastopore, or embryonic mouth, forms the mouth of the adult, and hence this great array of animal groups is referred to as the protostomes. Finally, a very simple type of larva, the trochophore (figure 7.8), which swims by means of bands of cilia, is very widespread in this line of descent. Because of the enormous numbers of species and of individuals in the Arthropoda, including as it does the Crustacea and the Insecta, the protostomes form a large part of the total bulk of animal life.

Only a few phyla comprise the second, or deutero-

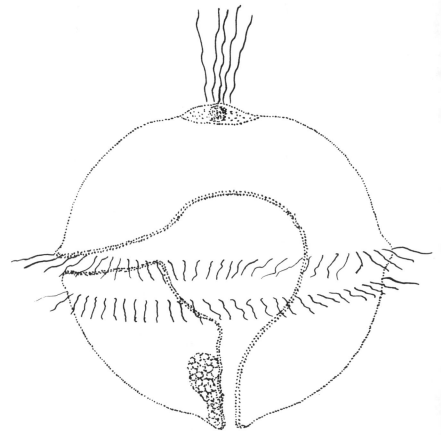

Figure 7.8. Trochophore larva.

stome, line of descent, but this line culminates in the great phylum Chordata, which includes a large portion of the dominant animals of the world and the only one which studies the others and himself, the only one which knows that he has a history. In addition to the Chordata, this line includes the phylum Echinodermata (figure 7.9), the sea stars and their allies, and several minor, wormlike phyla. The characters which unite them contrast to those of the protostomes. Cleavage is neither spiral nor determinate; mesoderm and coelom are formed at once as outpocketings of the embryonic gut; the blastopore of the embryo may become the anus of the adult, and a new mouth is formed, hence they are called deuterostomes. Finally, there is no larval type common to this assemblage.

The evolution of the phylum Chordata has been entirely consistent with that of the rest of the animal kingdom. It has been much disputed from which group of lower animals the chordates may have arisen, and it cannot be said that the question is settled yet. Unlikely as it may seem at first consideration, the balance of evidence favors the echinoderms. Echinoderms and chordates agree in all of the fundamental deuterostome characters. While the radial symmetry of echinoderms contrasts jarringly to the bilateral symmetry of chordates, still echinoderms have larvae which are bilaterally symmetrical, and it is almost certain that they were derived from bilaterally symmetrical ancestors. Further, the larvae of some echinoderms agree in detail with those of hemichordates, a small group of marine invertebrates which are closely allied to the chordates and are classified as chordates by some zoologists. There are also biochemical links between the echinoderms and the chordates. It is probable that a bilaterally symmetrical deuterostome of late pre-Cambrian time gave rise to the aberrant echinoderms, the more typical hemichordates, and the very progressive chordates.

The early adaptive radiation of the chordates resulted in three subphyla, of which only one, the Vertebrata, will

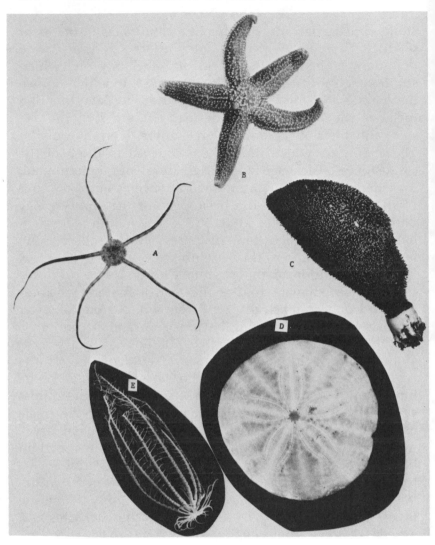

Figure 7.9. Representative echinoderms. A, a brittle star; B, a sea star; C, a sea cucumber; D, a sand dollar; and E, a sea lily.

be discussed here. These are the animals with backbones. They were first represented in the fossil record over 400 million years ago by the ostracoderms, small, armored fishes which, like their unarmored descendants today, the lampreys, lacked both jaws and paired fins. The expansion of the vertebrates proceeded by a series of adaptive radiations. A first series of radiations filled the waters of the world (figure 7.10). The diversification of the ostracoderms included the formation of the placoderms, a highly varied array of fishes which represented a series of natural experiments in the formation of jaws and paired fins. Early in their adaptive radiation, the fresh water placoderms produced the bony fishes (class Osteichthyes), while marine placoderms gave rise to the sharks (class Chondrichthyes). The latter are an only moderately varied class. Soon after their origin, they displaced the placoderms as the dominant fishes of the seas, only to yield this position to bony fishes, which had invaded salt water. The Chondrichthyes have since remained a moderately important group, while the placoderms have long since become extinct.

The adaptive radiation of the bony fishes, on the other hand, produced a startling variety, including two subclasses and a very large number of orders which collectively dominate the waters of the world. Early fishes commonly had lungs, that is, the last gill pouch did not break through to the outside but remained as a pair of blind pouches from which air could be respired. One order of lung fishes, the Crossopterygii, had a pattern of skull bones similar to that of the Amphibia, and the pattern of limb bones was also similar to that of the limbs of primitive amphibians (the dichotomous pattern, in which a single proximal bone, the humerus, is followed by parallel radius and ulna, with a similar pattern in the hind limb). Some fossils can be assigned to one group or the other (e.g., Crossoptergii or Amphibia) only with difficulty and with some uncertainty, and it is clear that the Amphibia arose from Crossoptergian ancestors.

With the advent of the Amphibia, a new wave of adaptive radiations began, one which filled the lands with vertebrate life. The amphibians themselves have never been dominant animals in the ecological web, but they soon gave

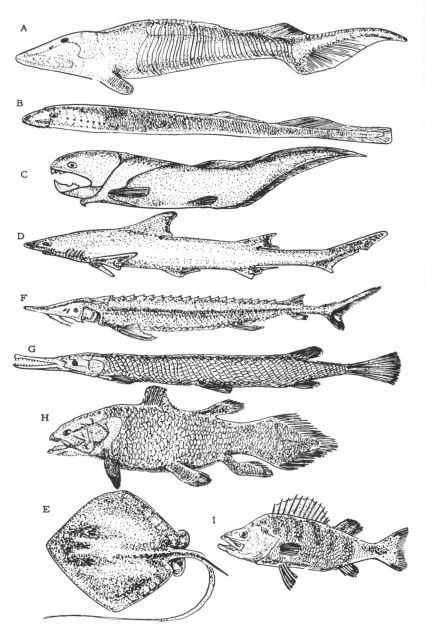

Figure 7.10. Representative fishes. A, an ostracoderm; B, a lamprey; C, a placoderm; D, a shark; E, a ray; F, a sturgeon; G, a garpike; H, the living crossopterygian; and I, a teleost. Reprinted courtesy of Willard Grant Press, from Dodson and Dodson, *Evolution: Process and Product*, 3d ed., 1984.

rise to the reptiles, which adapted to a wide variety of terrestrial and some aquatic niches. At the height of their development in the Mesozoic era (the age of the great reptiles), they comprised no less than sixteen orders which were adapted to exploit a wide variety of habitats, but only four orders have survived to the present. Early in their adaptive radiation, the reptiles gave rise to the mammals, and somewhat later to the birds.

The transition from reptile to mammal involved many structural changes which increased the efficiency of the animal. Prominent among these were simplification of the skull, simplification of the jaw and transfer of bones from the jaw suspension to the middle ear, with a consequent refinement of the sense of hearing. Teeth were reduced in number and differentiated into three types, incisors, canines, and cheek teeth (molars and premolars), with a great increase in efficiency resulting. The legs, which had projected at right angles to the body, were rotated to a position under the body, so that the latter could be lifted off the ground without working against a leverage. This alone would not be mechanically stable, because the long body, with its heavy mass of organs, would tend to sag between the limbs. Offsetting this, the vertebral column was arched between front and hind limbs, with the muscles and tendons arranged like the cables of a suspension bridge.

With all of this, the mammals remained an insignificant group as long as the great reptiles filled the principal ecological niches. Once the dinosaurs became extinct (for reasons unknown) at the end of the Mesozoic era, however, the adaptive radiation of the mammals was almost explosive. In all, some thirty orders were produced, of which about two thirds have survived to the present.

Most of the orders of mammals have specialized in one way or another for a specified mode of life. The insectivores are perhaps the most primitive of placental mammals. They have forty-four teeth, including the three principal mammalian types, with none developed more prominently than the others. Moles have limbs specialized for digging, but otherwise the skeletal structure of insecti-vores is primitive. Their diet is a mixed one, consisting of insects, worms, and other small invertbrates, as well as some roots, seeds, and other vegetable matter. The other orders are almost all characterized by specializations which at once make the animal highly efficient in some particular mode of life *and* restrict it to that mode of life. Thus bats are specialized for flight and for feeding on flying insects. The armadillo and its allies are specialized for digging and for eating the burrowing insects, worms, and other small invertebrates which they expose. Rodents feed by gnawing hard plant materials. Their incisors are much enlarged and they grow continuously to offset wear, and their other teeth are also profoundly modified. Ungulates (hoofed animals) are specialized either for grazing or for browsing, and their cheek teeth are specialized as grinding mills, while their limbs are specialized for running. Finally, the carnivores have canines which are modified for tearing flesh and cheek teeth which are modified to serve as shears. In all of these groups, the limb structure is also modified to facilitate the specific mode of life, as was indicated in figures 5.3 and 5.4.

One order is exceptional in this respect: the order Pri-mates. It would be misleading to say that there are no spe-cializations among the primates. Some of their specializa-tions will be discussed below. Yet it is true that this order has not been characterized by specializations which restrict them so stringently to a single mode of life, as has been the case in so many other orders. And it was from this order that man was to evolve.

CHAPTER EIGHT

The Primates and Man

MAN—"a little below the angels," yet so much a part of the animal kingdom! With all eucaryotes, he shares typical cellular structure, with DNA gathered into a nucleus which is separated by a membrane from the cytoplasm. He also shares the typical pattern of mitosis and meiosis and the fundamental biochemical pathways, like the Krebs cycle. Like all of the rest of the animals, he is unable to synthesize complex food from the elements, and so it is that all flesh is grass. With all of the Metazoa he shares multicellularity, and with most of them he shares tissues elaborated into organs and a coelom in which the major organ systems are contained. In common with the rest of the deuterostomes, his coelom is an enterocoel, and segmental organization is prominent, especially in the embryo. Further, man is a member of the phylum Chordata and of the subphylum Vertebrata. With all of the former, he shares a pharynx modified for respiration, a dorsal nerve tube, and, at least in the embryo, a notochord supporting the nerve tube. With the latter, he shares a vertebral column, a chondrocranium, paired eyes, and a ventral heart. As a member of the superclass Tetrapoda, he shares with amphibians, reptiles, birds, and mammals pectoral and pelvic appendages of a dichotomous construction and adapted to use on land. Finally, man is a mammal, and he shares with other mammals such traits as constant body temperature, at least a partial covering of hair, and the feeding of the young with milk.

Man, then, fits harmoniously into his niche in the animal kingdom on so many scores that it is difficult to attribute all of this to anything less than organic continuity, that is, to evolutionary origin of man from lower primates, and, through them, from the general tree of animal evolution. Nonetheless, the disparity in mental attributes is so great that many well-informed people have questioned whether man really does belong in one community with all of the rest of the animal world. Only man studies the world of which he is a part; only man *knows* that he has a history. It is therefore appropriate to ask how man measures up against the several evidences of evolution mentioned in chapter 5.

As a worldwide organism, man is not a good subject for biogeography. The minimum geographical requirement for relationship of two species is that their ancestors must have shared common territory at some time. The record of the paleontological remains of ancient man and subman will be reviewed below; for the present, suffice it to say that those areas in which probable ancestors of man lived were also areas rich in lower primates, so that this minimal requirement for common ancestry was met. The facts just summarized demonstrate that man fits harmoniously into the taxonomic system, and the facts of comparative anatomy fit as well. If the student learns the structure of almost any organ system, like the skeleton, in a lower tetrapod, he has no difficulty in identifying the same parts in man. Each is constructed on a basic plan which is simply varied in each group to adapt it to its special conditions of life, much as a composer varies a theme in the composition of a sonata. For an example, look again at the forelimbs of a series of tetrapods (figure 5.3). As we saw before, each is constructed upon the same plan, with such variations as are needed to adapt to the mode of life of each animal.

Human embryology is a rich store of evidence for the evolution of man, for almost every aspect of human embryology shows features which are understandable only as a legacy from the past. A few examples may be cited. At no time does a human embryo breathe by means of gills, yet every human embryo develops a series of gill slits, and, while the respiratory epithelium does not develop, the branchial circulation is complete and closely comparable to that of embryonic fish. Again, the most primitive vertebrates have a pronephric type of kidney, developed from the first few segments of the nephrogenic ridge. In fishes, this is soon replaced by a second kidney, the mesonephros, which is developed from an extensive series of segments of the nephrogenic ridge more posteriorly. Finally, in all tetrapods, the mesonephros is replaced by a third kidney, the metanephros, which is developed from a mass of unsegmented tissue at the posterior end of the nephrogenic ridge and from the ureteric bud. In the human embryo, all three kinds of kidneys are formed in sequence. A third example is provided by the very fine, silky hair, or lanugo, which the baby grows while in the uterus and with which some babies are born. This lanugo is much more like the hair of apes than it is like that of human adults. Even these few examples show that human embryology would be most enigmatical without the concept of human evolution.

A major example from human biochemistry was given in chapter 4, so it need only be recalled now. DNA was extracted from human cells, then heated to separate the strands, and the single strands were then trapped in a gel so that they could not reunite. DNA from other vertebrates was then marked with radioactive isotopes and broken into fragments. The fragments were then heated to separate the strands, and they were incubated with the gel containing human DNA. After a time, the gel blocks were washed free of uncombined DNA fragments, then the radioactivity was measured. The assumption is that retention corresponds to base sequences and hence to genes held in common by the two species being compared. Actually, the amount of radioactivity retained proved to be roughly comparable to the level of taxonomic relationship. This, too, bespeaks our evolution.

The major line of evidence to which I would like to direct attention now, however, is one which has been neglected up to the present: paleontology, the science of fossil remains of past life. This has unique importance, for a well-graded series of fossils is usually the only possible direct proof of a specific line of descent. First, let us review the taxonomy of the order Primates, of which man is a member.

The principal groups which comprise the order (figure 8.1) are tree shrews, lemurs, tarsiers, Old and New World monkeys, the great apes, and man. Each of these, as we know it today, is the product of a long history and cannot be ancestral to the others, yet they simulate an evolutionary sequence in a remarkable way. In the fossil record, the groups are much more difficult to separate clearly, and this too is evidence of evolution. The first three, tree shrews, lemurs, and tarsiers, are very much more primitive than the others, and they comprise the suborder Prosimii. (Present evidence tends to separate the tree shrews from the others, and it may be that they belong in a separate but allied order.) The rest comprise the suborder Anthropoidea. This suborder falls into three clearly marked superfamilies, the Ceboidea, or New World monkeys; the Cercopithecoidea, or Old World monkeys; and the Hominoidea, or great apes and man. Finally, the superfamily Hominoidea comprises three families: the Hylobatidae, or gibbons; the Pongidae, or great apes; and the Hominidae, the family of man.

The fossil record of the primates does not compare in detail with that of the best-documented groups, such as the horses, but it is a good record—good enough to leave little doubt of the fact of human evolution, yet not good enough to resolve controversy regarding the specific steps in the evolution of man. Let us begin with a very brief survey of the age of mammals, the Cenozoic era, which began some 63 million years ago, after the disappearance of the great reptiles. It is divisible into seven epochs. The Paleocene

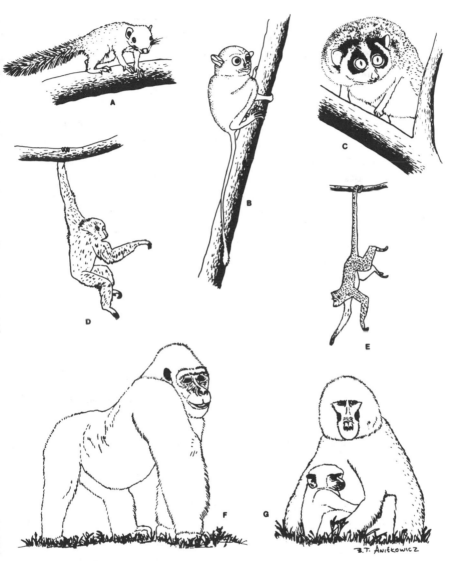

Figure 8.1. Representative primates. A, tree shrew; B, tarsier; C, slender loris; D, gibbon (note brachiation); E, spider monkey (note prehensile tail); F, gorilla; and G, baboon. Not drawn to scale: A–C, squirrel-sized; D and E, the size of medium-sized dogs; F, the giant among primates; and G, the size of a large dog.

was characterized by archaic mammals, the first natural experiments in this new series. It continued for about 5 million years. Then followed the Eocene, which began about 58 million years ago and continued for 22 million years. The Cenozoic era and its subdivisions are summarized in table 7.1.

Tree shrews, or animals very similar to them, appear in the record in the Paleocene, while lemurs and tarsiers appeared in the Eocene. Although the Eocene tarsiers were quite varied, some of them showing quite progressive, monkeylike traits, the record is too scant for the construction of a good phylogeny. A good morphological series, however, suggests the probability that a good phylogenetic series awaits only a more complete exploration of the fossil record. Such a morphological series from a tree shrew through lemur and tarsier to a New World monkey is shown in figure 8.2.

Anthropoid apes first appear in the fossil record in the Oligocene, which began some 34 million years ago and continued for 12 million years. They are known from a baker's dozen of mandibles and a larger number of isolated teeth, all of which have been found in El Fayum province of Egypt. Teeth are among the most frequently fossilized structures because of their great hardness. It is fortunate that they are also among the most useful structures for identification of mammals. Their major features are readily diagnostic for the orders of mammals, and their minor characteristics are useful for diagnosis of genera and species.

These oligocene hominoids fall into at least five genera, and it is possible that they are distributed among all three of the hominoid families. They ranged from the size of a squirrel monkey to that of a gibbon. They had the dental formula characteristic of the higher primates, that is, two incisors, one canine, two premolars, and three molars in each half-jaw. In general, the canine teeth were small, in contrast to the tusks of modern great apes. Three genera,

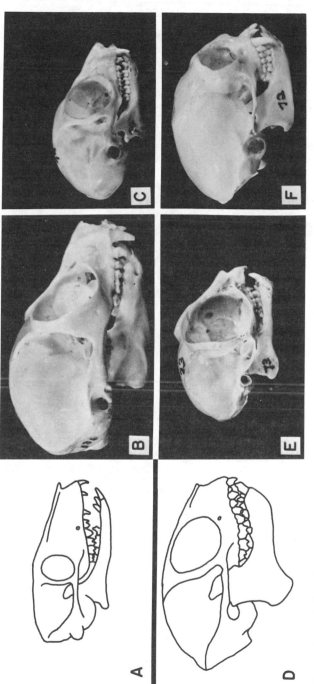

Figure 8.2. Skulls of primates showing morphological (but not phylogenetic) transition from a tree shrew (A) through two lemuriforms (B and C) and two tarsiers (D and E) to a primitive monkey. Note progressive enlargement of the cranium and reduction of the muzzle from A to F. A, *Tupaia*; B, *Nycticebus*; C, *Galago*; D, *Necrolemur* (a fossil tarsier despite its name); E, *Tarsius*; and F, *Callithrix*.

Aegyptopithecus, Parapithecus, and *Oligopithecus,* have been assigned to the family of the great apes, the Pongidae; two, *Aeolopithecus* and *Propliopithecus,* have been assigned to the Hylobatidae; however, *Propliopithecus* was once considered to be the earliest recognizable member of the family Hominidae, our own family. A sampling of these fossils may be illustrated. First, a lateral view of the jaw of *Aegyptopithecus* (figure 8.3) shows the three lower molars and the second premolar. Unfortunately, the rest of the jaw is missing. It shows the low-crowned, relatively unspecialized structure which is typical of anthropoid cheek teeth. The crowns of the same teeth show four cusps per molar and a rather simple pattern of wear. Next, the mandibles of *Aeolopithecus* (figure 8.4) diverge in a V form, a very primitive character. In pongids, the cheek teeth are generally parallel, while in hominids the teeth form a gently curved U. The molars and the second premolar are again simple, typical hominoid teeth, but the first premolar is a sectorial, cutting tooth, and the incisors are rather protruding.

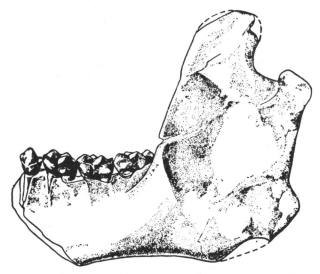

Figure 8.3. Jaw of *Aegyptopithecus,* lateral view. Reprinted by permission of Macmillan Journals Limited from E. L. Simons, *Nature,* (1965), 205 (4967): 137

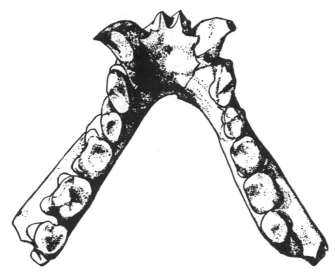

Figure 8.4. Jaw of *Aeolipithecus,* superior aspect. Reprinted by permission of Macmillan Journals Limited from E. L. Simons, *Nature* (1965), 205 (4967): 137.

A rich array of hominoid fossils is known from the Miocene epoch, which began about 22 million years ago and continued for some 17 million years. From the early Miocene of east Africa, a wide variety of pongid fossils has been found. Most of these were originally assigned to the genus *Proconsul,* a highly varied group ranging in size from rather small animals to great brutes approaching the size of a gorilla. They are now usually united with *Dryopithecus* of Europe and Asia. The skull of *Dryopithecus* resembles that of the Old World monkeys, but the teeth already show moderate specializations in the direction of the great apes: large molars and tusklike canines. The limb bones are lighter than those of modern apes, and they do not show specialization for brachiation. A word about brachiation is perhaps needed, because it plays an important role in discussions of the origin of man. Brachiation is locomotion by arm swinging through the branches of trees, with the power supplied by the arms and shoulders. The brachiatorial adaptation is best seen among living primates in the gibbon, and to understand it one should watch these extraordinarily graceful animals at play in a zoo. The arms are much longer than the legs, and the hand is developed as an elongate hook, with the thumb much reduced. It is possible to brachiate without these adaptations. Many monkeys do, and "the daring young man on the flying trapeze" does it quite well, too. But all of the great apes have the brachiatorial adaptations well developed. *Proconsul* at most showed only moderate trends in that direction and is often referred to as a "prebrachiator."

Later in the Miocene and in the Pliocene, there is a scattering of anthropoid remains throughout the Old World. They are called dryopithecines from the type genus, *Dryopithecus*. *Dryopithecus* was a widely distributed ape which approached the size of a chimpanzee. It is known mainly from skulls and teeth, some of which suggest the chimpanzee, some the gorilla, and still others the orangutan. It is quite probable that all of these modern great apes are derived from dryopithecine ancestors. Around a dozen genera have been described, but it is probable that some of these are not valid. Thus, E. Simons has shown that the differences between *Ramapithecus* from India and *Kenyapithecus* from east Africa are probably insufficient to justify specific distinction, let alone generic. He attaches great importance to this because he believes that *Ramapithecus* lies in the direct ancestry of man. Only a very few dryopithecine limb bones have been discovered, but these indicate absence of brachiatorial specialization. During the Pliocene, however, the pongids did become highly specialized brachiators.

A particularly interesting fossil was found in the Pliocene of Italy in 1872. It was described as a fossil ape under the name of *Oreopithecus*, then forgotten until it was restudied in the 1950s and 1960s by J. Hürzeler, who recognized hominid characters. He then went to the coal mines of Tuscany, where the original find was made, and succeeded in finding more fossils, including a nearly complete skeleton. Hominid characters include dental formula and morphology, the structure of the elbow, the broad ilium and short, oblique pubis, and large lumbar vertebrae. Hürzeler and others who have examined the fossils believe that the hominid characters are so numerous that they cannot be explained by coincidence; they do not believe that *Oreopithecus* was in the direct line of human ancestry, but they do believe that he was a collateral member of the family Hominidae and a close relative of our actual ancestors. They regard this as proof that the family Hominidae must have separated from the Pongidae at least as early as the Miocene.

Three hypotheses are possible regarding the time of separation of the hominids from the pongids. According to the brachiator hypothesis, the hominids separated from the pongids *after* the development of the brachiatorial specialization, so that despecialization was required. Under this hypothesis, the hominids must have originated in the Pliocene, perhaps even in the late Pliocene. The prebrachiator hypothesis suggests that the hominids branched off before the origin of this specialization, hence probably in the Miocene. Finally, there is the protocatarrhine hypothesis, according to which the hominids branched off in the Oligocene, when the pongids and the cercopithecine monkeys were first separating. There are well-qualified proponents for each of these theories, but the first has gained favor recently because of new fossil evidence and because of new data from biochemistry. Final judgment is not yet possible.

Whatever the origin of the Hominidae, they are abundant throughout the Pleistocene. From the earliest Pleistocene of Africa, there have been found a great and varied array of fossils of strongly hominid character. They were first assigned to several genera, but only one assignment, *Australopithecus,* is still considered valid, although several species are recognized. At one time, E. Mayr treated them all as one species and assigned them to our own genus as *Homo transvaalensis,* but he subsequently reconsidered and

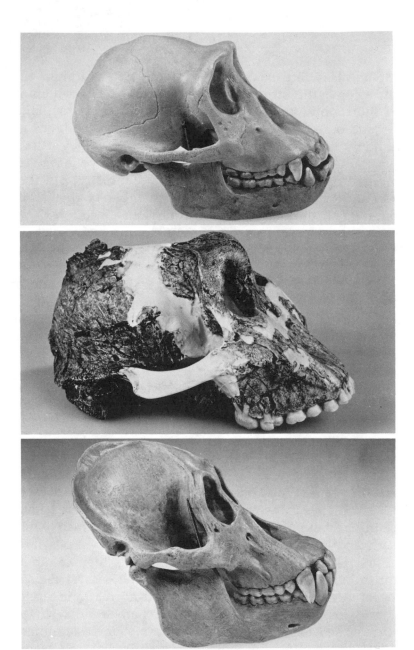

Figure 8.5. Skulls of chimpanzee, australopithecine, and orang utan from top to bottom. Note that the cranium is relatively larger and the face flatter in the australopithecine than in the apes. Both changes are in the human direction. Specimen of *Australopithecus boisei* loaned by Dr. J. S. Cybulski and the National Museum of Canada.

recognized the validity of the genus *Australopithecus*. The skull of *Australopithecus africanus* is about the size of a chimpanzee skull, but the differences are significant (figure 8.5). The cranium is much larger, the brow ridges smaller, and the face less prognathous. The teeth (figure 8.6) form a gently curved arch, in contrast to the dental arcade of the apes. The skeleton indicates that these little men—four feet was a good adult height—habitually walked erect. There is no indication of brachiation. It has been much debated whether they made tools, but they almost certainly used tools—the odd stick or stone which could be used without fashioning. Similar remains have been found at widely scattered places in the Old World. If these men (or near men) were not our actual ancestors, they must have been very closely similar to them.

A wide array of australopithecines has been found, with ages ranging from less than a million years to nearly 4 million years. The oldest of these, *A. afarensis*, is represented by an extensive array of very primitive fossils which were discovered and described by D. C. Johanson and his collaborators in the Afar region of Ethiopia. They believe that the descendants of *A. afarensis* branched into two lines, one of which first produced *A. africanus* around 2.5 million years ago and *A. robustus* about a million years later. This line has not left descendants in the modern world. The sec-

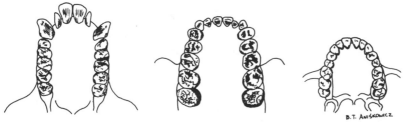

B.T. ANISKOWICZ

Figure 8.6. Toothrows of orang utan, australopithecine, and human, from left to right. In most instances, the australopithecine dentition would be much smaller than the human, but this drawing was made from *Australopithecus boisei*, a species with massive jaws and teeth. Specimen of *Australopithecus boisei* loaned by Dr. J. S. Cybulski and the National Museums of Canada.

ond line was represented by a species which L.S.B. Leakey called *Homo habilis*. He regarded it as the earliest member of the genus *Homo* (but this has been disputed by others, who regard it as an advanced australopithecine). Finally, *H. habilis* gave rise to the early members of *Homo erectus*, a species which is clearly cogeneric with our own species.

The next important series of fossil men was first found in the early mid-Pleistocene of Java, then from somewhat later deposits in China (Teilhard's work as a paleontologist was especially concerned with the Chinese fossils), and finally from a few widely scattered sites across the Old World. These were first described under the names *Pithecanthropus* and *Sinanthropus*. They are now generally recognized as true men and are referred to the species *Homo erectus* (figure 8.7). These men were of moderate stature, and they stood erect, or nearly so. Limb proportions were much as in modern man. The forehead was retreating, and the jaws were moderately prognathous and lacking a chin. The teeth were large by modern standards, but their structure was entirely human. While the cranial capacity was small by modern standards, it was much greater than that of *Australopithecus*, which in turn was larger than that of the largest gorillas. The Chinese fossils are associated with crude stone tools and with fire.

Perhaps the most storied of the later human fossils are the Neanderthals, first found at Gibraltar in 1848. Then eight years later, a skull cap and a few more bones were found in the Neander Valley of Germany. They were at first thought to be the remains of a Napoleonic soldier, but they soon achieved fame as *the* prehistoric man! This man had very heavy bones, a massive eyebrow ridge, a receding forehead, and a cranial capacity which was large even by modern standards. The teeth and jaws were massive, and the chin was receding. Until recently, he was believed to have had a stooped posture, but this was probably an error. It was based upon one remarkably complete skeleton, but it has now been shown to have been that of an arthritic

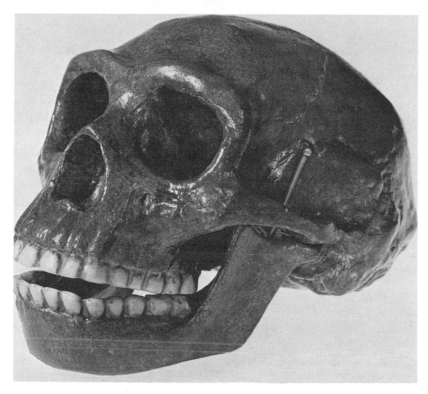

Figure 8.7. Skull, Peking Man.

man. Average stature was about five feet. The hands and feet were disproportionately large. The Neanderthals were expert toolmakers.

The classical Neanderthal fossils have all been found in southwestern Europe in deposits of the last ice age, which began about 120,000 years ago. They appear to have become extinct about 25,000 years ago. Widely scattered finds from all parts of the Old World, however, show some Neanderthaloid characteristics and some characteristics of more modern men. Some of these are of great age—up to as much as a quarter of a million years, hence approaching *Homo erectus* in antiquity, and probably derived from the latter. These are sometimes referred to as "generalized Neanderthals," in contrast to the extreme Neanderthals of later date. It seems probable that, as early as the second interglacial period, much of the Old World was inhabited by a rather modern type of man belonging to our own species, *Homo sapiens*. These ancient men, even as today, were highly variable, and the range of variation included Neanderthaloid traits. As the last glaciation set in, those with the more extreme Neanderthaloid characteristics were isolated from the rest in southwest Europe. Developing in isolation, and with much inbreeding, they evolved the extreme, classical Neanderthal habitus, essentially as a subspecies. Meanwhile, the main population to the east and south developed along more modern lines to form *Homo sapiens* as we know him. They moved into the Neanderthal territory late in the last Ice Age, and they gradually replaced the Neanderthals. The fossils of these later men are not distinguishable from modern Europeans, and they are called Cro-Magnons, from the French cave in which their remains were first found. It was the Cro-Magnons who were the artists of the caves of France and Spain. Their remains gradually blend into history.

Very briefly, this is the record of human paleontology as it is now known. While it is not adequate to fix the specific steps in the descent of man, and while some important questions remain controversial at every stage of it, it is complete enough to leave little room for doubt regarding the fact of human evolution. We saw at the beginning of this chapter that evidence leading to much the same conclusion was to be found in such different disciplines as taxonomy, comparative anatomy, comparative embryology, and comparative physiology and biochemistry. In general, none of these is an absolute proof, admitting of no other possible interpretation, even though any of them would be anomalous under any but an evolutionary interpretation. The concurrence of so many independent probabilities is actually the strongest argument for the fact of human evolution.

Man, then, is a part of nature. He belongs in one community with the animal kingdom, with the deuterostome series, as a part of the phylum Chordata and the subphylum Vertebrata. With the amphibians, reptiles, birds, and mammals, he is a tetrapod. Finally, he is a mammal and a primate.

CHAPTER NINE

Hominization

WHEN SHAKESPEARE wanted to convey the idea that Hamlet's father was thoroughly admirable, fully deserving to wear the crown, he climaxed his description with the sentence, "He was a man, all in all." "All in all"—that is most inclusive, yet people rebel at the suggestion that it might be inclusive enough to take in gill slits. Many people, confronted with the evidence that man is part of nature and one of the late products of animal evolution, conclude that man is *nothing but* an animal: that his aspirations and ideals are illusions; and that he may as well revert to the amorality of the jungle. Charles Darwin was not among those who drew this conclusion, for he wrote in the *Descent of Man,*

> Man, with all his noble qualities, with sympathy which feels for the most debased; with benevolence which extends not only to other men but to the humblest living creature; with his godlike intellect, which has penetrated into the movements and constitution of the solar system—with all these exalted powers—man still bears in his bodily frame the indelible stamp of his lowly origin. (1871:405)

It was Darwin's difficult task to expound man's lowly origin to a society which regarded this as blasphemous, yet he did it without losing his appreciation of the uniqueness and greatness of man, as shown by the above quotation.

Teilhard liked words which suggest development, becoming, evolution, as opposed to fixity. Thus, he replaced cosmology by cosmogeny. Man, too, he thought of in terms of development from a subhuman or prehuman past to his present condition, which is in turn in process of development toward a future which can only be guessed but which will certainly differ in important ways from man as we know him. For this great process which has been in progress for millions of years, which is continuing still, and which will continue into the indefinite future, Teilhard used the word *hominization*. He used the word especially in relation to the *within*, the psychic aspect of man, but the present chapter will be concerned with the *without*, the more conventionally scientific aspect of the phenomenon of man. Two important processes of hominization will be discussed: the development of erect posture, and the development of the brain.

ERECT POSTURE

A distinguished professor of my acquaintance likes to tell his classes that the greatness of man depends upon his great brain and his great toe. The great toe was, of course, simply selected as a representative of many modifications throughout the body which are adaptive to erect posture. Erect posture was of fundamental importance for the development of man, for it freed his hands from locomotion and for handling objects, for making and using tools, and, eventually, for writing and for all of the myriad activities which comprise or implement culture—and culture is a distinctively human phenomenom.

The beginnings of erect posture are associated with the arboreal habit, although not with brachiation. Tarsiers run up trees trunk-erect, and so do many monkeys. Many arboreal monkeys sit with trunk erect. None of the great apes can stand erect more than very briefly without a hand hold, yet the gibbon, in which the brachiatorial adaptation is most perfect, can run erect along a horizontal branch, high above the jungle floor.

Because of the great importance of erect posture, it may be worthwhile to go into some detail on the specific anatomical modifications which permit it. The great toe was already mentioned in this connection: in apes, it is opposable, which makes the foot a good grasping organ, but it also leaves the foot less firm than if the toes were all bound parallel, as in man. Thus, greater mobility has been sacrificed in order to gain strength to bear the entire weight of the body, unaided by the forelimbs. Similarly, the ankle bones are larger and heavier in man, for much the same reason. In apes, the arm bones are longer than the leg bones, while the reverse is true in man. Actually, man is the more primitive in this, as in many other respects, for the limb proportions of apes are adaptive to brachiation. Further, the long bones of the legs are straight in man, or very nearly so, while they are gently curved in the apes. The net effect of the changes in man is one of greater stability when standing erect. For much the same reason, the trunk of man is shorter relative to the legs. The hip bones of apes are long and narrow, like those of other four-footed mammals, while those of man are broad, forming a basin which supports the viscera when he stands erect. The knee and hip joints are normally somewhat flexed in apes, but in man they are extended straight when standing erect. The curvature of the spinal column of apes is a single, sweeping, outward curve, like that of other four-footed animals. This tends to throw the animal off balance when standing erect. The spinal column of man has four curves which alternate in direction, thus averaging out to a straight line, yet the springlike curves act as a shock absorber, which protects the brain against the shock of walking over a hard surface. Finally, the occipital condyles of apes are near the posterior end of the skull and are directed backward, while those of man are near the center of the base of the skull and are directed downward. Thus, the adaptation for erect posture has affected every part of the skeleton. The viscera, too, have been affected in many ways which may not be immediately obvious. One example will suffice to represent them. In four-footed animals, including the lower primates, the abdominal viscera are suspended from the dorsal body wall by mesenteries. In the early embryo, these are much the same whether in man or ape. Soon, however, the mesenteries of man develop a series of adhesions, the net effect of which is to prevent the collapse of the viscera into the pelvis during erect posture.

Not enough is known about the paleontological development of these adaptations, but the process may have started as early as *Oreopithecus*, some ten million years ago, for the hip bone of this early hominid was already quite broad—far more manlike than apelike. In *Australopithecus africanus* and in early members of our own genus, these modifications were already quite far advanced. The limb bones were nearly straight, the hip bone broad and basinlike, and the occipital condyles set further forward than in any living ape, though not as far as in later men. There is not much room for doubt that these little men habitually stood erect. In *Homo erectus*, the occipital condyles were still further forward, approaching, but not quite reaching, the condition of modern man. In all of the later fossils, this adaptation is essentially modern, although its refinement may still be in progress.

Erect posture, then, is a very basic human adaptation which began very early in hominid history and was substantially complete very early in human history.

DEVELOPMENT OF THE BRAIN

The history of the brain of man is somewhat parallel to that of his posture, but it lagged behind in the early part of his history. It is far more difficult to assess, because we are interested in the *quality* of the brain, and this is not fossilized. Indeed, usually the only thing available is the skull, and from this the size of the brain is estimated. But size of the brain and intelligence are not closely correlated. Among living men, the smallest brains are always associated with feeblemindedness, but the largest human brain known also belonged to a feebleminded man. Within the broad range of normalcy, there seems to be very little correlation between brain size and brain quality. Nonetheless, it seems probable that there is a minimum brain size necessary for normal human intelligence, and there has been a progressive increase over the range of human evolution. There has been a limited tendency toward expansion of the brain throughout the evolution of the primates, but only in man has this been a dominant characteristic. There is no indication that the Miocene ancestors of man were the possessors of larger brains than their pongid cousins, but by the time the South African men appeared, they already had appreciably larger brains than any pongid. The australopithecines appear to have had a cranial capacity averaging around 600 cc. and ranging up to 800 cc. This is somewhat larger than that of the largest gorilla, but it is proportionately very much larger. It must be remembered that a cranial capacity of 600 cc. for a 275 kg. gorilla is quite modest compared with the same cranial capacity for a little man of perhaps less than 45 kg.

Whether the australopithecines had a culture is debatable. R. A. Dart, who first discovered their remains in the early 1920s, believed that they did. He described a culture based upon tools fashioned very simply from bone, teeth, and horn. Most anthropologists have been very skeptical. Over a period of many years, L. S. B. Leakey assembled a collection of very simple stone tools from the Olduvai Gorge of east Africa, but the toolmaker of this Oldowan culture remained unknown. Then, in the early 1960s, Leakey found advanced australopithecine-type fossils in some of the same sites with Oldowan tools. He described this fossil as *Homo habilis*, and he believes this to be the oldest known species of man. This evaluation of the fossils is controversial. J. T. Robinson, who has seen the material and is profoundly familiar with the australopithecines, says that these fossils are within the range of variability of the latter and so should not comprise a new species. As a minimum, the finds do indicate that late members of *Australopithecus* were beginning to develop a culture.

Homo erectus had a decidedly larger cranial capacity— around 900 cc. in the Java fossils and well over 1,000 in the the later Chinese fossils. In the later fossils of *Homo sapiens*, the cranial capacity is substantially modern. For modern man, the average is around 1,350 cc. There are no cultural remains directly associated with the Javanese fossils, but a very primitive culture, including stone tools and fire, has been found in association with the Chinese fossils. In the case of *Homo sapiens,* the development of increasingly complex cultures is his most striking characteristic, and the point need not be labored.

It appears, then, that the major expansion of the brain of man began later than did the adaptation to erect posture, yet it progressed with amazing rapidity. I believe that it represents a major change in mode of life, like the change from fish to amphibian, for the early hominids changed from a brute life, dominated by instinct, to a rational life, in which cleverness was the principal defensive and offensive weapon. In the earliest stages, the hominids must have been poor competitors on the brute level, while still not clever enough to gain much advantage. Thus a very strong selective force must have favored rapid development of the new faculties.

FUTURE TRENDS

We have discussed the evolution of the physical basis for psychosocial evolution, but we still have not assayed to enter into the latter. Yet it is in the psychosocial order that most scientists expect the most important aspects of the future of man. The basis for this was well stated, in Teilhardian fashion, by Julian Huxley:

> All reality is . . . a single and comprehensive process of evolution. But this comprehensive process falls naturally into three main sectors. The first, is the inorganic or cosmic sector . . . resulting in the evolution of elements, nebulae, stars, and planetary systems; the second is the organic or biological sector, operating by automatic natural selection superposed on physicochemical interaction, and resulting in the evolution of plant and animal organisms—from fungi and flowers to monkeys and medusae; the third is the human or psychosocial sector, operating by mind-accompanied psychosocial pressure superposed upon natural selection, and resulting in human societies and their products—from machines and works of art to sciences and religions. . . . In the psychosocial phase, evolution is predominantly cultural. (1963:1–2)

P. B. Medawar added, "We must not distinguish a strictly biological evolution from social, cultural, or technological evolution. Both are biological. The distinction between them is that one is genetical and the other is not" (1960:92).

Nonetheless, the present chapter has been concerned only with the physical evolution of man, and certainly man's physical evolution will continue as long as he survives. Some predictions of the physical future of man have been published. R. C. Andrews (1939), a former director of the American Museum of Natuural History, tried to predict the far distant future of man. He saw the man of that distant time as a mental giant whose physical features would reflect long absence of any selection in favor of brute power but also long selection in favor of mental abilities of a very high order and of the ability to manipulate skillfully and accurately the machines which would do most of his work.

Quite different was the prediction of Ales Hrdlicka (1929), once the dean of American anthropologists. He started from the assumption that only short-range prediction was feasible and that this was best identified in the recent past. In this way, he found certain trends in the human remains of the past five thousand years, and he used these to predict the physical characteristics of man of five thousand years in the future. Very briefly, he expected no change in the size of the brain, but he did anticipate increased efficiency of its organization. Correlated with this, he expected increased efficiency of the sense organs. Otherwise, he predicted an extensive series of minor changes affecting all parts of the body. Some of these would refine the adaptation to erect posture still further. Others included such things as thinner skull bones, more prominent nose, further reduction of hair, loss of the wisdom teeth and perhaps of some other teeth, and some changes in the pattern of diseases to which man is subject. In all, it is not a very exciting prospect, and in fact it tends to reinforce the opinion that it is in the psychosocial sphere that the future evolution of man will be centered. This will be the subject of chapter 11.

Man, then, does have a uniqueness and a greatness not found in any other species, for only man has entered the third great sector of evolution, the psychosocial sector. There is a biological basis for this, particularly in erect posture and in the great development of the brain, but it goes beyond this. Th. Dobzhansky has summarized much of the import of this chapter with his usual brilliant clarity:

Ostensibly there is a basic clash in human nature. Mankind is a biological species which belongs to the animal kingdom. But man is also the creator and the creature of his society and of his cultural heritage. And, finally, the inspiration of the mystics sees man in still another light—that of the Son of God. The intellectual history of mankind can be written in terms of shifting emphasis on one or the other of these aspects of human nature. And the history of human error could well be portrayed in terms of attempting to understand everything, instead of something, about man by investigation of only one of these aspects to the exclusion of the others. In particular, the study of evolution has often been handicapped by this purblindness. . . . It is a demonstrable fact that human biology and human culture are parts of a single system, unique and unprecedented in the history of life. Human evolution cannot be understood except as a result of interaction of biological and of social variables.

CHAPTER TEN

Some Evolutionary Generalizations

HAVING REVIEWED, if sketchily, the grand sweep of evolution, we may now try to see generalizations in it. In the whole process, nothing is more basic than reproduction. As a minimum, reproduction increases the number of living things and hence supplies pressure for selection. It also leads to association of organisms. In procaryotes, this may not go beyond the simple association resulting from juxtaposition of the sister cells, still colonies of bacteria or blue-green algae may have definite morphology, which suggests that the characteristics of the colony, as well as of the individual, are genetically determined. Among the Protozoa, colonies of genetically determined type are widespread, especially among the flagellates, and, as discussed in chapter 7, it is not improbable that it was this process which led to the origin of the first metazoans. But metazoans, too, form associations which extend from simple aggregates of related individuals to the complex societies of insects, birds, and mammals, the latter culminating in human societies.

SOME ASPECTS OF REPRODUCTION

One result of reproduction is the profusion of life. In chapter 5, some examples of the prodigality of nature were discussed. A bacteriologist, commenting upon this, said that, if a bacterium like the colon bacillus, which may divide every twenty minutes, were to reproduce at maximal rate for twenty-four hours, it would cover the earth a foot deep. This may not be too unreasonable an estimate, for it would amount to something on the order of 2.32×10^{21} cells, an almost inconceivably large mass! As Teilhard put it, "Life advances by mass effects, by dint of multitudes flung into action without apparent plan . . . there is . . . a great deal of biological efficiency in the *struggle for life*. . . . . 'Survival of the fittest by natural selection' is not a meaningless expression, provided it is not taken to imply either a final ideal or a final explanation" (p. 109).

Another result of reproduction is what Teilhard called the *ingenuity* of life. Had the first cells and all of their descendants reproduced without change, not only would life have remained stultifyingly uniform, but it would have *ended* with the exhaustion of the primitive stockpile of organic compounds. But in fact, mutation occurred from the start, introducing variants, novelty. Then as now, the overwhelming majority of mutations were undoubtedly deleterious, and their prospective fate was elimination by natural selection. But whenever a mutation occurred which adapted the organism to a new mode of life, or even to a somewhat different mode of life, then life expanded and diversified in the new direction. This exploration of every possible pathway for development, an exploration carried out by large numbers of individuals varying in every imaginable way, Teilhard called *groping*, combining "the blind fantasy of large numbers with the precise orientation of a specific target. It would be a mistake to see it as mere chance. Groping is *directed chance*" (p. 110). The result was the exploitation of the many modes of life open to procaryotes. Some developed chemotrophic mechanisms and became producers, capable of synthesizing at least some of their nutritional requirements from the elements. Some developed chlorophyll, so that they could tap the radiant energy of the sun. All of the photosynthetic bacteria metabolize sulfur compounds, but the blue-green algae release oxygen into the atmosphere. Some bacterial mutants were produced which were capable of exploiting this new element in the atmosphere, and thus aerobic metabolism was introduced. Some became parasitic upon one or another of the more progressive species. Still others became predators. And some, using the system of symbioses described in chapter 7, moved up to a new order of complexity and became eucaryotes, thus opening far broader possibilities for the future.

The evolution of the procaryotes was accomplished by mutation and selection unaided, but with the eucaryotes, sexual reproduction was added (Teilhard refers to it as *conjugation*). This greatly increased the rate of evolution because, in sexual reproduction, two different lines of descent are brought together at every generation, and their various characteristics (or, rather, the genes which determine those characteristics) are reshuffled into new combinations. In this way, the number of character combinations which is tested by natural selection in each generation is raised to a maximum, and hence each species approaches effective adaptedness far more rapidly than would be possible in the absence of sexual reproduction.

Another consequence of the profusion of life is what Teilhard calls its "indifference." "Life passes over a bridge made of accumulated corpses, and this is a direct effect of multiplication" (p. 111). Death is the end of every life cycle, often long before that cycle has run its potential course. One thinks of the lines in Tennyson's "In Memoriam," "so careful of the type she seems, so careless of the single life." In one sense, reproduction is the antidote for death, for it assures the continuation of life. Yet it does this at the expense of production of great numbers, many of which only begin their life cycles. Teilhard's statement that "life is more real than lives" (p. 111) is certainly true if one equates reality with long duration. Only with the appearance of mind can this indifference be replaced by solicitude.

RAMIFICATION OF THE LIVING MASS

In the diversification of living things, no process is more fundamental than adaptive radiation. As Teilhard put it,

> The formation of a verticil is explained . . . by the phylum's need to pluralize itself in order to cope with a variety of different needs or possibilities. . . . The concept of fanning out . . . involves a forest of exploring antennae. And when one of these chances upon the fissure, the formula, giving access to a new compartment of life, then instead of becoming fixed or merely spreading out in monotonous variations, the branch finds all its mobility once more. (p. 118)

In any radiation, a particularly successful line of descent will tend to serve as a center for a new radiation, and thus a maximum number of modes of life are tested, and organisms are almost inevitably evolved to exploit whatever modes of life are open to them.

When animals are considered from an evolutionary point of view, it is quite clear that a line of descent is a basic unit of consideration, as basic as the taxonomic categories introduced in chapter 5. Lines of descent are especially clear in the study of paleontology, Teilhard's profession, and, in common with many paleontologists, he called them *phyla*. Phylum will not be used in that sense here, as it has already been used to designate the major subdivisions of the animal (or other) kingdom, the largest groups within which relationships are at all clear. These are, of course, lines of descent, but in a special and broadly inclusive sense.

The relatively uniform ancestor of such an adaptive fan Teilhard called a *peduncle,* while the fan itself (an array of related but differently adapted organisms) he called a *verticil.* Such peduncles and verticils occur at every taxonomic level from the species (where subspecies are the rays of the verticil) through genera (where the species are the rays of the verticil) and families (broken up into genera) and so on up to the entire world of life (which is divided into three kingdoms, which are very broadly adaptive to different orders of life). The world of life as a whole includes three broadly contrasting and complementary types: producers, consumers, and decomposers. The producers are organisms which have enzyme systems which permit them to synthesize organic compounds (food) from the inorganic elements. The green plants are the principal producers in the world today, but chemosynthetic bacteria make some contribution, and in the remote past chemosynthetic bacteria were the only producers. Consumers are organisms which must use already elaborated organic compounds. They eat producers, or they eat other consumers which do eat producers. The entire animal kingdom is made up of consumers, some herbivores which feed directly upon plants, others carnivores which feed upon herbivores. Finally, the decomposers attack dead plants and animals, as well as other organic wastes, decompose them, and return their substances to the inorganic stockpile upon which the producers draw. The decomposers are mainly bacteria and fungi. Among the three sorts of organisms, the cycles of the elements are maintained. The necessity of the producers is obvious, but it is sometimes necessary to remind people that, in the absence of a rich array of decomposers, all life would soon come to an end, for all available organic compounds would soon be locked into the bodies of dead plants and animals.

All of the taxonomic entities are, then, the products of adaptive radiation. In the "forest of exploring antennae" (p. 118) of each such radiation, adjacent types may differ by only one or a very few genes. Why, then, do not the various groups blend one into another in such a way that no taxonomic pattern can be seen? In part, many of the potential genetic combinations are by chance not formed. Of the vast number which are in fact formed, only those which are reasonably adaptive in the conditions under which they occur will survive long, while the maladaptive ones will soon disappear. Of those that are successful, some continue their progressive adaptation when conditions change, while others become extinct because they fail to produce mutations which are adaptive to the new conditions. Extinction has been the fate of the great majority of species which have ever lived. One of its effects is to prune back the branches of the tree of life so that the taxonomic pattern stands out more clearly. It may further be mentioned that extinction has two very different meanings. It may be the epitaph of failure. Thus the dinosaurs were a highly specialized array of reptiles which dominated the earth for many millions of years. When conditions became unsuited to their survival, however, they failed to produce mutations which were suited to the new conditions and so became extinct and left no descendants. But extinction may also be the hallmark of success. The cynodont reptiles were partly contemporaneous with the dinosaurs, and they too became extinct. The cynodonts, however, were succeeded by their own descendants, the adaptively superior mammals, which resulted from the production of fortunate mutations in the cynodonts and their preservation by natural selection. Thus extinction may mark the end of a line of descent, or it may be a necessary byproduct of the origin of new and superior types. The latter then begin a new round of adaptive radiation.

In principle, then, each fan of adaptive radiation takes its origin within an earlier one. Should not these peduncles make visible the actual origin of new species, genera, and higher groups? No, said Teilhard, for at their origins, they are not yet sharply differentiated from their predecessors, and they would be clearly recognizable as something new only in contrast to their more strongly differentiated descendants. But by the time the latter have evolved, the peduncles have already disappeared. He notes that it is the same in all fields and asks where are the first Romans, or Greeks, or even automobiles, which originated so recently?

THE TREE OF LIFE

We speak of the tree of life, but actually it has more the form of a shrub, because new groups generally branch off not from the late, specialized members of ancestral groups but from the early, generalized members. This has been true throughout the world of life, but a few examples will be selected from among the vertebrates.

Almost as soon as the placoderms were formed early in the Paleozoic era, they gave rise to the sharks and bony fishes. These two groups came to dominate the waters of the world, while the less progressive placoderms continued to diversify as a minor group until their extinction at the end of the Paleozoic. Amphibians were derived from bony fishes, and bony fishes have specialized for every conceivable aquatic habitat. Yet it was not from any of these late, specialized fishes that amphibians arose, but from the primitive, lobe-finned, lung fishes (crossoptergians), which were common in the mid-Paleozoic. The Amphibia in turn gave rise to reptiles so early in their history that at the very origin of the Amphibia some fossils could be assigned to one class or the other with about equal justification. (In this case, do we have the actual peduncle? Perhaps!) For a final example, the reptiles reached their peak of development and profusion during the Mesozoic era, but it was not any of these which gave rise to the mammals, rather it was the cynodonts, a group of reptiles which branched off at the end of the Paleozoic, before the great specialization and dominance of the reptiles.

The "tree" of life, then, is really a shrub. Without repeating chapter 7, we may sketch in some of its main features. The first great adaptive radiation produced the vast array of procaryotes, the simplest of which are on a level of complexity far above that of the most complex of polymers, yet the procaryotes themselves are all on the same general level, granted that they diversified to form a balanced ecological community of producers, consumers, and decomposers. One result of this was to make the life of the early earth not merely a collection of innumerable organisms but a true biosphere of interrelated, interfunctioning organisms.

Further advances awaited some invention which would permit a genuinely higher order of complexity, and this was achieved by the series of intracellular symbioses which culminated in the eucaryote cell. The eucaryote cell combines the complexities of several originally different procaryotes and adds new features not found in any of those. The newly evolved eucaryotes immediately began a new adaptive radiation which again led to the three major ecological types. Producers were represented by a half a dozen phyla of algae, all capable of photosynthesis, and so liberating oxygen into the atmosphere as well as producing food. Consumers were represented by the myriads of kinds of protozoans, some primary consumers, others secondary consumers, including parasites as well as predators. Finally, decomposers were represented by two phyla of fungi. At this level, as among the procaryotes, evolution produced and is continuing to produce a wide variety of organisms of each of these major ecological types. Some of these are adapted to radically different habitats, as fresh water, marine, or parasitic. Others represent relatively minor differences, as adaptation to stagnant, slowly flowing, or briskly flowing waters. The net result was to cover the earth with a wide variety of organisms filling all the ecological niches open to small eucaryotes.

Further development of the plant kingdom will not be followed here. Protozoa exist in great variety, and they range in levels of complexity from cells of minimal eucaryote characteristics to the most complicated ciliates, which have analogs of many of the organ systems of higher animals and which are surely the most complicated of cells. But the small size of the protozoans places limits on the level of complexity they can attain. Probably the more complex ciliates have approached or even reached that limit. Again, further evolution of higher levels of complexity could only be achieved by the invention of a new type of organization, in this case, the multicellular or metazoan type. The sponges, which have never progressed beyond the cellular level of organization, are a side issue. The first great radiation of metazoan evolution resulted in a group of phyla at the tissue level of construction, exploiting a wide variety of marine and fresh water consumer niches. The next major radiation led to the organ grade of construction, with a whole series of acoelomate and pseudocoelomate phyla, but very early in this radiation the coelomates arose, whether from one peduncle or two is unknown. In either case, one major coelomate radiation produced the protostomes, culminating in three of the greatest phyla of the animal kingdom, the Mollusca, the Annelida, and the Arthropoda, the latter comprising nearly a million species! The other main radiation of coelomates produced fewer phyla, and only two of these are major phyla, the aberrant Echinodermata and the Chordata. The latter, however, has unique interest, for it includes man.

Most of this great array of phyla quickly evolved classes which were broadly adapted to quite different modes of life. Thus, in the phylum Mollusca, the class Pelecypoda, the bivalves, is adapted to life on the bottom of fresh water or marine bodies or to burrowing. In either case, they feed upon plankton, the minute plants and animals which float upon the water currents. But the class Cephalopoda, the squids and octopi, are adapted to active swimming and predation upon moderate-sized to large fishes.

At the lower levels of orders, families, genera, and

species, the same sort of adaptive radiation continues, producing a magnificent wealth of life, with similar ecological
niches being occupied by members of many groups at all
levels of the animal kingdom. Teilhard's own example of
the adaptive radiation of the mammals at the levels of orders and families may be reviewed. At the outset, there are
three orders which feed primarily upon insects and other
small invertebrates. These are the order Insectivora (shrews
and moles), Chiroptera (bats), and Edentata (armadillos and
anteaters). The first are terrestrial or burrowing insectivores, the Chiroptera are flying mammals which catch insects in flight, and the last are equipped with powerful
claws for digging up small invertebrates (armadillo) or with
a long sticky tongue which can be plunged into an anthill
to collect fresh food (anteater). Some of the Insectivora are,
in fact, omnivorous, for moles eat plant roots as well as
insects. The herbivorous mammals are represented by several orders, the evolution of which has been rather complex. The rodents are a highly varied array of gnawing animals—rats (many of which are omnivorous), mice,
squirrels, beavers, muskrats, etc. These are adapted to
feeding in a very wide variety of habitats. The lagomorphs
(rabbits and hares) are a much less varied group of grazers.
The two great orders of herbivores are the Artiodactyla and
the Perissodactyla. The Artiodactyla are herbivores with an
even number of toes (two or four). There are five principal
families of artiodactyls: the Suidae, or swine, which tend
to be omnivorous; the Camelidae, comprising camels, lla-
mas, and alpacas; the Cervidae, or deer family, primarily
browsers; the Bovidae, or cattle, primarily grazers; and
Proboscidea, or elephants, grazers and browsers. The order
Perissodactyla includes three principal living families. The
tapir family is a small group of South American browsers.
Better known is the rhinoceros family. But much the best
known of the perissodactyls is the family Equidae, the
horses, which are specialized for grazing and for running.
In addition, the order also includes two families of extinct

perissodactyls, the Titanotheridae and the Chalicotheridae.

Surprising as it may seem, when the herbivores are traced back in time, they approach the early carnivores. The order Carnivora includes a wide variety of flesh-eating mammals which feed upon the herbivores and insectivores. Large cats and wolves feed primarily upon the larger artiodactyls and perissodactyls. Smaller cats, foxes, weasels, and other small carnivores feed upon rodents, lagomorphs, and insectivores. Bears are also carnivores, but, although they do take fish and some terrestial mammals, they are omnivorous, and some bears are very nearly vegetarians. The Cetacea, comprising whales and porpoises, were derived from early carnivores, and they feed mostly upon fishes and marine invertebrates. Surprisingly, the largest whales are primarily plankton feeders, straining enormous quantities of sea water for the small crustaceans which it contains.

We have touched only upon the principal orders of mammals, yet it is sufficient to show that they include numerous representatives in each of the main ecological niches open to consumers—primary consumers which feed upon plants, secondary consumers (carnivores) which feed upon the herbivores, and omnivores which feed upon both plant and animal sources. Such a widely varied group, Teilhard called a *biota,* but perhaps it is more explanatory to call it a *balanced ecological community.* Teilhard noted that most of the major groups tend to produce such biotas. The net result is that, at every level, every ecological type is represented by a considerable number of variants. Why should natural selection favor such multiplicity? Why not just one or a few types at each level? The answer may be found by looking again at a relatively impoverished biota. In chapter 5, the case of the arctic hare was described. These animals may reach enormous population densities, and a whole series of carnivores depends upon them as their principal or exclusive source of food. But every eight to ten years, the hare population is nearly destroyed by an epidemic of shock disease, and this leads to widespread starvation and death among their predators. In a more typically diversified community, in which each herbivore can feed on any one of a number of plants and each carnivore can prey upon any one of numerous animals, disaster to any one species merely results in some shifts in the dietary habits of the other members of the community. To put it another way, a diversified living community is a buffered community. It is stable, whereas a community of a minimal number of species is unstable. Like a diversified investment program for a financier, a highly diversified biota is the best insurance that evolution can provide for its own successful continuation.

SOME GENERALIZATIONS FROM THE RECORD

Some generalizations can be drawn from the record. I shall begin by treating certain aspects on which Teilhard and I are in agreement, then I shall pass to other aspects which I am forced to see rather differently than he did.

NUMBERS

Numbers vary inversely from the most inclusive taxonomic groups through the less inclusive to the individual organisms. There are only three kingdoms of organisms according to the system which seems best to me. Traditionally, two kingdoms have been recognized, but systems of four or five kingdoms are commonly advocated, and one current author recommends only one.

Whatever the system of kingdoms used, they include some forty to fifty phyla, and again there is no universal agreement among specialists on just how the phyla should be delimited. Most phyla include several classes, and some include a fairly large number of classes. As one goes down the taxonomic hierarchy, the number gets larger at every level, until finally no one knows how many species there are, but it is currently fashionable to estimate something on the order of two million. And how many individuals in a species? Of course, this is highly variable, ranging from species like the whooping crane, which is teetering on the edge of extinction, with about one hundred birds as the entire world population, to the enormous populations of some insect species and of the small crustaceans, which are so abundant that whales can be well nourished upon them. This great multiplicity at once provides the competition which gives natural selection its force and the many species in similar ecological situations which gives the system elasticity and stability.

VOLUME

Under this heading, Teilhard wished to raise the question of the relative importance of the various groups in the world of life. As an antidote for the fact that this discussion is centered on man and therefore dwells primarily on the animal kingdom, let me begin by saying that the plant kingdom is of preeminent importance even for animal life, because no animal is a producer, hence all flesh is grass. Further, the fungi (plants) and bacteria (mychotans) are essential to animal life because their role as decomposers is essential if the elementary cycles upon which all life depends are to be continued into the future. Concentrating on the animal kingdom, however, are some groups clearly more important than others? There are a few phyla which can be discounted as of little consequence in the bulk of life. An example is the Phoronidea, a small group of marine tube worms comprising only about a dozen species, and none of these has very much effect on the other life in its habitat. Most phyla are in fact great assemblages of organisms, comprising biota or series of biota in the Teilhardian sense, yet their overall importance in the world of life is of roughly similar magnitude. Three phyla are of out-standing importance, having produced more species than the others, and commonly these species dominate the habitats in which they occur. The first of these is the phylum Arthropoda, made up of crustaceans, spiders, insects, and several lesser groups. Collectively, there are nearly a million species of arthropods, and over half of these are members of one order of insects, the beetles. The second is the phylum Mollusca, including such animals as chitons, clams, snails, and octopi, numbering around 80,000 species or more. And the third is the phylum Chordata, including the vertebrates and a few lesser relations. They are less prolific in species than the Mollusca, yet the dominant animals of the waters, lands, and skies are mainly vertebrates. Among the most recently evolved vertebrates one finds the class Mammalia, comprising some 4,400 species, hardly a competitor *quantitatively* for some of the groups of insects. Teilhard describes it as "a poor little lobe, a belated offshoot on the tree of life . . . *quantitatively*" (p. 134).

DURATION

This was one of Teilhard's favorite concepts, as well it might be for a paleontologist, who sees animal groups progressing from an origin in the past through a historical development and perhaps to their extinction. The major development of the mammals has occurred in the past 65 or 70 million years, but their first beginnings occurred some 200 million years ago. The tetrapods have been evolving for some 300 million years, and the vertebrates for at least 400 million years. Even this, however, is a short span compared with the total duration of life, which began more than 3 billion years ago. Since Darwin, time has become one of the fundamental dimensions of life.

The rates of evolution have been highly variable. In general, the rate is slow during periods of geological and climatic uniformity, rapid during periods of rapid change in the physical world. At any time, however, some groups evolve more rapidly than others. For example, the lampshells are a minor group which is adapted to plankton feeding on subtropical and temperate tide flats, probably one of the most stable of habitats. They are known in the fossil record over a range of about a half-billion years. Over this enormous reach of time, they have persisted almost unchanged. At least one genus, *Lingula,* has persisted throughout that time, and it is even possible that some of the same species are still present. On the other hand, the mammals have come to prominence only in the last 70 million years, yet they have diversified into about 30 orders and a very large numbers of species, of which about 4,400 are still extant.

IRREVERSIBILITY

Many times during the long history of life, advanced organisms have returned to an ancestral habitat. This gives selective value to traits of the ancestors, and it raises the question of whether evolution might be reversible. Many reptiles and mammals, such as the plesiosaurs and seals, have reverted to a marine habitat. They have assumed a streamlined, fishlike form, with the limbs shortened, webbed, and finlike. Yet the skeleton of those limbs always shows a clear reptilian or mammalian pattern, each contrasting strongly to the skeleton of a fish fin. Other organs similarly show a superficial convergence toward the fish type while remaining in basic pattern true to their own class. The result of many such studies is the conclusion that the major steps in evolution are not reversible, a fact which is often called Dollo's law. This might be expected on theoretical grounds, for major evolutionary steps are made up of many smaller steps, each based upon chance mutations which were favored by natural selection. That such a sequence should be exactly reversed would be extraordinarily improbable, if not actually impossible.

EVOLUTION AND PROGRESS

In the early post-Darwinian days, there was a widespread faith that evolution must necessarily be "onward and upward." Progress was seen as inevitable. This, however, was a mistake. Evolution can be retrogressive, and it obviously has been in the case of the origin and evolution of parasitic groups. Evolution is a matter of continuous selection for mutations which tend to improve the adaptation of each species to its conditions of life. But because those conditions are continually changing, there is generally a lag, and any species finds itself with Alice in the looking glass, constantly obliged to run as fast as possible in order to stand still.

COMPLEXITY AND EFFICIENCY

It is obvious that the general movement of evolution has resulted in the development of new structures and systems and in increased complexity. The simplest eucaryote is vastly more complex than any procaryote. Some protozoans are more complex than the simpler metazoans, but metazoans are typically far more complex than are protozoans. One could continue this progression much further. Accordingly, one tends to think of an advanced animal as a complex one, yet advance is often achieved by means of simplification: increased efficiency may be obtained by reducing the number and complexity of parts. The teeth of fish are generally very numerous and indefinitely replaceable. They are less numerous in amphibians and reptiles. In mammals, they reach a low in numbers along with a maximum in specialization and efficiency. Again, the reptilian skull is the prototype of the mammalian skull, which far surpasses the former in efficiency. This increase in efficiency, however, has been obtained by elimination of some bones and fusion of others, so that a much simplified structure results. For a third example, the sacrum of mammals is formed by the fusion of three to five originally separate vertebrae, thus strengthening the attachment of the hind limbs to the axial skeleton. Simplification, then, has been a very real component in the progress of evolution. Nature has wielded Occam's razor with a free hand.

CAUSAL FACTORS IN EVOLUTION

As the causal factors in evolution were discussed at some length in chapter 6, they can be summarized tersely here. In general, the interplay of mutation, Mendelian inheritance, and natural selection are sufficient to account for the major facts of evolution. Population structure influences the effectiveness of selection, and various isolating mechanisms also play an important role. Finally, a number of accelerating mechanisms have been proposed which may catalyze the evolutionary process. These range from systemic mutations, through coincidence of direction of selection and predominant direction of mutation, to severe selection pressure favoring a major change, such as the transition from fish to amphibian.

Teilhard recognized the importance of these, but he also felt that Lamarckian inheritance might—and probably did—play a role in evolution, and he was fully committed to the belief that orthogenesis played a major role in evolution. In both of these respects, his thinking went sharply counter to that of most modern students of evolution. Let us therefore examine these ideas carefully, considering Teilhard's reasons and the question of whether these ideas are in fact essential to his major thesis.

LAMARCKISM

Lamarckism is the idea that the environment induces those variations which are best adaptive to it and that such adaptations, acquired during the lifetime of the individual (as opposed to mutation of genes) are then inherited by the offspring. Some Lamarckians (an extremely rare breed among modern biologists, and nonexistent among geneticists) envision the environment as impressing the adaptive character on the organism without regard to the activity of the latter, while others think of adaptation as an active response on the part of the organism. It is probably the latter aspect which appealed to Teilhard for he said in a footnote, "I shall be accused of showing too Lamarckian a bent . . . of giving an exaggerated influence to the within." He then opts for an interplay of Darwinian and Lamarckian forces, for the footnote continues, "An essential part is left to the Darwinian play of external forces and to chance. It is only really through strokes of chance that life proceeds, but strokes of chance which are recognized and grasped—that is to say psychically selected. Properly understood the 'antichance' of the neo-Lamarckian is not a mere negation. On the contrary it appears as the *utilisation* of Darwinian chance" (p. 149).

Thus, it was because Lamarckism seemed to offer a directive role in evolution to the within that Teilhard favored it. On the other hand, Teilhard emphasized that many properties become important only when a certain threshold is crossed. Ice becomes water if its temperature is raised above 0°C, and steam above 100°C. Matter shows the properties of life when its complexity is raised to the cellular level. He emphasizes ascending levels of consciousness throughout the development of the animal kingdom. Might it not be that it is only when the latter reaches the human level that the Lamarckian type of inheritance becomes possible? Teilhard himself suggests this in a footnote: "Even if the Lamarckian view of the heritability of acquired characteristics is biologically *vieux jeu*, and decisively refuted, when we reach the human level and have to reckon with history, culture, etc., 'transmission' becomes 'tradition' " (p. 178). It is now quite generally understood that cultural evolution is the dominant phase of human evolution today and that cultural evolution, while it is based upon biological (genetic) evolution and interplays with it, nonetheless has laws of its own which are not genetic laws. This might very well be considered as a form of Lamarckian inheritance, and Teilhard seems to infer that this is enough for his purposes. And, if the human level of intelligence (to be discussed in the following chapters) is a minimal threshold for the Lamarckian phenomenon, then there is no reason why it should be expected or found except in human cultural evolution.

At least brief mention should be made of the reasons for which biologists generally reject Lamarckian inheritance (below the cultural level). Many experiments have been made upon a very wide variety of plants and animals to test the inheritance of acquired characteristics. Most of these have given negative results from the start. One major series of experiments on the inheritance of learning in rats (an acquired characteristic par excellence) seemed to give positive results at first, but repetition of the experiments under more carefully controlled conditions led to negative results once again.

Studies on mutation have also failed to show any Lamarckian guidance of the mutation process. Under any experimental or natural conditions, the overwhelming majority of mutations are harmful: they represent loss or impairment of some structure or function. Only a very small fraction of mutations is even potentially useful to the organism, and these are not necessarily useful under the condition in which the organism lives. Teilhard suggested that it is only through such strokes of chance that life proceeds, but through "strokes of chance which are recognized and grasped—that is to say psychically selected" (p. 149). In terms of cultural evolution, this can be accepted, but at lower levels, Darwinian natural selection, working in the manner described in chapter 6, is sufficient to explain the results.

Finally, there is now a theoretical basis for the exclusion of Lamarckian inheritance below the cultural level. Molecular biologists have shown that there are three kinds of "informational macromolecules," giant molecules whose structure encodes hereditary information. These are DNA, RNA, and protein. DNA is the primary one of these, and its basic function is self-reproduction, so that identical strands of DNA are passed to the progeny (mutation results from occasional mistakes in the self-copying of the DNA). A second function of DNA, however, is to make copies of itself in RNA (which differs from DNA in small but important chemical details). The RNA copies of the DNA then diffuse into the cytoplasm, where they attach to structures called ribosomes, and there the messenger RNA serves as a pattern upon which amino acids are assembled to synthesize protein molecules. Because most protein molecules are enzymes, which control the basic processes of life, this chain of reactions occupies a central position in the processes of life. Notice that it is a directional process running from DNA to RNA to protein, and in terms of protein the characters of plants and animals are expressed. The latter may be modified by environmental conditions, but as there is no mechanism whereby a modified protein can change the RNA upon which it was constructed, the inheritance of acquired characteristics would seem to be impossible.

ORTHOGENESIS

Orthogenesis is the idea that evolution follows a predetermined course to an inevitable end. Although Teilhard was fully committed to this idea, nowhere does he specify the nature of the directive force. He seems simply to have accepted it as a fundamental property of matter, a "law of directed* complication, the mature stage of the process in which we get first the micromolecule then the megamolecule and finally the first cells" (pp. 108–109). Nonetheless

*In the English editions, "dirigée" has been translated as "controlled." I think that "directed" may be better.

his statements have some ambivalence relative to orthogenesis. He states enthusiastically that "orthogenesis is the only dynamic and complete form of heredity. The word conceals deep and real springs of cosmic extent. . . . Thanks to its characteristic additive power, living matter (unlike the matter of the physicist) finds itself 'ballasted' with complications and instability. It falls, or rather rises, toward forms that are more and more improbable." Continuing the quotation, Teilhard revealed the reason for his commitment to orthogenesis: "Without orthogenesis life would only have spread; with it there is an ascent of life that is invincible" (pp. 108–109). To paraphrase, for reasons which will become apparent in succeeding chapters, Teilhard was convinced that there is a fundamental direction to evolution, and orthogenesis seemed to provide the basis for that direction.

On the other hand, Teilhard made several statements comparable to the following: "So as to overcome the improbability of arrangements of ever increasing complexity, the involuting universe, considered in its prereflective zones, proceeds step by step by dint of billionfold trial and error. It is this process of groping, combined with the twofold mechanism of reproduction and heredity . . . which gives rise to the extraordinary assemblage of living stems forming . . . the tree of life" (p. 301). It seems evident that "billionfold trial and error" and a directed process such as orthogenesis are mutually exclusive. If one holds true, the other is wrong. Teilhard tried to harmonize them by defining groping as directed chance, the organism trying everything in order to find something specific. Is it not more probable that natural selection simply eliminates the less adaptive variants, while favoring the expansion of the more adaptive variants? This would automatically direct each line of descent toward ever more refined adaptation to its conditions of life. Because those conditions themselves are constantly changing, however, this also provides for ever continuing evolution.

What is the positive evidence for orthogenesis? It was first proposed because certain fossil series seemed to suggest goal-oriented evolution. The mole-rats (genus *Siphneus*), which Teilhard studied in the Miocene and Pliocene of north China, comprise such a series. Teilhard followed their fossils through about ten million years of evolution, during which time they formed three distinct lines of descent. Yet, all three lines showed parallel changes: total size increased progressively; the crowns of the molar teeth became ever higher; and the cervical vertebrae gradually fused. Clearly, this was oriented evolution, and no doubt this study influenced Teilhard in favor of orthogenesis, yet the data are as readily interpreted on the basis of similar responses to similar selective forces. More famous is the horse series, which began in the Eocene with the small, browsing *Hyracotherium* and proceeded through half a dozen neatly spaced genera to the horses of the present day. The series seemed to suggest that horses knew from the start where they were going and took the most direct steps to get there. When the horse series was explored more fully, however, it proved to include some twenty-odd genera, most of which were not in the direct line of descent to modern horses, and some of these showed quite contrasting specializations. Clearly, the history of the horses was based upon typical adaptive radiation, the antithesis of orthogenesis, but our view of it is distorted by the facts that only one genus has survived to the present and that the record was very incompletely known for a long time. Other supposed cases of orthogenesis have suffered a similar fate upon fuller study of the fossil record.

Some paleontologists have suggested that orthogenesis may be uniquely a phenomenon of macroevolution (i.e., evolution on a geological scale, as opposed to the microevolution which geneticists study). While it would be difficult to exclude this possibility completely, still the trend of modern thinking on evolution has been toward the uniformitarian concept that the same basic processes are operative at all levels of biological evolution.

Teilhard's most critical point, however, was that "without orthogenesis life would only have spread; with it there is an ascent of life that is invincible" (p. 109). Whether evolution is directional has remained a controversial question up to the present. Many biologists, like G. L. Stebbins, favor the viewpoint that, because the mechanism of adaptive radiation by means of mutation and selection is an opportunistic one, groups expanding where they can and contracting where they must, any appearance of direction in evolution is illusory. Simpson's viewpoint is generally quite similar, yet he finds a tendency toward greater awareness and individualization. Others, such as J.B.S. Haldane, and J. Huxley have found a tendency toward higher levels of organization and of awareness or consciousness. Teilhard saw the development of consciousness as the major thrust of evolution. He saw evidence of this in the phylogenetic development of the nervous system, and he wrote that *"it proves that evolution has a direction"* (p. 146). This is, then, a controversial question which various biologists resolve on the basis of differing definitions of direction. However many organisms may have remained at lowly levels of biological organization, some have risen to higher levels, and man is here, studying all of the rest. For the present discussion, the question is, could these higher levels of biological organization, including the human level, have been attained in the absence of orthogenesis?

I think that question can be answered in the affirmative on the basis of the inherent potential of natural selection. Life originated and proliferated on the procaryote level. The manner in which natural selection favored the development of more versatile, more productive metabolic systems was discussed in chapters 4 and 5. Once the variety of ecological niches open to procaryotes was largely filled, evolution could only monotonously produce more variants on the same theme until a threshold was crossed to form the eucaryote cell. Immediately, this opened a vast range of possibilities on the protozoan level (I deliberately neglect plant evolution here, although animal evolution depends upon it absolutely). Natural selection favors diversification because it increases the total quantity of life which can survive in a given area.

When the ecological niches for protozoans were filled, a major advantage could be gained only by mutation to a metazoan type of organization, and hence selection favored this and then led to diversification of the simpler sorts of metazoan organization by the usual process of adaptive radiation. And so it continued, with natural selection favoring not only diversification within each level of organization but also the crossing of thresholds to new levels of organization, for in this way the total mass of life can be greatly increased and more complex, better buffered, and more stable ecological communities can be developed. And so it is that at the leading tip of the most successful lines of descent there are organisms with highly developed nervous systems, acutely responsive to the environment in which they live.

EVOLUTION AND ENTROPY

As discussed in chapter 3, one of the fundamental laws of physics is the law of entropy. This is the proposition that, in any physicochemical reaction, some energy is lost as heat, with the result that the total amount of available energy in the reacting system is reduced and order is gradually replaced by disorder. Physicists have predicted that this inexorable process of increasing entropy (which is decreasing order) must finally lead to the death of heat, a cold and lifeless universe. The course of evolution from the most elementary physicochemical levels through the world of life to man has run counter to this general trend of entropy: it has run from simpler to more complex levels of organization. Teilhard spoke of "the law of complexification" as a descriptive law which summarizes one of the major aspects of evolution.

The law of complexification is paradoxical in that it runs against the current of entropy. How is this possible? The law of entropy is strictly valid only in a closed system, that is, a system which receives no energy from the outside and contributes no energy to an outside receiver. As far as is known, the universe as a whole is such a closed system, but the earth certainly is not. The earth is bathed in a prodigal outflow of energy from the sun, and it is this that has powered the progress of evolution at all levels. In the earliest stages of chemical evolution, compound formation was probably strictly random, but as soon as the first autocatalytic compounds were formed, a sort of incipient natural selection would have favored the proliferation of these macromolecules. And as soon as the cellular threshold was crossed, typical Darwinian natural selection, as described above, could only result in the diversification and ascent of life. Indeed, natural selection has sometimes been defined as a mechanism for the generation of very high degrees of improbability. Evolution, then, runs counter to the current of entropy because the biosphere is not a closed system. Rather it is the beneficiary of the flood of solar energy, because the biosphere is prepared to exploit that flood of energy through the mechanism of natural selection.

CHAPTER ELEVEN

Thought
and the Noosphere

HAVING REVIEWED the grand sweep of evolution from primeval matter to man, Teilhard returned to the problem of direction of evolution, and he asked whether there might not be some standard by which this question could be evaluated. Before taking up his discussion of this problem, it may be well to review and extend somewhat the two aspects of matter, the without and the within, which were first introduced in chapter 3.

The ordinary physical properties of matter comprise the *without*, the world of mass, velocity, temperature, emission of light—the whole gamut of properties which physicists study. In addition to this, however, Teilhard proposed that there must be a *within* of matter, an aspect in which are found the possibilities of spontaneity. At the atomic and molecular levels, the within is not detectable, but as the organization of matter becomes more complex, the within becomes relatively more prominent, and at the cellular level it becomes visible as life, with all of its properties. In the highest animals, and especially in man, it is the within of matter that is the seat of psychic properties. Teilhard proposed this because he believed that it was required for scientific symmetry, for psychic properties could not emerge at higher levels unless they had been present, at least in rudimentary form, in the matter from which the first living organisms were constructed. Teilhard proposed that we are dealing with a threshold phenomenon, a change of state with the continued development of a specific property. Just as H_2O is liquid water at 99° and becomes gaseous steam on crossing the threshold of 100°, so the within of matter is undetectable even in very complex polymers but displays the basic properties of life when it crosses a threshold to reach the cellular level of complication.

Energy also shows two aspects, which Teilhard called tangential and radial energy. Tangential energy is characteristic of the *without* of matter, and accordingly it is the ordinary energy of the physicist, completely governed by the law of conservation of energy and the law of entropy. Radial energy is the psychic energy of the *within*. It is undetectably small in quantity at the atomic and molecular levels, but it increases proportionately at more complex levels of organization. Let me clarify this by an example. Proteins are large polymers made up of amino acids, which are already fairly complex molecules composed of carbon, hydrogen, oxygen, and nitrogen and, in two of the twenty amino acids, sulfur. Each atom has its component of radial energy, an undetectably small quantity. An amino acid of perhaps 20 atoms has radial energy somewhat in excess of the sum of that of its component atoms, because the higher complexity of the compound is characterized by radial en ergy based upon the arrangement, the order of the compound. A moderate-sized protein of, let us say, 150 amino acids, might include on the order of 3,000 atoms in a highly specific and complex arrangement, and its radial energy would be significantly greater than the sum of the radial energies of its component atoms. Finally, at the cellular level of complexity, the radial component becomes identifiable because it has crossed a critical threshold. At the level of simple cells, then, radial energy is detectable, and it becomes increasingly prominent as animals become more complex, until finally in man it is the dominant form of energy. Teilhard believed that radial energy was *not* subject to the physical laws of conservation and entropy. The two kinds of energy are clearly interrelated, but not in any simple way. Nourishment of the body (providing tangential energy) is necessary for thought (the specifically human aspect of radial energy), yet the slice of bread which supports sublime thoughts in one instance may subserve only trivialities in another.

Because evolution tends to produce ever higher degrees of complexity, as we saw in chapter 10, it also tends to produce ever more concentrated radial energy, and thus consciousness. Teilhard referred to this as the *law of complexity-consciousness,* and he regarded it as one of the most important of evolutionary generalizations.

ARIADNE'S THREAD

In Greek mythology, Ariadne gave Theseus a ball of thread, which he unrolled as he wandered through the labyrinth, seeking the Minotaur, a fearsome beast, which he slew. Had he not unrolled Ariadne's thread, he would have died in the labyrinth, unable to find his way out, but the story tells us that he simply followed the thread to the exit. Teilhard, in pondering the question of whether there was a direction to evolution, sought a comparable way to follow the true direction of evolution, if there be one. "The essence of the real," he wrote, "could well be represented by the 'interiority.' . . . In that case evolution would fundamentally be nothing else than the continual growth of this 'psychic' or 'radial' energy" (p. 143). We have seen that interiority and radial energy increase with the complexity of the animal, but the total complexity of an array of animals, let us say a lobster, an octopus, and a shark, is very difficult to compare. Is there in animal morphology any specific indicator of levels of radial energy? Teilhard thought that he could recognize such an indicator in the nervous system.

To test this, he applied this standard to the animals he

knew best, the higher vertebrates. Reptiles, as represented by the dinosaurs, had very small brains, actually smaller in some dinosaurs than the swelling at the base of the spinal cord which controlled the hind limbs. Mammals were derived from reptiles, and in general mammalian brains are much larger than reptilian brains. In marsupials, however, the brain is only a little larger and its surface is smooth. The archaic placental mammals which evolved early in the Cenozoic era were only a little more advanced, but all more recent mammals have distinctly larger brains, and the surface is generally thrown into folds, which permit a much larger number of nerve cells, with greatly increased numbers of connections among them. The order Primates is outstanding among the other mammalian orders in this respect (the great development of brain in man and his immediate forerunners was already reviewed in chapter 9).

In this limited survey, then, the nervous system does seem to serve as Ariadne's thread to guide us through the taxonomic-evolutionary labyrinth. Teilhard was so enthusiastic that he wrote,

> From the moment that the measure . . . of the evolving phenomenon is sought in the elaboration of the nervous systems, not only do the countless genera and species fall naturally into place, but the entire network of their verticils . . . rises up like a quivering spray of foliage . . . correspond[ing] exactly to the classification of systematic biology, but it confers on the tree of life a sharpness of feature . . . which is incontestably the hall-mark of truth. (p. 145)

Is so strong an endorsement as this really justified? To test this, it may be best to review the animal kingdom, very briefly, from the standpoint of nervous systems. One does not expect a nervous system in a one-celled animal, nonetheless, the neuromotor system which controls the ciliary beat of ciliate protozoans simulates a nervous system and may be highly complex. Sponges and mesozoans have no nervous system, and coelenterates have a simple nerve

net with little or no tendency to centralization. The flatworms show a clear advance, for they have a centralized
nervous system with a concentration of nerve cells forming
a "brain" and two nerve cords, one on each side. Associated with the brain are organs of special sense, a pair of
eyes and a pair of "auricular" lobes, which are actually organs of chemical sense. Thus the flatworms show the beginnings of the important process of *cephalization,* the concentration of the central nervous system and the sensory
organs at the anterior end of the body to form a head. In
higher groups (but not in the flatworms), the mouth is also
located here.

Thus far, we have seen a steady rise in complexity of
the nervous system from the most primitive phyla, which
have none, through the coelenterates, with their diffuse
nerve net, to the flatworms, which have a simple centralized nervous system with the beginnings of cephalization.
But what of the many invertebrate phyla which arose from
the flatworms, or from similar ancestors? Except for the
highest of them, they have diversified in many other ways,
while their nervous systems have remained at the same
general level or have even regressed. Teilhard wrote, "We
are dealing with only one event, the grand orthogenesis of
everything living toward a higher degree of immanent
spontaneity . . . over all of that like a simple sheath, we
find the veil of tissues and the architecture of limbs" (p.
151). Yet, if this were altogether true, could a radiation of
a dozen or more phyla be formed with no significant variations in the nervous systems? It seems more probable that
what evolution has done in this vast realm of life is to explore a maximum number of ecological niches and assure
that the total web of life has the variety upon which the
elasticity and viability of the system depend. Perhaps "a
higher degree of immanent spontaneity" is best understood as part of such a total system—even as the most important part, as it is the part which holds promise for the
future.

Among the protostomes, three phyla are outstanding for the development of the nervous system—the Annelida, the Arthropoda, and the Mollusca. In the annelids, there is a pair of solid, closely apposed nerve cords running the length of the body, just inside the body cavity and on the ventral (lower) surface. Along the length of these cords, there is a mass of nerve cells (a ganglion) in every segment of the body, and from these there arise two pairs of nerves, which serve the various structures of the body, segment by segment. At the anterior end, there is a cluster (or two clusters) of large ganglia which comprise the brain. There may be organs of special sense in the head region, and of course the mouth is located there. Thus, there is a high degree of cephalization. All in all, this is much the highest degree of development of the nervous system which we have yet seen. Nonetheless, within the present context, the importance of the annelids lies in the fact that they gave rise to the arthropods, the great phylum which culminated in the insects, the most successful of all groups if the number of species produced be the standard, and a highly successful group by any other standard. The arthropod nervous system is essentially the annelid system, but more highly developed.

More highly developed, but only within rigorously limited bounds. The psychic development of insects has been based upon instinctive responses which are largely invariant. There is little to suggest approach toward capacity for thought. Teilhard described them as "a multitude pathetically involved and struggling in a blind alley" (p. 153). Although they are a very ancient group, they have produced no really new type since the Paleozoic era. They have specialized for the exploitation of small size, and Teilhard suggests that higher levels of psychic activity may require brains of larger size than the insect body can accommodate.

A secondary peak among the protostomes was reached by the cephalopod molluscs—the octopus, squid, and their allies. In general, the nervous systems of molluscs are rather retrogressive, but the cephalopods have large brains, and they are capable of rather complex behavior. Psychological experiments have proven that they are capable of distinguishing different geometrical patterns, and they can acquire conditioned reflexes. Thus, the cephalopods are more flexible than the insects, yet they seem to have stopped considerably short of the threshold of thought.

The deuterostomes have produced the other major summit—one might say *the* major summit—of nervous development in the mammals. Curiously, the phylum to which the Chordata is most closely related, the Echinodermata, shows much retarded development of the nervous system, really a rudimentary system. Even in the most primitive chordates, however, some of the salient features of the organization of higher nervous systems appear. Thus it is based upon a hollow nerve tube, which runs the length of the body and gives off a pair of nerves in each segment of the body. In fishes, this is clearly divided into a nerve cord enclosed within the vertebral column and a large, complex brain of several lobes within the skull. The major sense organs—eyes, ears, and nose—are all located in the head region, in close association with the brain, so that cephalization is highly developed. In the spinal region, there is still one pair of nerves for each body segment, but in the head region the relationship of nerves to segmentation is not clear. There are, however, ten so-called cranial nerves which arise directly from the brain.

The situation is quite similar in the amphibians, and in the reptiles it differs mainly in that two more cranial nerves have been added. The nervous development of mammals, especially the Primates, was reviewed above. Suffice it to add here that the great development of the mammalian brain has occurred predominantly in the part called the neopallium, in which the higher centers are located. Clearly, this is the most complex of nervous systems in the entire animal kingdom, and it is just the sort of climax which Teilhard sought, a fitting place for the rise of thought.

This discussion began with the question of whether Teilhard's enthusiastic evaluation of the nervous system as Ariadne's thread was fully justified, whether in fact it does lead to a classification with "a sharpness of feature which is . . . the hall-mark of truth" (p. 145). A review of the major groups of the animal kingdom shows that some of the critical transitions are indeed marked by significant advances of the nervous system, but in other cases this is not true. Whole groups of phyla or classes may be at comparable levels of nervous organization. Genera and other lower groups were not discussed above because to do so was not practical. In general, closely related genera are not significantly different in their nervous organization, although it may be that such a clear difference did set off the genus *Homo* from its immediate predecessor. Thus, the criterion of nervous organization may function as Ariadne's thread for those critical parts of the taxonomic system in which Teilhard was most interested, but it lacks the generality he ascribed to it.

THE RISE OF CONSCIOUSNESS

Structure and function necessarily develop hand in hand, and where nervous systems are concerned, psychology is an important aspect of function. We have direct knowledge of consciousness only for one species, our own, but we infer it for many of the higher animals because they react so much as we do in many situations. In the lowest invertebrates, with no nervous system or only a nerve net, consciousness must be extremely dim, if it is recognizable at all. Among the many groups whose nervous systems are organized at the flatworm level, consciousness seems to be at a somewhat higher level, yet it must still be very dim.

In the higher annelids and most especially in the insects, invertebrate psychism reaches its peak. As mentioned above, however, the psychology of insects seems to have been locked into a rigid pattern of instinctive reactions which precluded consciousness of the sort we experience. In the cephalopods, we may recognize something more akin to consciousness and adaptability as we know them, but still on a very elementary level.

Another way to look at this is from the viewpoint of loss of consciousness, which we call sleep. Sleep is an urgent necessity for man. It is not fully understood by any means, but it is a complex function, with two types of sleep alternating. In slow sleep, the brain waves (electrical currents produced by the brain and detectable by an apparatus essentially identical to the electrocardiograph) show a slow and regular rhythm, and dreaming does not occur. In REM (rapid eye movement) sleep, the brain waves are more rapid and less regular, dreams occur, and the eyes move rapidly, as though following the action of the dream. It is doubtful whether sleep occurs in any of the invertebrates. There are simply cycles of activity and inactivity. This may also be true for fishes. Even amphibians lack certain brain centers which, in mammals, are associated with sleep. Reptiles appear to have the neurological centers needed for both types of sleep, but it is not clear to what extent sleep of reptiles is comparable to that of man. Do they, for instance, dream? Lower mammals, on the other hand, clearly do have both kinds of sleep. It is a common observation that dogs, for example, may quiver and make sounds suggestive of various activities while sleeping.

There has, then, been an ascent of consciousness paralleling the rise of complexity of the nervous system in the animal kingdom, with both reaching maximal expression in man. Sleep is necessary for deep rest only when consciousness is highly developed.

We have seen before that any property developing over a wide range tends to pass through a critical point, resulting in a change of state. A curve may change direction, as when a population grows at a continuous rate until a certain density is reached, then the growth curve levels off. Mass of an object remains apparently constant over a very wide range of acceleration, but as its speed approaches the speed of light, the mass increases enormously. At low temperatures H_2O is a solid, but if the temperature is raised above 0° it becomes liquid, while above 100° it becomes a gas. Such changes of state at critical points are thus well known to science. One of Teilhard's major arguments is that some of the most important properties of organisms result from just such changes of state at critical points in the progressive increase in complexity (complexification) from the atomic level through compounds and polymers, cells, and the many metazoan stages to man.

Let us review some critical points in the history of life which may be understandable on this basis. The first is the origin of life itself. Teilhard pointed out that the simplest of cells is far more complex than the most complex of polymers, and he suggested that the properties which we recognize as life may be the result of a change of state attendant upon crossing this threshold of complexity. The within, with its radial energy, has become sufficiently prominent to be overtly expressed. There has been a long step toward consciousness.

Let us consider some other possible examples which Teilhard did not discuss. A probable example is the origin of the eucaryote cell by a series of symbioses, as described in chapter 4. Any eucaryote cell shows an order of complexity which surpasses that of any procaryote cell by a margin which may rival that by which procaryote cells surpass the most complex of polymers. The development of the entire plant and animal kingdoms depended upon the prior origin of the eucaryote cell. Similarly, such critical points may be represented by the origin of multicellularity, of tissues, including nervous tissue, of organs, of the coelom, and of cephalization. Each of these in turn was a landmark in the history of morphology, and each resulted in a major adaptive radiation of whole phyla. For a similar reason, the origin of the dorsal nerve tube in the early chordates might be so considered, for it led to the basic pattern of the vertebrate nervous system, with all of its potentialities. Finally, one might include that combination of mutations which made possible the invasion of the land by early amphibians, an event which resulted in a series of adaptive radiations which produced the whole array of tetrapods, including the mammals. In all of these cases, threshold effects are highly suggestive, but it must be admitted that critical experimental tests of the hypothesis would be very difficult to devise.

Teilhard added one more case which is highly important for his argument. Remember that any property steadily increased over a long range tends to pass a critical point with a change of state. The within, consciousness, has, according to Teilhard, been developing for some billions of years from the atomic level through the various molecular and polymeric levels to cellular, multicellular, vertebrate, and finally mammalian levels. The higher mammals often show at least the rudiments of rational behavior. The central nervous systems, especially the brains, of mammals show a degree of complexity of organization which is without precedent in the entire animal kingdom. In the primates especially, the evolution of the brain is accentuated. Might they not be near a threshold on the other side of which is thought?

THE ORIGIN OF THOUGHT

As we saw in chapters 8 and 9, the step to man was not a great one in terms of morphology. It required a bigger (and probably better) brain and erect posture. The hands, freed from locomotor functions, could become grasping organs, and they were modified to permit accuracy of manipulation as well as a power grip. This released the jaws from their old prehensile function and permitted a relative reduction of the jaw musculature. The jaws were foreshortened, and the eyes moved forward on the reduced face, so that they could converge upon an object held in the hands, the gesture of reflection, according to Teilhard. Other morphological changes were no greater than these.

All morphological changes considered, the step to man was a rather minor one, yet its consequences have been enormous and without precedent. Was it merely a minor change in degree, like the transition from one species to another in the evolution of the horses, as the morphological facts would suggest? Or does man represent a new *kind* of life? Teilhard suggested that this question could be answered only by consideration of the within. Seen from this viewpoint, and against the background of the above discussion, the step to man appears as the crossing of a threshold in the development of complexity-consciousness, resulting in a change of state from simple consciousness of surrounding objects to thought, rationality, and reflection.

Teilhard saw reflection, the ability of the conscious individual to consider himself as an object, as the heart of the problem. Clearly, the higher animals know much, but they do not and they cannot *know that they know.* Thus, the individual tends to become a *center* about which he mentally organizes the world and puts it in perspective. "Abstraction, logic, reasoned choice and inventions, mathematics, art, calculation of space and time, anxieties and dreams of love—all these activities of inner life are nothing else than the effervescence of the newly formed center. . . . Because we are reflective we are not only different but quite other. It is not a matter of change of degree, but of change of nature, resulting from a change of state" (p. 165). And such a reflective center is a *person,* capable of free choice, responsible for his acts, capable of good and evil.

For all of this, the same old biological processes continue much as they had for billions of years, just as though nothing had happened. The physiology of man differs only in minor details from that of other mammals. The genetics of man is identical to that of all of the rest. The same evolutionary processes of mutation, selection, and adaptive radiation continue as before, but here there is a difference which is not fully explained yet. A typical mammalian species in its adaptive radiation forms an array of geographically replacing subspecies, some of which in the course of time become good and distinct species. It may be that two or more species of australopithecines were contemporaneous, but it is also debatable whether they had passed the threshold to thought (it is even debatable whether they should be assigned to the genus *Homo*). At later times, however, there never has been more than one species of man at a time. There has been a degree of cohesiveness in man not shown by other species.

This is not to say that there has been no adaptive radiation in man: there has been, but it has not led to formation of a cluster of species.

The old evolutionary processes interact with the new phenomenon of thought. The latter resulted in the development of cultures, which were transmitted by speech and by other means of communication. Such traditions may be said to be inherited, but it is not genetic inheritance. On the contrary, tradition bypasses the genes and operates via the processes of learning. As learning is an acquired character par excellence, cultural or traditional inheritance may be said to be Lamarckian. While evolution by means of mutation and selection is typically a very slow process, cultural or psychosocial evolution may proceed with startling rapidity, as indeed it has for the past several generations. Cultural evolution also shows properties which might be called orthogenetic, for people and societies do work toward predetermined ends. It was partly because Lamarckism and orthogenesis are so clearly demonstrable in cultural evolution that Teilhard favored them in animal evolution generally. Relying on his principle that nothing could emerge at higher levels which was not present, at least in rudimentary form, at lower levels, he considered that the clear emergence of these phenomena at the human level was strong inferential evidence for their presence at lower levels. It seems at least as probable, however, that, in strictly Teilhardian terms, the emergence of these properties is a result of a change of state upon crossing the threshold of thought. Indeed, the latter alternative seems much more probable in view of the serious evidence against Lamarckism and orthogenesis at lower levels.

Cultural evolution has not, as is sometimes said, replaced biological evolution. Rather it has supplemented it. Just as biological evolution supplements but does not replace physicochemical evolution, so cultural evolution works in harmony with biological evolution. While cultural evolution may be very much more rapid than genetic evolution, it can only proceed within limits which are genetically determined. For example, a society in which science, engineering, medicine, law, and other learned professions play prominent roles can only be produced by a population in which the general level of intelligence is high enough to include many who meet the requirements of these professions and to produce at least a few creative geniuses capable of the brilliant achievements which are responsible for the progress of these professions. Thus, the genetically determined characteristics of the brain serve as the basis of cultural development. On the other hand, a society in which a premium is placed upon such abilities also acts as a selective force to favor those mutations which facilitate cultural achievement. Thus there is an interplay between genetic and cultural evolution which enriches both. It is this combined effect of the two levels of evolution which is responsible for the continuing development of man, which Teilhard referred to as *hominization*.

NOOGENESIS AND THE NOOSPHERE

The origin of reflective thought by the crossing of a critical threshold in the organization of the brain, together with the further development of this new property as well as its consequences, Teilhard called *noogenesis*. The word was deliberately chosen to indicate that it is a continuing process, an evolution, consistent with the whole history of a world in evolution, rather than a single event accomplished once for all time. This is the most recent in a long series of such evolutionary processes. It began with cosmogenesis, the evolution of the physicochemical universe, one aspect of which was geogenesis, the evolution of the earth. The latter reached its climax in biogenesis, the origin and evolution of life. This in turn included psychogenesis, which finally resulted in man. And now the last and highest of this sequence—noogenesis.

Geologists have long agreed that the earth consists of an inner, metallic core, the barysphere, surrounded by the rocky lithosphere. This in turn is surrounded by the liquid hydrosphere and the gaseous atmosphere. Biologists have long recognized a biosphere, the total living community, spread out over and near the surface of the earth. Because of the complex web of interdependence among all living things, and because all are interrelated genetically due to evolution from common ancestors, Teilhard referred to the biosphere as a living membrane, a fifth layer spread over the entire earth. Carrying the same reasoning one step further, then, Teilhard suggests that the origin of thought, of mind, added one final layer to the earth, the *noosphere*. "The earth gets a new skin," wrote Teilhard. "Better yet, it finds its soul" (p. 182). He believed that the origin of the noosphere was an event comparable in importance only to the origin of life itself.

NOOGENESIS IN THE PALEOLITHIC

Teilhard liked to say that "man came silently into the world" (p. 183), meaning that there was no radical change in the world of life immediately after the origin of man or for a long time afterward. Life went on much as though he were just another primate rather than a really new kind of life. The adaptive radiation of early man and his immediate ancestors was reviewed in chapters 8 and 9, and that need not be repeated here. More important in the present context are the evidences of culture, which comprise the record of noogenesis. There is a possibility that culture first appeared fairly early among the australopithecines. A few anthropologists believe that they developed a culture based upon simple tools fashioned from skin, bone, and horn. Probably the majority opinion is that the evidence for this culture is inadequate. Simple pebble tools however, have been found in association with those late australopithecines which L.S.B. Leakey has described under the name *Homo habilis* and which he regarded as the first true men. No cultural remains have been found in direct association with Java man, but this may not be significant, because the fossils were recovered from a lake deposit, and the remains may have been carried into the lake by a stream from some unknown campsite. With the remains of Peking man, however, abundant stone tools and the charred wood of ancient campfires were found.

The record of *Homo sapiens* is rich in cultural remains, except for its earliest, mid-Pleistocene representatives. Even the Neanderthals were expert makers of stone tools, and they buried their dead, so it seems clear that they had religious practices. But the Cro-Magnon men of southwestern Europe had a rich culture, the remains of which we can still admire today. They were, of course, expert craftsmen in the making of stone tools. The remains of countless campfires attest to their use of fire. But it is primarily their art which shows the richness of their culture. The plethora of paintings which adorn many of the caves of southwestern Europe has become well known in the present century, first through the researches of Teilhard's friend, Père Henri Breuil, later through the work of many others. Many of these show a high order of artistic skill: sense of form, sensitive use of color, even clever exploitation of the contours of the rock upon which they were painted. The remains of shell jewelry have also been found in their caves and in their graves, as well as carvings on reindeer horn and small stone statuettes. Some of their paintings depict religious ceremonies which suggest those of primitive peoples of today. Teilhard referred to this exuberant outflow of art as "these flowers of a consciousness not merely reflecting upon itself, but rejoicing in so doing" (p. 201), and the metaphor rings true.

Throughout the Paleolithic age, the human population seems to have been sparse. The economy was based upon hunting and gathering fruits and vegetables. The men were typically nomads who traveled in family groups or in small tribal groups still based upon blood relationship, essentially extended families. Thus, noogenesis was in full swing by late Paleolithic time, yet the noosphere was spread rather tenuously over the surface of the globe, and there was little or no communication and cohesion between different groups of men.

THE NEOLITHIC METAMORPHOSIS

After long ages of Paleolithic culture, marked by the fashioning of unpolished stone tools and a loose, nomadic social organization, a radical change took place. Hunting gave way to herding of domesticated animals, and gathering of wild fruits and vegetables gave way to cultivation of the soil. Permanent settlements were formed for the first time, and the development of civilization was in progress. This time of great change is called the Neolithic period, meaning new stone age, because craftsmen of this time learned to polish their implements.

The Neolithic transition was amazingly rapid. Teilhard wrote that "in a matter of ten or twenty thousand years man divided up the earth and struck his roots in it" (p. 203), but it now appears that this was much too generous a time allowance. The diagnostic features for the Neolithic are polished stone, pottery, agriculture, and permanent settlements. The last glaciation retreated about eleven thousand years ago, and the resulting improvement of the climate provided the opportunity for the development of agriculture, an opportunity which men of the time were quick to exploit. The remains of domesticated dogs, found in the region of the Caspian Sea, have been dated by the radiocarbon method, which has shown that they lived about 9000 BC. The earliest villages known, found in the Iranian highlands, are of about the same age. The earliest known pottery is substantially later.

Arbitrarily, we designate as historic time the last six thousand years or so, for which there are written records, and back of that is prehistoric time, including the more recent Neolithic and the more ancient Paleolithic ages. This leaves only about five thousand years for the entire Neolithic. Teilhard pointed out, however, that much of historic time might be regarded as a prolongation of the Neolithic, for trends which began in the Neolithic were simply continued, elaborated, and recorded in the documents of history.

An agricultural economy will support a larger population than will a hunting–gathering economy. It may be, as Teilhard suggested, that growing density of population in the late Paleolithic provided part of the stimulus for the invention of agriculture. Certainly, once agriculture was established, growing density of population provided pressure for its continuing development and improvement. As the population grew more dense, groups tended to coalesce and form larger groups. Societies became complex, and organization developed on several different planes. Tribal organization blended into villages, then city-states, then larger, geographically based political units. Concepts of property developed as the land was divided and as villages were built. This necessitated the development of concepts of rights and duties, of law, and of judicial authority and structures. Religions were developed, as well as morals, marriage, and the family. The importance of mind, of psychic factors, is obvious in all of these developments. From this time on, psychic factors may be regarded as more important than somatic factors in the development of man.

A time of such profound change produced many new needs and hence stimulated very fundamental inventions and the beginnings of research. The wheel and the plow were invented in Neolithic times. Almost all of the plants and animals upon which we depend today were, within a fairly short time, selected and domesticated. The art of pottery was developed to a high degree, as was weaving. Soon the first rudiments of metallurgy were discovered, and this resulted first in the Bronze Age and later in the Iron Age. Most portentous of all, writing was invented, and this not only made the transmission of culture very much more efficient but also constituted the transition to historic time.

Had the expanding Neolithic populations been living on the flat earth which was once imagined, extending off indefinitely in every direction, they might have simply spaced out more widely and each group developed uninfluenced by the others. On our round earth, however, there was no possibility but that the neighbors be forced into contact and interaction. Among lower animals, competition may lead to elimination of the weaker competitor, but in man there is almost always at least partial assimilation, and a conquered people may have profound influence upon the conqueror. Thus, there may be cultural hybridization as well as genetic hybridization. To take one example (necessarily from historic rather than Neolithic times), the Romans conquered the Greeks, but as Greek slaves were then the teachers of the Romans, Roman culture bore a strong Greek stamp. And further, there was much interbreeding as well.

Finally, Teilhard emphasized that all of this early human history (and later history as well) is still *natural* history, because man, his works, and his complex societies are still parts of nature. In this connection, I would like to quote P. B. Medawar, a distinguished biologist who has been highly critical of Teilhard, yet he wrote, "The biologist has much to learn from human biology, and chiefly this lesson: that the distinction he has been wont to draw between Nature, on the one hand, remote and wild, and, on the other hand, Man and his works, is one that damages his understanding of both" (1964: vi). However unique man may be in nature, then, he is still very much part of it.

THE MODERN WORLD

Thus, the Neolithic metamorphosis was extended into historic times, and history is its logical prolongation through ancient and medieval times. Many things suggest, however, that modern man is experiencing a change as fundamental as that of his Neolithic ancestors, and that change has been in progress at least since the time of the Renaissance. Let us discuss some of the indications of this change, drawing examples from economic, sociopolitical, and scientific spheres.

THE ECONOMIC SPHERE
One of the major effects of the Neolithic metamorphosis was to establish the arable field as the basis of the economy. So fundamental was this that it determined also the character of the family and of the emerging states. And so it remained until recent times. In a sense, the arable field will always have fundamental importance unless synthetic food production should someday replace it. Nonetheless,

the relative importance of the arable field has declined dramatically. In Neolithic times, almost everyone earned his living by agriculture or by trading in agricultural products. As recently as the middle of the nineteenth century, well over half of the population of the United States lived by farming, but today the farm population is a minority.

This is partly a consequence of the industrial revolution. Since Neolithic times, fire, usually of wood, had been the only source of chemical energy, and muscle, whether of man or of his domestic animals, had been the main source of mechanical energy, although water wheels and windmills made small contributions. During the industrial revolution, new fuels were tapped, and better ways of using their energy were invented. The wood fire was largely replaced by coal, and more recently, petroleum and its by-products have gone far toward replacing coal. Electricity was discovered, and its importance has grown steadily since the mid-nineteenth century. Finally, atomic energy has become available very recently.

The energy of these new fuels was soon channeled into more productive machines. The steam engine was invented, then the internal combustion engine and the electric motor. These were harnessed to an ever increasing array of machines which now do a very large share of the world's work and which provide a standard of living for the ordinary laborer which in many respects far exceeds that of the kings of only a few centuries ago.

Small family-run businesses, comparable to family-run farms, at first dominated the urban economic scene, but these have been largely succeeded by ever larger corporations run by boards of directors. Their businesses are ever more diversified, and their scope is commonly international, even worldwide. In the modern economic world, the stock certificate may often be more important than the arable field.

THE SOCIOPOLITICAL SPHERE

Changes have also been great in the sociopolitical sphere, as the very size of the units suggests. The earliest villages consisted of a few families, probably rather closely related. By early Hellenic times, these had become the classical city-states. These gradually united to form national states based upon common language, culture, and religion, and empires were based upon conquest. In the modern world, there have been some significant experiments looking toward an international state. The old League of Nations and the current United Nations, as well as the British Commonwealth of Nations (which is *not* the old British Empire) and the more informal association of French-speaking nations, might all be regarded as experiments looking toward a comprehensive world state of the future.

There has also been a radical change in the form of government. There is little known about the government of ancient Neolithic societies, but as they merged into history, they were generally ruled by kings whose power was absolute. In surviving Neolithic societies, there is generally a tribal organization under a powerful chief. Although some of the Greek city-states developed highly democratic governments for the free citizens, they were based upon slavery. In general, ancient and medieval history saw the development and strengthening of monarchical government, together with its corollary, a system of nobility to extend the royal power throughout the realm. In modern times, democratic government has largely replaced the old autocratic monarchies, either totally by abolishing the monarchy or through constitutional government in which the crown is the formal symbol of government only, with the actual power being entrusted to elected officials.

In early societies, master–servant relationships were the norm, and positions were often hereditary. While it cannot be said that this has been totally changed, still the democratization of society has proceeded very far in recent generations. One important factor in this has been the growth of education. Formal education was once largely restricted to a favored few, but now there is universal education in all developed countries. Such massive programs of education inevitably are beset by difficult problems, and in most societies the school systems are severely criticized. Nonetheless, it is noteworthy that they generally do try to assist their students to rise to the highest level of socio-intellectual achievement which the student is capable of attaining. In spite of all of the criticism, it is fair to say that their overall success rate has been quite creditable, as judged by the numbers of men and women who have risen to positions above those of their recent forebears.

Another factor in the democratization of society has been the rise of the trade unions. Considerably less than a century ago, the typical laborer had almost no bargaining power with his employer. The employer could dictate the terms of employment, and a worker who protested, or who joined a union, was quite likely to find himself unemployed. Today, workers in most major industries are strongly unionized, and their leaders can bargain with employers as equals, and sometimes they may be stronger than the employers.

THE SCIENTIFIC SPHERE

The explosive development of science has been one of the most characteristic aspects of the modern world. The old alchemy developed into chemistry. Most of the elements were discovered during the past two hundred years. Inorganic reactions were the first to yield to research, but the development of organic chemistry was not far behind, and in recent years biochemistry has caught up with the older chemical disciplines. Modern physics began with Renaissance studies in mechanics and optics, then electricity was investigated, radioactivity was discovered, and finally atomic physics came to the fore. Biology was a growing chaos until Linnaeus undertook the study of the world of life. He stimulated a century of biological exploration which greatly enriched the fund of biological data but also showed that the Linnean system was inexplicable. Darwin filled this breach with the theory of evolution. Only a little later, Mendel discovered the fundamental laws of inheritance, while the main facts regarding cells were being discovered by many biologists. Today, cell biology, genetics, and evolution have combined forces with physics and chemistry to give a very profound understanding of the processes of life.

In a few short lines, one cannot review the entire recent history of science. Suffice it to say that the histories of other sciences, such as geology, astronomy, and mathematics have been comparable to those of chemistry, physics, and biology. Recent history has, indeed, witnessed the rise of science from obscurity to a position of dominance in the modern world. And, of course, it is primarily applied science which supports the high standard of living in the developed countries of the world.

In the modern world, then, more people share in a higher standard of living than ever before. In the sociopolitical sphere, there is more freedom, more education, more opportunity to share in making the decisions which effect one's self than ever before. In the scientific sphere, we have in the past few generations achieved an unprecedented knowledge of and mastery over the forces of nature. And yet, in spite of this brilliant record of successes, modern man is looking to the future not with confidence but with anxiety.

NEW DIMENSIONS

Post-Renaissance science has totally changed our conception of the spatial and temporal dimensions in which we live. Less than two hundred years ago, our forebears thought of the earth as the center of a tidy little universe created especially for man only six thousand years before. Astronomical research, which began with Copernicus,

showed that in fact the earth is a middle-sized planet re-
volving around the sun, an average star which is part of a
great galaxy hundreds of light years across. Further, our
galaxy is only one of a large number in an immensity of
space which staggers the imagination. More or less concurrently, the microscope revealed the hosts of microbes, then
physics and chemistry carried dimensions still further down
to the molecular, atomic, and even subatomic levels. Man
seemed to live in an ill-defined mid-region between the
infinitely small and the infinitely large.

Time was originally just a convenient scale on which
to locate consecutive events, and its total duration was only
a brief six thousand years up to the present. Astronomy,
biology, and geology all showed that there was an immensity of time comparable to the spatial immensity of the
universe. Current estimates of the age of the universe range
from four and a half to twenty billion years. Further, these
showed that time is historically irreversible. Nonetheless,
the two immensities of space and time seemed more or less
unrelated at first, but evolutionary biology showed that they
are joined "in the irreversible coherence of all that exists"
(p. 217). Each organism has its place in space *and* time.

The early evolutionists thought of themselves as essentially outside of evolution, its most recent product, but essentially completed, especially as regards the mind. Teilhard pointed out that this is an untenable position: nothing
is outside of evolution, and certainly not the mind. Biogenesis must be continued as noogenesis. In fact, Teilhard
defined "modern man" as one who sees all things, including himself, in terms of evolution. Of course, he acknowl-
edged that many of our contemporaries are not modern by
that definition.

RETROSPECT

In the preceding chapters, we have followed evolution
forward from the creation of the universe to man, to hom-

inization and noogenesis. At this point, Teilhard invited us to look back. Looking back, he believed that he could see, in the grand sweep of evolution, a triple unity: unity of structure, unity of mechanism, and unity of movement. Let me discuss each of these unities briefly.

At every stage in evolution, we have seen adaptive radiation, with the resulting structure of peduncles and verticils. This is continued into the psychosocial evolution, the noogenesis, of man, where it appears as the complex of races, nations, cultures, and other ramifications of human society. Teilhard believed that this continuation in human society of the old structural pattern of the species and subspecies of lower animals proved that the social phenomenon is the culmination of the biological phenomenon, not its antithesis, as has so often been asserted. Once again, we must insist that *human history is natural history.*

Under unity of mechanism, Teilhard spoke of groping and invention, but, as we saw in chapters 6 and 10, we may substitute mutation and selection. We saw that, although these may be supplemented by various secondary processes, they are found throughout the world of life, and their power to generate very high degrees of improbability (successful organisms) has been demonstrated. These processes continue in man, but groping and invention in a much more literal sense also occur in the psychosocial evolution of man. Faced with a problem, we do in fact try a variety of potential solutions until we find one which works. "The spirit of research," wrote Teilhard, "is the permanent soul of evolution" (p. 223), a fine statement which appeals very strongly to a scientist. Yet I must also note that the type of purposeful groping and invention which are under discussion are probably possible only after crossing the threshold of thought.

Finally, Teilhard saw unity of movement in "the rise and expansion of consciousness" (p. 223). It is a fact of observation that this has been a major movement of evolution, but, as developed in chapter 10, it has not been a continuous movement, and it may quite possibly be one aspect of the ecological diversification which has occurred at all levels of biological evolution. Yet this does not negate Teilhard's beautiful poetic insight: "Man is not the center of the universe as once we thought in our simplicity, but something much more wonderful—the arrow pointing the way to the final unification of the world in terms of life. Man alone constitutes the last-born, the freshest, the most complicated, the most subtle of all the successive layers of life" (p. 223).

In man, the age-old mechanism of genetic inheritance is combined with the new, cultural inheritance to give possibilities for the direction of his own evolution. Hence, in a very real sense, we hold the future of evolution, the future of life, in our hands. The future depends upon how we use that power, and this leads directly to the problem of action.

THE PROBLEM OF ACTION

Man, then, has arrived at the present after several hundred years of extraordinary successes. He has crowned it all by the discovery that not only is he a product of evolution but, in Julian Huxley's brilliant phrase, "he is nothing else than evolution become conscious of itself" (p. 220). The future of evolution depends upon how man uses his gifts of genetic and Lamarckian (cultural) inheritance to build the future. Yet, in the face of this magnificent challenge, modern man is worried, more worried than any of his ancestors. Why?

THE MODERN DISQUIET

Perhaps, as Teilhard suggested, anxiety is a direct consequence of reflection, and therefore it is as old as man himself. But few will deny that the anxiety of modern man runs deeper than that of his forebears. Only a few generations ago, people believed almost universally that they lived at the center of a rather small universe which had been recently created especially for them. All things were under the Providence of God, and they could entrust themselves to His care without reserve. This belief was based upon Scripture and the traditions of the Church. The Reformation tended to divide men into two camps which emphasized one or the other of the two, yet the long-range effect was to cast doubt upon the reliability of both. The investigations of Galileo cast further doubt upon the old beliefs because, erroneously, the geocentrical system had been treated as a truth of faith. That it was demonstrated to be wrong cast doubt on the entire deposit of faith. Meanwhile, modern science developed and its technological applications began to provide a more abundant standard of living for an ever greater proportion of humanity. While we still have a long way to go in this respect before poverty can be only an unpleasant memory, still men who no longer felt the need to pray for their daily bread no longer felt the need to pray. And when Darwin published the *Origin of Species* and the *Descent of Man*, it seemed as though God were no longer necessary even as our Creator. Of course, the old faith still survives, and for many it is stronger than ever for having been relieved of unnecessary burdens, but for large sections of modern humanity, faith is no longer possible, or it is held in a tentative fashion which does not offer substantial hope. Those who have been emancipated from the fear of hell have also been deprived of the hope of heaven.

Teilhard proposed two causes of the modern anxiety which are more immediately related to his thesis. The first he called the sickness of space-time, by which he meant that one may feel utterly lost and insignificant when he realizes the awful chasms of space and time which extend to seeming infinity on either side of his brief moment of life.

He also proposed a cure, and that is an appreciation of our role in evolution.

> What matters the giddy plurality of the stars and their fantastic spread, if that immensity (symmetrical with the infinitesimal) has no other function but to equilibrate the intermediate layer where, and where only in the medium range of size, life can build itself up chemically. What matter the millions of years and milliards of beings that have gone before if those countless drops form a current which carries us along (p. 227).

"No other function" may be too strong a restriction on the great bulk of the universe, but this does not gainsay the fact that, in an evolving universe, there is an especial importance to that one middle-sized body on which evolution is known to have crossed the threshold from the physiocochemical to the biological phase of evolution. And in the realm of life, only man has crossed the threshold to the psychosocial evolution, which is noogenesis. Thus, a man who can think of himself as "the arrow pointing the way to the final unification of the world in terms of life" (p. 227) should not be overwhelmed by the sickness of space-time.

Teilhard's second cause of the modern anxiety is more fundamental. He called it the sickness of the dead end. Even if one has learned to view all of reality in terms of evolution in its three great phases and to think of man as the leading edge of this great creative process, he may still have nagging doubts whether there will be a suitable outcome for evolution. After the grand progression from cosmogenesis through noogenesis, could evolution simply stagnate and abort, so that it would all come to naught? This, Teilhard felt, was the most painful source of the modern anxiety. Perhaps it is simply a restatement of the discussion of religious doubts with which this section began.

I do not suggest that these three factors are an exhaustive explanation of the modern malaise. Undoubtedly, additional factors from every aspect of culture are involved, but these are the ones which are most germane to the present discussion.

According to Teilhard, the modern disquiet has resulted in a crisis in evolution. Now that evolution has become conscious of itself, it can progress to a still higher level only if man acts to achieve the higher level. And man will do that only if he believes that to do so is worthwhile, that a suitable outcome for evolution is possible. The crisis in evolution consists in this, that large numbers of people are asking whether the game is worth the candle, and not a few are answering in the negative. Despair in the economic sphere led to strikes in the nineteenth century, and in the twentieth century strikes have become an important tool in labor–management relations. Teilhard asked whether the present century might not see strikes in the noosphere. I think that this question can be answered in the affirmative: the widespread anti-intellectualism, the hippie phenomenon, the drug culture, the modern philosophies of despair, and the desperate interest in occult philosophies and religions might all be considered as strikes in the noosphere. They represent forlorn and pathetic inability to find satisfying meaning in life, that is to say, the strikers lack confidence that there will be a satisfactory outcome for evolution.

Teilhard suggested that such strikes could be settled and man could then act for a satisfactory outcome of evolution only if two conditions be met: first, people must be assured that there is a future, a survival for us; and second, they must be assured that to reach that satisfactory outcome we need only continue in the direction in which the lines of evolution take on their maximal coherence.

CHAPTER TWELVE

Omega

IN THE PRECEDING CHAPTERS, I have reviewed the course of evolution from the origin of the physical universe up to the present. In general, I have tried to present the essential scientific facts and to reason from them inductively, in the ordinary scientific fashion. In the attempt to see not only what has happened but also what it means, it has occasionally been necessary to leave scientific procedure and reason deductively or to use propositions which are not amenable to experimental test. In some instances, I have called attention to these extrascientific passages. In other instances, I have considered it sufficiently obvious that I need not repeat over and over a dull and unnecessary warning.

In the chapters that follow, we shall be dealing with the future (survival, as Teilhard called it). While I shall continue to stick to established facts as far as possible, I must also rely on the Teilhardian principle that every evolutionary movement has its origin in the past and its extension into the future. It should be obvious that the speculative element in these chapters will be far greater than in the preceding ones. Indeed, it will now be predominant.

MEGASYNTHESIS

Since the beginning of the evolutionary process, the within has been gathered into ever larger units, beginning with atoms and proceding through molecules, polymers, cells, metazoans with more and more complex nervous systems, and now man. We have seen that human societies are in the process of grouping into ever larger, more organized units. Could there be a megasynthesis in progress, tending to make an organic reality, a unity, of mankind? There are some facts which point in that direction.

Teilhard asked why there should be unification, and he answered it by formulating two equations which had emerged out of the study of evolution: "Evolution = rise of consciousness; Rise of consciousness = effect of union" (p. 243). As we have seen, it is true that the rise of consciousness has been a major aspect of evolution. It has not, however, been a universal aspect, and it may be that this equation is somewhat overenthusiastic. As for the second equation, we have seen in the preceding chapters that Teilhard has made a fairly good case for consciousness as resulting from increasing complexity, especially of the central nervous system. If it is legitimate to define complexity as the union of many parts to form a coordinated whole, then the equation is valid.

CONFLUENCE OF THOUGHT

We have seen that, at every level in the evolution of the world, units at the same level react upon one another. As Teilhard liked to say, they interpenetrate one another. And while the obvious result is an increase in complexity of the without, a correlative result is an increase in the radial energy of the within. At the human level, this interpenetrability leads to the vast complex of social phenomena whereby both individuals and whole societies interact, influence one another, and modify one another. Thus, their radial energies are combined, and the whole is greater than the sum of its parts. This natural tendency is intensified by two factors: the roundness of the earth and the development of modern transportation and communications.

Were the earth a flat surface of more or less indefinite extent, as our ancestors once imagined, early man, as he became more numerous, could have simply spread out more widely so that populations would have remained sparse and there would have been minimal mutual interaction and stimulation. In fact, once the land was generally occupied, there was no alternative on this round earth but that we become more densely packed. Individuals, families, and tribes fused to form more complex societies, and societies interacted, fused, and rebranched to form the complex maze of societies, states, cultures, and religions which make up the human verticil today.

The pace of this interaction has been much quickened and intensified by the development of modern communications and transportation. Only a few generations ago, the great majority of people lived their entire lives within a few miles of their birthplaces. Only a century ago, Jules Verne's *Around the World in Eighty Days* seemed wildly visionary, yet today satellites circle the globe in little more than eighty minutes! At least in the more highly developed countries, people of today are as mobile as their ancestors were sedentary. As a result, the man of today meets and interacts with people over a wide area, whereas his ancestors of only a few generations ago spread their influence (and were in turn influenced) only over a radius of a few miles.

The effect of modern communications has been even more profound, for by means of radio and television the more distant parts of the world may be brought into immediate contact. The result is that very large numbers of people wield influence which is truly worldwide, and everyone in the mainstream of modern life is subject to worldwide influences. Further, our needs must be satisfied on a worldwide basis. Neolithic man required only his daily bread, and this was provided by a single field. But Teilhard pointed out that modern man "demands his daily ration of iron, copper, and cotton, of electricity, oil, and radium, of discoveries, of the cinema, and of international news" (p. 245). Of course, the list could be extended indefinitely, and the whole world is the field which must provide them.

All of these pressures work together to concentrate and intensify the energies of consciousness. The social phenomenon represents a new order of complication, a supraindividual complication, in the organization of living matter, and hence it should again result in a new level of the radial energy of the within. Man, of course, is not the first animal to develop social organizations. The social organization of bees and termites may be highly complex, but they are confined to the progeny of a single mother. Schools of fishes and herds of various mammals may involve a broader sample of the population, but their organization is very simple and probably serves mainly for protection against predators. Only man has evolved the complex, multipurpose societies which are a matter of everyday experience to us.

As a typical mammalian species becomes widespread, it splits up into a verticil of subspecies, and some of these usually separate off to become good and distinct species. Man is the most cosmopolitan of all species. There is no habitat from which he is completely excluded, and he thrives in all but the most inhospitable parts of our globe. Yet, although he has formed the most complex of verticils, made up of races, cultures, nations, and all of the rest, he has remained one, single, worldwide species. How has this been possible? Teilhard suggested that thought may be the cement which binds together the parts of the human verticil and keeps the whole species one great unit. Henceforth, then, formation of verticils is subordinate to a *convergence* of the differentiated lines to form a unity.

MANKIND

There is, then, a serious possibility, even probability, that the dream of the prophets of the eighteenth century of a unified mankind is in process of realization. Surely the developments of the intervening two centuries have given us a degree of economic, social, political, and cultural interdependence which they could scarcely imagine. And if an evolutionary All is in process of formation, how should it be conceived? Generally, it has been conceived in very vague terms, but some have thought of it as a sort of nascent giant, with specific organs and functions; others as a legal entity, a sort of super United Nations; Teilhard, however, believed that it must be conceived as a genuinely new biological category, a collective, which could only be defined in terms of *mind*. Accordingly, he pictured the future of mankind in terms of two attributes: knowledge and unanimity.

Man's appetite for knowledge is a consequence of crossing the threshold of reflection, and it is as natural to him as is his appetite for food, for the breath of life, or for sleep. Strangely, this distinctively human appetite has not always been accorded the respect it deserves. It has often been regarded as "idle curiosity" or as speculative pleasure in the consideration of the "static" world around us. In an evolving world, however, thought and the acquisition of new knowledge may become highly creative, a conscious participation in the great creative process which is evolution. From this point of view, Teilhard pointed out, "unconsciousness is a sort of ontological inferiority or evil, since the world can only fulfill itself insofar as it expresses itself in a systematic and reflective perception" (p. 248). Failure to recognize this is the fatal error of all those philosophies and religions which find their ideal in the extinction of the individual personality by merging it with an impersonal All, as a drop of water merges with the ocean.

The alchemists sought the philosopher's stone for the transmutation of base metals into gold. Now our objective should be not to *have* more but to *be* more. Teilhard suggested that a first approximation of the future of knowledge might be "the establishment of an overall and completely coherent perspective of the universe" (p. 248). He hoped that this might result in "mastering . . . the ultimate energy of which all other energies are merely servants, and thus, by grasping the very mainspring of evolution, seizing the tiller of the world" (p. 250). And he predicted that, should we achieve this, we would find less difference than people had thought between research and adoration. However far we may progress in knowledge, there will remain the problem of how to give each person his full value by grouping them in an organized unity. That is the problem of unanimity.

The grand sweep of evolution, from primeval atom to man, has been characterized by ever increasing complexity and hence by ever increasing consciousness and radial energy. Below the human level, however, tangential energy has always been predominant, and hence the end result has been an evolutionary shrub, the end points of which comprise a multitude of divergent lines. In man, the situation is quite different: having crossed the threshold of reflection, radial energy is now predominant, and the grains of thought (thinking persons) tend to converge and form a single thinking membrane stretched over the entire earth. We saw above that many pressures tend to reinforce this natural convergence of thought. Thus the noosphere tends to form a "single closed system in which each element sees, feels, desires and suffers for itself the same things as all the others . . . a harmonized collectivity of consciousnesses equivalent to a sort of superconsciousness . . . the plurality of individual reflections grouping themselves . . . and reinforcing one another in the act of a single unanimous reflection" (p. 251).

Of course, this stage is still very much in the future. The lack of human unanimity is painfully obvious. Yet this view of the future of the noosphere, to which Teilhard was led by the conviction that the convergence of the noosphere must continue into the future, also suggested to him a simple explanation for some of the troubles of the modern world. The planetization of man, that is, the formation of a single worldwide community of mankind, began as early as the Neolithic, and it has long since reached a level of physical contact and socio-economico-cultural interdependence at which no part of the human community could continue its development except in relation to all the rest. Because of the unprecedented level of productivity in the noosphere, including the invention of modern machinery, "we are witnessing *a formidable upsurge of unused powers.* Modern man no longer knows what to do with the time and the potentialities he has unleashed" (p. 252). Teilhard suggested that these were symptoms of an approach to a critical threshold on the far side of which is the next great level of noogenesis.

OBSTACLES

Teilhard saw several obstacles before that threshold—discouragement, repulsion, and materialization. The past few centuries have witnessed great successes in almost every aspect of life—mastery of nature, achievement of democracy, rising standard of living, personal freedom, and others. Yet discouragement is widespread. Was it not in the eighteenth century that Condorcet and the other prophets of the Enlightenment wrote that we were on the threshold of a golden age? The nineteenth century lived in expectation of early fulfillment of that prophecy, but the twentieth century saw those hopes dashed by two world wars, the most dreadful ever, separated by an economic depression which shook the confidence of men everywhere in their ability to cope with modern life. The idea of mankind seemed to be a utopian dream best forgotten. Or is it? Man has been nearly two million years in the making since the australopithecine days, and all of recorded history is much less than 1 percent of that time. Shall we be discouraged, then, if a dream is unrealized after only two hundred years?

Great movements are slow. Let us have patience commensurate with the greatness of the end sought.

Opposing the convergence of thought are some forces of repulsion, which make it difficult for the grains of thought to converge. One of the most important of these is egotism, whether of an individual or of a race. On an individual basis, the person may feel that he can achieve a degree of excellence alone which is closed to others. On a racial basis, whatever our race may be, it seems to us clearly to be the one to which the future belongs, and others may be trampled if they get in the way. We shall return to this below. For the present, suffice it to say that racism is a vicious counterevolution promoted by disillusionment.

By materialization, Teilhard referred to those many forms of organization, or regimentation, which largely remove the incentive for thought and so encourage life on a purely material, tangential plane. These reach their extreme in the totalitarian societies in which the right to think is, as far as possible, restricted to the leadership. The result, as Teilhard expressed it, is that "we get the crystal instead of the cell; the anthill instead of brotherhood" (p. 257).

Discouragement, repulsion, materialization—all of these result from insufficient appreciation of the value of the *person* and of the role of *personalization* in the evolving world.

THE PERSONAL UNIVERSE

Primitive peoples saw a personality in every rock and rill, and the ancient Greeks deified all the forces of nature, yet modern man tends to impersonalize or depersonalize everything. Teilhard attributed this partly to analysis, a marvelous instrument for scientific discovery, but one which "allows one soul after another to escape, leaving . . . a pile of dismantled machinery" (p. 257); and partly to the new perspective of the universe, in which the beginning and the end both appear as cold and lifeless matter, with personality as only an evanescent intrusion. Nonetheless, the perspective of evolution, if it is to be consistent from its remote beginnings through the present and into the future, leads to quite a different view.

We have seen that one of the major movements of evolution is an ascent toward consciousness. Therefore, to be entirely consistent, it should culminate forward in a supreme consciousness. For the curve of hominization to end in reduced consciousness or in loss of personality would be contradictory. Therefore, if as developed above, mankind is in process of evolving a biological collective, then that collective must be hyperpersonalized and capable of hyper-reflection. To paraphrase, this hyperpersonal biological collective which Teilhard proposed is clearly the same as the biological macrocosm which I envisioned many years ago and which in the preface to the present volume I described as having "a life and a consciousness as far beyond ours as ours is beyond that of our component cells." This was an intuitive insight based on the evolutionary facts reviewed above, and I am inclined to leave it at that. Teilhard, however, prepared a carefully reasoned reply to those who feel that the All must be impersonal. This evolutionary All, the genesis of which we have reviewed, is an extrapolation from individual, thinking persons. Now any person tends to put all things in a perspective about himself as a center; in fact, Teilhard often used *center* as a synonym for *person*. Further, in a sort of second-degree act of centering, a person also centers his ideas of himself and of other persons upon himself, and thus he is brought into association with all other centers. The result could only be a hyperpersonal unity after the crossing of the next great evolutionary threshold. Returning to the intuitive approach, could the All be *less* than its parts? As the parts are reflective persons, the most highly developed products of evolution up to the present, an impersonal, nonreflective All would in fact be less than the sum of its parts. The evolutionary All, then, is necessarily hyperpersonal rather than infrapersonal.

This description of the biological macrocosm finds a clear precedent in a passage from J.B.S. Haldane's "Essay on Science and Ethics," which Teilhard quoted:

> We do not find obvious evidence of life or mind in so-called inert matter, and we naturally study them most easily where they are most completely manifested; but if the scientific point of view is correct, we shall ultimately find them, at least in rudimentary forms, all through the universe.
> Now, if the cooperation of some thousands of millions of cells in our brain can produce our consciousness, the idea becomes vastly more plausible that the cooperation of humanity, or some section of it, may determine what Comte calls a Great Being. (p. 57)

The natural universe of space and time has, as we have seen, evolved consciousness, which has matured into convergent personality. Because the universe both engenders and contains convergent personality, *it follows that the universe itself must be convergent and personal in nature, and this convergence must lead to a final unity*. If we follow the radii of convergence in the right direction, then, they must finally meet and fuse, even if outside space and time, in the supreme consciousness, the supreme personality, which Teilhard called the *Omega point*. The immensity of the universe gives some clue to the depth, the richness, and the intensity of this supreme personality. To see the universe in this revealing perspective, it is necessary to look beyond our souls (forward toward pure radiality) rather than behind our bodies (backward, toward predominate tangentiality). Then, as Teilhard put it, "In the perspective of a noogenesis . . . far from being mutually exclusive, the Universal and the Personal . . . grow in the same direction and culminate simultaneously in each other" (pp. 259–260).

THE BIOLOGICAL COLLECTIVE AND THE OMEGA
POINT

It is important to point out that the biological macrocosm and the Omega point are not the same thing. The latter is the supreme personal principle of the universe, which it transcends; the former is the hyperpersonal extrapolation of human personalities, and its close union with Omega is its most important property. As we have seen, personality is convergent; the personal centers organize in relation to each other and mutually converge; and Omega is the center toward which all other centers converge, "a distinct center radiating at the core of a system of centers" (p. 262). This distinction is an important one to which I shall return.

UNION OF PERSONS

When mankind crosses this final threshold, then, there will be a union of persons to form a biological macrocosm with a life and a consciousness as far beyond ours as ours is beyond that of our component cells, and this collectivity will converge with Omega, so that, in a sense, each person may be said to be added to Omega. But how? Many Marxists and other materialists have suggested that the sacrifices required of men are justified by the legacy which we leave to posterity in our material works, our works of art, and our intellectual achievements, all of which enrich mankind. The durability of these, our best works, is the only sort of immortality for which we may hope. As Teilhard's book and the present one have both emphasized the great importance of these cultural productions of noogenesis, we cannot be accused of deprecating them, yet I must agree with Teilhard that they are "only the shadow of ourselves" (p. 261). It is the reflective centers themselves, our inmost personalities, which must unite to form the biological macrocosm by convergence with Omega. Only center-to-center union, by radial energy, will suffice.

At this point, an important Teilhardian principle applies. Are we to think of each personality as losing its identity in the collective, as a drop of water is lost in the sea, or as a grain of salt is dissolved? Not at all: *union differentiates.* Each personality will not only remain distinct within the great unity but will be most uniquely, most fully itself in uniting with Omega. In a crystal, the repeated parts are so many identities, but in a living union, the parts are differentiated. Thus in a population of the protozoan *Amoeba,* there is a limited, although important, range of variability, but all of the cells are easily referable to a single type. In the human body (or in that of any other highly evolved animal), the billions of cells are referable to a series of clearly differentiated types (epithelial, muscular, vascular, connective, and nervous), and each of these is again divisible into a number of more or less well marked subtypes. Again, the members of any species of solitary insect are much alike, but social insects, such as termites, are differentiated into several castes which perform different functions in the colony, and which may be so different in structure that a casual observer, seeing them for the first time, might very well believe that they belonged to different species. And in man, where the social phenomenon reaches its present maximum as a consequence of noogenesis, how vast is the variety of abilities, social functions, and personalities! As a final example, a good marriage is the most complete, the deepest, and the most satisfying of human unions, yet it is in this union that each partner realizes himself fully. Union differentiates, and hence we may expect that each consciousness will reach its maximal intensity in union with Omega. Thus, the pantheistic expectation of the mergence, or submergence, of the person in the All is an illusion which results from failure to recognize the differentiating effect of union.

ISOLATIONIST SOLUTIONS

Above I referred to the efforts of some people to organize their lives in isolation, either individually or in racial groups. In some cases, they may be sincerely convinced that, in isolation from the rest of humanity, they can achieve a degree of excellence which is closed to others. We are now in a position to understand why such isolationist solutions to the problems of life are inherently perverse: the direction of the evolution of man is toward convergence and union, while all isolationist solutions lead to fragmentation and plurality. Maximal personality results from maximal union, and all mankind is needed. The differentiated persons and races will complement one another. That union, however, must be center to center, by radial energy, and this brings us to the problem of love.

LOVE AND ENERGY

We know love in man in many forms—love of man and wife, parental and familial love, love of friends, social solidarity, patriotism, and all of the rest. However, love is not a uniquely human passion, and we recognize it readily in other mammals in such basic biological phenomena as sexual union, parental instincts, and social structures and loyalties. As one goes further down the evolutionary tree, these features become less and less distinctive. Finally, there remains only the drive to unite for reproduction, and then even this becomes imperceptible. At this point, Teilhard returned to the same argument he used to establish the existence of the within at the physicochemical level of evolution: if we know the property at a more highly evolved level, then in order to maintain scientific symmetry and coherence, it is necessary to postulate a related property, at least in an inchoate form, at lower levels. Teilhard associated love primarily with radial energy, and he did believe that, in its most primordial and unevolved form, it must be inherent in all matter as a simple propensity to unite. Like the postulate of the within of all matter, this proposition would not seem to be amenable to experimental test. Whether one judges it valid or invalid must be decided on much the same basis as the evaluation of the within. In either case, it would seem to be clear that love becomes increasingly important in the more highly evolved animals, and in man, it provides the strongest motivations, together with its perversion, hate.

At the conclusion of the preceding section, it was stated that the union of persons must be center to center, by radial energy, and Teilhard believed that only love could achieve this. But it was also stated that all mankind is needed for the biological macrocosm, in union with Omega. Are we capable of loving everyone, or will the effort to love everyone end by loving no one? Man shows his aspirations to the universal in his response to many phenomena—the beauty of nature, great music, poetry, and other great works of art. Nonetheless, it is difficult to love pure number or an abstract All, and these aspirations to the universal are often swamped by the many divisive factors discussed above. What is necessary to overcome these divisive factors is the realization of the *present reality* of Omega, with whom we can establish a direct center-to-center union, thus bringing us into union with all other centers which are united to Omega.

THE ATTRIBUTES OF THE OMEGA POINT

Teilhard then undertook to define what seemed to be the necessary attributes of Omega. Because the function of Omega is to attract and maintain within its radius the reflective grains—persons—of the world, it must be present now, loving and lovable. Only love can achieve the universal synthesis of mankind which is necessary if evolution is to be satisfactorily completed, and without this actually present focal point for center-to-center union by love, the convergence of thought would lead to naught. For this property, Teilhard's French word was *actualité*. While this has been rendered in English, almost letter by letter, as *actuality*, the meaning in English is not very close to the French. "Presence now", if a little awkward, is perhaps closer to Teilhard's meaning.

The second attribute Teilhard called *irreversibility*, by which he meant *immortality*. Nonliving matter is characterized mainly by tangential energy, and it is fully subject to the law of entropy. In all organisms, the level of radial energy is significant, but in those below the threshold of thought, this radial energy is largely resorbed into the tangential upon death, and again it follows the law of entropy. But Omega is pure radial energy and is independent of entropy. As Teilhard wrote, "What is the use of detecting a focus . . . in the van of evolution if that focus can and must one day disintegrate? . . . Omega must be independent of the collapse of the forces with which evolution is woven" (p. 270). And thus we have the third property of Omega, *autonomy*.

In the history of evolution, we have seen a sequence from cosmogenesis through geogenesis and biogenesis to hominization and noogenesis. Noogenesis produces reflective persons which converge upon the Omega point and will do so much more after the final threshold of the biological collective is crossed. So, in a sense, Omega is the culmination of the series. Yet Omega, as we saw above, is outside space and time, and so is transcendent to all series. This *transcendence* is the final property of Omega.

During most of the great extent of evolution, the within of matter, with its radial energy, has been expressed principally in animal consciousness of varying degrees. But being predominantly tangential and unable to attach to a higher center, they disintegrate into the tangential upon death. But once the threshold of reflection was crossed in hominization, personal centers resulted, and center-to-center contact became possible. The reflective particle which is in center-to-center contact with Omega escapes into pure radiality and is liberated from its tangential envelope. The tangential envelope of the world goes on dissipating itself in entropy, but the radial nucleus, in union with the transcendent Omega, moves against that tangential tide to a climax of transcendent personality. Thus, "the universe is a collector and conservator . . . of *persons*" (p. 272) rather than of material particles, as had been thought.

CHAPTER THIRTEEN

The Ultimate Earth

EARLY IN THIS BOOK, we reviewed the evolution of the primitive earth, and we saw that physicochemical evolution culminated in the formation of a stockpile of polymerized organic compounds, then crossed a threshold of complexity-consciousness to give rise to the first living cells. Biological evolution, rooted in and building upon physicochemical evolution, then elaborated and diversified the biosphere to produce the astonishing wealth of living forms, teeming in every habitat from abysmal depths to alpine peaks, from equator to poles. One of the major movements of this great adaptive radiation has been the production of ever greater degrees of complexity, especially of the nervous system, and this has been accompanied by rising levels of consciousness (the within, with its radial energy). When we reached the modern world in our review, we found that in one species—our own—the development of complexity-consciousness had crossed another critical threshold and man had become capable of reflection, capable of knowing himself, capable not only of knowing but of knowing that he knows, capable of organizing ideas of the world about himself as a center; in short, personalization had begun. And now the within and radial energy had become predominant!

Now, however, we have glimpsed up ahead a universal psychical center, transcending time and space, which sustains consciousness and toward which all consciousnesses converge. While noogenesis has up to the present been achieved in strict association and correlation with physico-chemico-biological evolution, the fact that consciousness, the most highly evolved expression of radial energy, is converging toward point Omega, which is pure radiality, outside the framework of space and time, requires that evolution achieve its climax through dissociation of the tangential (physical) and radial (psychic) components. And this brings us to the idea of the end of the world, the end of life on this earth, and the final phase of the phenomenon of man.

CATASTROPHIC PREDICTIONS TO BE SET ASIDE

From a physical point of view, the end of the world may be expected to be the death of heat—maximal entropy. While this appears to be inevitable, it also appears to be extremely remote. Physical considerations suggest that the "life" of the universe ahead will be considerably in excess of the duration of the past. The more critical question is, will life on earth be cut short by some catastrophe long before the chilling of the universe forces it?

There has been no dearth of catastrophic predictions. Teilhard specifically discussed collision with a comet, a universally destructive earthquake, and a universal repudiation by men of the task of ascending higher toward union. The last is a possibility which arises from the fact that man is, in Huxley's phrase, "evolution become conscious of itself" (p. 220). Had he written thirty years later than he did, Teilhard might have developed the last in terms of an atomic holocaust or an ecological disaster. Teilhard was inclined to dismiss a catastrophic end of the world as possible but too improbable for serious consideration, but he also believed that it would not happen "for higher reasons" (p. 275): the irreplaceability of man.

It has been suggested that, if man were to disappear, another thinking species would take his place. But from what source? One distinguished paleontologist who is a student of dinosaurs has noted that the brain was significantly larger in one line of these reptiles than in others, and he has wondered whether, in the absence of the mammals, these might not have produced types comparable in brain power to the mammals. Yet it was only after the disappearance of the great reptiles that the expansion of the mammals occurred. Another mammal? In general, their specializations bind them so narrowly to their specific modes of life that hominization would seem to be out of the question. Another primate? This would seem to be a better possibility but still not a very strong one. While the expansion of the brain has been a major feature of primate evolution, nonetheless only the great apes show any signs of an approach to the threshold of thought, and not a close approach at that. Further, they seem to be in even more imminent danger of extinction than are we. So man may well be irreplaceable as a thinking species.

Teilhard approached the problem from a different viewpoint. Since the early ages of the earth, life has not again arisen. And similarly, only once has life crossed the threshold of thought. Perhaps in both cases only once have a unique set of conditions been fulfilled. The future of the noosphere thus depends solely upon man, and since noogenesis is the climax of the entire evolutionary process, its failure now would amount to abortion of the universe, an absurd end. Therefore, man must not fail—he must reach the goal. Perhaps that is too strong a conclusion, but the success of evolution over the ages and up to the present should offer a basis for reasonable optimism regarding the future. Nonetheless, there is an important difference: as improbable as the products of evolution may have been up to the present (and they are superbly improbable thermodynamically), their production has been controlled by natural selection, which is a mechanism for the production of high degrees of improbability, and hence it could scarcely have failed. Natural selection still plays a considerable role in the continuing evolution of man, but now that evolution has become conscious of itself, the conscious cooperation of man is necessary for further success, and hence failure is a real possibility.

That failure is possible should occasion neither despair nor resignation: on the contrary, it should inspire us to work all the harder for the success which can be ours if only we give our full cooperation and effort to the great evolutionary movement toward fuller consciousness, fuller personality. Up ahead there awaits the threshold to the superpersonality of the biological macrocosm and that perfect union with Omega in which every personality will be fully realized, fully differentiated; the supreme improbable from a thermodynamic point of view, yet the fitting climax to a process which has always run counter to the stream of entropy, producing ever greater degrees of improbability. Thus, the great stability is not at the base in the elementary particles, which are subject to entropy, but at the top in personality, which escapes from entropy.

THE APPROACHES

In the meantime, it is reasonable to expect a long future for man. Thermodynamically, the earth may be expected to remain habitable for a far longer period than its duration up to the present. Some groups of organisms have had extremely long duration, even on a geological scale. Thus, the lampshell, *Lingula,* has been on the subtropical and temperate tide flats for some 500 million years. Extinct genera of pelecypod molluscs have had an average survival of about 80 million years. Mammals of the order Carnivora have, so far, had an average survival of about 8 million years and a maximum of about 20 million years, although it cannot be said that these figures may not be exceeded in the future. If one includes the earliest hominids which could possibly be assigned to the genus *Homo,* man is still less than 2 million years old, and thus a rather young species.

Further, noogenesis, the pace of which has long been quickening, marks man as a really new *kind* of life. Thus the probability is good that he has a long future. During this long future, evolution will continue, both the genetic evolution of which man is a recent product and cultural evolution, which is now very strongly predominant. The two are, of course, intimately interrelated. The continuing progress of noogenesis is constructing of all minds in concert, *mind*. Along what major lines will the advance of noogenesis occur? Teilhard saw three: the organization of research; the concentration of research on man; and the conjunction of science and religion. To these, I would like to add some notes on sociopolitical organization.

SOCIOPOLITICAL ORGANIZATION OF MANKIND

As we saw in chapter 11, there has been a long-continued trend toward ever larger sociopolitical units, starting with the family and extending through the many sorts of international associations and a quasi-government (the United Nations) which characterize the modern world. This trend may be expected to continue and culminate in true world government, not by conquest of any superpower over the rest but by mutual consent of the peoples of the world. Such a world government is presaged by many aspects of the modern world. One of these is the world consensus which resulted in the organization of the United Nations itself. The British Commonwealth of Nations is another step in this direction, the European Common Market is a third example, and of course there are many other international associations of states with more or less limited purposes. Commonly, these are treaty organizations based on defense, but they generally include provisions for trade and cultural exchange and often for cooperation in many other spheres, such as agricultural development, scientific research, and health services. International organization of science is well advanced, and this has perhaps been the most successful bridge between East and West. Finally, both labor and business are becoming increasingly international in organization. Many, perhaps all, of these things may have to be radically changed before they can serve the world-state of the future, but their true significance may be that they are experiments toward that future. "The Age of Nations is past," wrote Teilhard. "The task before us now, if we would not perish, is to build the earth" (1965).

What will be the form of that world government of the future? I suspect that we will evolve better institutions than any we now have. The economic system may include some of the better features of both capitalist and socialist systems, but it will be so much improved that it will not be readily interpretable in terms of any present economic system. Politically, we may expect the world government to be democratic, deriving its power from the consent of the people and exercising that power in their interests, but again it will be so much improved over all present models as to be not readily interpretable in terms of any of them. While such a government will ensure the worldwide coordination of the affairs of men, it will protect individual freedom and will encourage local and regional autonomy in matters of local and regional concern. Culturally, a world culture may emerge, but it must promote and encourage regional cultures. Union differentiates.

ORGANIZATION OF RESEARCH

Teilhard's discussion of the "present" organization of science is based upon the fact that he completed *The Phenomenon of Man* in 1940. He wrote, "We behave as though we expected discoveries to fall ready-made from the sky. . . . Less is provided annually for all the pure research all over the world than for one capital ship" (p. 279). During World War II, massive government support of military research was a major arm of the war effort, and after the war the governments of the leading powers continued to support research, not only military and other applied research but also pure research in a great many fields of science. Granted that applied fields such as medicine and engineering were especially favored and that continuation of support for pure science was sometimes in doubt, still the situation was vastly improved over that which prevailed when Teilhard wrote.

Teilhard looked forward, however, to a world in which organization and support of pure research would be universally recognized as one of the primary obligations of government; a world in which the man in the street would give more admiration to scientific discovery than to all of the spectacular equipment of war; "a world in which, as happens already, one gives one's life to be and to know, rather than to possess" (p. 280). Such is the world of research which Teilhard saw in the future of noogenesis.

CONCENTRATION OF RESEARCH ON MAN

The future, then, will be an era of science, but more specifically, Teilhard expected it to be an era of human science, in the spirit of Alexander Pope's line, "The proper study of man is man." Needless to say, however, Teilhard did not think of this in a narrow sense. In this era of human science there was to be room for all of the sciences, but man would constitute a focal point. He believed that man could well serve this function for two reasons. First, man represents the most highly synthesized state of matter, the most complex state in the Teilhardian sense. Second, man is at present the most mobile point in evolution because of the rapid evolution of the noosphere. One might add a third reason, which is perhaps only an elaboration of the first. Because the sociocultural evolution of man (noogenesis) is rooted in and based upon biological evolution, and because the latter is rooted in and based upon physicochemical evolution, it follows that the study of man, broadly conceived, includes all of nature.

Why not, then, leave all of the old disciplines just as they were? Because they have too frequently been conceived in isolation, without relation to cosmogenesis or any other aspect of evolution, without relation to man or human welfare. Teilhard thought of man and human welfare as the organizing principle for the science of the future, but he could not think of this as narrowing the scope of science because man is the present terminal member of an evolutionary sequence which includes all natural phenomena. But as science concentrates ever more upon man, it "will find itself increasingly face to face with religion" (p. 283).

THE CONJUNCTION OF SCIENCE AND RELIGION

E. McMullen has pointed out that modern science arose out of the Judaeo-Christian tradition, which over a period of two thousand years had built up an intellectual climate in which science could develop. Key points include confidence that nature would prove to be intelligible; that knowledge of nature may be won by hard work, involving careful manipulation and observation; and that it is worth the effort involved. In all of these respects, the Judaeo-Christian tradition contrasts strongly to various others, and McMullen makes a strong case for the proposition that it is because of this that modern science arose when and where it did.

Nonetheless, science had no sooner become established than conflicts began to arise between science and the religion which had prepared the way for science. McMullen cites two principal factors, the changing ideas of the dimensions of the universe and biological evolution, both of which have been discussed at length in these pages. In the most bitter form of this conflict, proponents of each side have tried to eliminate the other. Others have worked for a dualism in which science and religion would coexist as two immiscibles. After several hundred years of such "solutions," neither science nor religion has eliminated the other, and dualism is generally considered to be intellectually a failure. Teilhard believed that both approaches were fundamentally wrong: it is synthesis of science and religion that is needed, for "the same life animates both" (p. 283).

Much of the conflict arose between the earlier, analytic findings of science and the cosmology associated with religious positions which were formulated in the days of fixity. Both science and religion have had to accommodate the idea of evolution, and it has not always been the religious who have accommodated the more reluctantly. As long as we look backward toward the earlier stages of physico-chemico-biological evolution, it may be possible to engage in pure science. But as soon as we look to man and the future and add synthesis to analysis, we find convergence, developing unity, and the need for a supremely attractive personal center. Teilhard therefore believed that the research of the future would necessarily blend with adoration, because "religion and science are the two conjugated faces or phases of one and the same act of complete knowledge—the only one which can embrace the past and future of evolution so as to contemplate, measure, and fulfill them" (pp. 284–285).

THE ULTIMATE

By pushing ahead in the four directions discussed above during the very long ages which probably remain at his disposal, man may build a great future for himself. Until man, each species was limited by its specializations to achievement of a very limited sort. In man, artifice largely replaces structural specialization; and the same individual can vary his action indefinitely without loss of freedom. The most important of the specializations of man is the great development of the central nervous system, which has carried him over the threshold of reflective thought and initiated noogenesis. In a relatively brief time, the results of this new kind of evolution have been great enough to change the face of the earth radically. Given millions of years to operate, the potential of noogenesis must be beyond present imagination.

Will the biological macrocosm be achieved during the progress of noogenesis, while man is still in full possession of the earth? Indeed, has it been achieved now? This question is not as simple as it might seem at first for, as suggested in the preface, it is extremely unlikely that the individual cells of our bodies have any awareness of their contributions to the whole or even of the existence of the whole. By comparison, if the convergence of man has, in fact, proceeded far enough to cross the threshold for the formation of the superconscious, superpersonal biological macrocosm, if all minds have in concert formed *mind*, would we, its components, necessarily be aware of it? Not necessarily, even though we would owe a heightened level of consciousness and personalization to that fact. Nonetheless, when one considers the divided and vexed condition of humanity today, that goal seems rather remote. But can one say that this may not be achieved while man is still in possession of the earth?

Teilhard approached this question somewhat differently. Noogenesis is proceeding with ever closer association of the grains of thought; this results in the formation of the various societies, nations, races, etc. which make up the human verticil; their continuing convergence requires an autonomous and supreme focus to bind the separate personalities in an association of love, an association which is facilitated by the curvature of the earth and by the convergence of thought (which Teilhard sometimes called psychic curvature). Now, when a sufficiently large number of people are closely related radially (by love), this convergent movement will attain such an intensity that mankind as a whole will be obliged to converge upon a single point, the Omega point, and this will be the fulfillment of the spirit of the earth and the end of the world. The within was, in elemental matter, unrecognizable within its tangential envelope; in any organism, it is recognizable, and in the more complex animals it may become quite prominent; in man it is predominant; and in the final union with Omega, which is God, the within will be freed from its tangential envelope.

And what will be the condition of man as he approaches that dénouement? Teilhard sketched two alternatives. According to the first, man may have progressed far toward elimination of both the physical and moral evils which have always beset him, and the final convergence upon Omega would take place in peace, a fitting climax to the phenomenon of man as we have sketched it.

The second alternative, however, is more in keeping with traditional apocalyptic thinking, and it is suggested more strongly by the present state of the world. Branching might occur for a final time, with the true radial cement of love bringing part of mankind to convergence upon Omega, while the perverted radial force of hate brings the rest to an antifocus. "Ecstacy in concord; or discord; but in either case by excess of interior tension: the only biological outcome proper to or conceivable for the phenomenon of man" (p. 289). "The only universe capable of containing the human person is an irreversibly 'personalizing' universe" (p. 290).

In concluding this survey of the phenomenon of man, Teilhard wrote, "In this arrangement of values I may have gone astray at many points. It is up to others to try to do better" (pp. 289–290). I hope that, in attempting some revisions which seem to me to be necessary, I have done him honor.

CHAPTER FOURTEEN

The Christian Phenomenon

TEILHARD WROTE his chapter with the above title with some hesitation because he feared that it would be dismissed as simply the work of a confirmed believer. And while he was indeed that, he tried to write objectively as a naturalist. I write with perhaps even more hesitation because I am not only a confirmed believer but I lack even Teilhard's competence in theology (and it should be pointed out that he was *not* a theologian, although of course he had had theological training as a seminarian). The present chapter, then, will be primarily a restatement of Teilhard's, with certain additions which seem to me to be necessary.

CHRISTIANITY AND EVOLUTION

A theme which runs throughout *The Phenomenon of Man* is this, that every evolutionary movement has its origin in the past, its expression in the present, and its extension in the future. The present convergence of the noosphere, which was illustrated in many ways in the preceding chapters, seemed to require the formation of a hyperpersonal biological macrocosm. Because this appears to be the climax of the entire evolutionary process, it seems necessary that the universe itself must be basically personal and convergent, the center of convergence being the Omega point, outside time and space, and providing the focus and attractive center upon which all individual consciousnesses tend to converge. But if all of this is really correct, and not just vain ideology, then this great presence should in some way be revealed all around us.

Teilhard tried to show that the Christian phenomenon does, in fact, meet the requirements of the manifestation of Omega around us. He analyzed this in terms of three characteristics of Christianity: its creed; its existence-value (which I will call pervasiveness); and its power of growth. To these, I would like to add a fourth, its relationship to history.

CREED

Those who know Christianity only superficially may find it terribly complex, but it is basically "an extremely simple and astonishingly bold solution of the world . . . the uncompromising affirmation of a personal God: God as providence, directing the universe with loving, watchful care; and God the revealer, communicating himself to man on the level of and through the ways of intelligence" (pp. 292–293). Because of this, the faith is open to and easily allied with "everything that is great and healthy" (p. 293). In Old Testament times, this faith may have seemed to be peculiar to one people, but Christ commissioned his apostles to preach it to all peoples, and they have ever since been striving to serve the whole world. So Christianity is personal and universal. But how are these two traits united in its theology? "Is the Kingdom of God a big family? Yes, in a sense it is. But in another sense it is a prodigious biological operation—that of the Redeeming Incarnation" (p. 293). For, to unify His creation, God immersed Himself in it, "and then, from this vantage point in the heart of matter, assuming the control and leadership of what we now call evolution, Christ . . . as man among men, put himself in position . . . to purify, to direct and superanimate the general ascent of consciousnesses. . . . And when he has gathered together and transformed everything," St. Paul tells us, "God shall be all in all." And it is with this union of persons with God, the Center of centers, that the Christian faith culminates. The close correspondence of Omega and Christ is obvious.

PERVASIVENESS

Some of the major philosophers have produced systems which rival in amplitude the perspectives of the Incarnation, yet they have remained ideologies which have enriched the noosphere without showing any tendency to build up a large following. Christianity, on the other hand, "addresses itself to every man and to every class of man, and from the start it took its place as one of the most vigorous and fruitful currents the noosphere has ever known. Whether we adhere to it or break off from it, we are surely obliged to admit that its stamp and enduring influence are apparent in every corner of the earth today" (p. 295). All of this is a matter of quantitative extension, but there is also a qualitatively new factor in the pervasiveness of Christianity, and that is Christian love. In chapter 12, I raised the question of whether the infinite and intangible can be lovable, even whether man in general, as opposed to specific persons, can be lovable; or does loving everyone lead to loving no one? Granted that many nominal Christians are not discernibly touched by this sublime emotion, two thousand years of history have witnessed untold numbers of mystics, martyrs, clergy, nuns, and laity from every walk of life who "have drawn from its flame a passionate fervor that outstrips by far in brightness and purity the urge and devotion of any human love" (p. 295). Let us take just two examples to represent many thousands. St. Francis of Assisi is a legendary example of a man whose love embraced all creation because it was all God's work, even to the humblest living creature, and he offered all back to God through

Christ. And in our own time, Dr. Thomas Dooley gave up the promise of a comfortable and lucrative medical practice in the United States in order to devote not his professional services but his entire life to the impoverished peoples of southeast Asia because he saw in them Christ's people and he embraced them in Christian love. Teilhard believed that, if this love were extinguished in the souls of the faithful, "the enormous edifice of rites, of hierarchy, and of doctrines that compose the Church would instantly revert to the dust from which it rose" (p. 295).

Teilhard regarded it as a matter of the utmost importance for the science of man that "a genuine universal love has not only been conceived and preached, but has also been shown to be psychologically possible and operative in practice" (p. 296).

POWER OF GROWTH

The creeds of the great world religions were all formed in the days of fixity, and they are cast in the idiom of that time. The rise of the modern scientific outlook, with its great dimensions in space and time and its evolutionary perspectives, caused a severe crisis for all. For the great religions of the Orient, this has been a catastrophe. They find their strength today in those people who have not yet integrated into the scientific culture, or in those Westerners who renounce their scientific-technological heritage and seek refuge from it in a guru.

Christianity, too, was severely shaken by the scientific revolution, but it shows every sign not only of recovery but of being better, truer, stronger for the experience. Teilhard pointed out that "to live and develop the Christian outlook needs an atmosphere of greatness and of connecting links" (p. 296), and these were not adequately provided by the old static conception of the world. But as the development of modern science has revealed the great dimensions of space-time and the interconnectedness of all things in one great evolutionary system, Christians, though at first badly frightened, are beginning to see that the full dimensions of the Incarnation are only now becoming clear, as "Christ invests himself organically with the very majesty of his creation. And it is in no way metaphorical to say that man finds himself capable of discovering his God in the whole length, breadth, and depth of the world in movement. To be able to say literally to God that one loves him, not only with all one's body, all one's heart, and all one's soul, but with every fiber of the unifying universe—that is a prayer that can only be made in space-time" (p. 297).

Thus, modern science, especially evolutionary science, has made Christianity alive to its true dimensions, and now Christianity may repay the debt. Teilhard tried to show that the hope of progress on earth requires "the primacy and triumph of the *personal* at the summit of *mind*. At the present moment Christianity is the *unique* current of thought . . . where faith and hope reach their fulfilment in love. *Alone*, unconditionally alone in the world today, Christianity shows itself able to reconcile, in a single living act, the All and the Person" (p. 297). Thus, it is Christianity which provides the necessary personal focus at the summit.

RELATIONSHIP TO HISTORY

Writers as different as E. McMullen and Th. Dobzhansky have pointed out that, among the great world religions, Christianity is almost unique in its historical orientation. Greek thought emphasized eternal essences, which left history more or less accidental. Oriental religions have generally made an uneasy truce with the material world as a whole, and of course with history, which is a sequence of events in the material world. Judaism, on the other hand, was alone in the ancient world in stressing the importance of time and history. The world had a beginning, as did man himself. But man had fallen, and so he must work out his salvation in time, in history. The goal of history was the coming of the Messiah, and it was the destiny of the Jews to prepare the way for His coming. All of this, Christianity inherited from Judaism. To this it adds that, at the central time in history, God was made man and lived among men as Christ the Messiah. The immediate effect of this was antihistorical because the early Christians felt that, with the coming of Christ, the main part of history had been accomplished and the end of the world should be near. As centuries passed, however, it became apparent that history had by no means run its course, but on the contrary, history was the arena in which men must work out their salvation through the application of the redemptive Incarnation and sacrifice of Christ to each soul. Thus, Christianity is radically historical, and hence evolutionary, by nature.

SUMMING UP

Teilhard summarized all of this in three points, which may be paraphrased briefly. First, because Christianity has its roots in the past and has developed ceaselessly through history, it shows the characteristics of an evolving organism, or line of organisms. Second, its major trend is toward a synthesis based upon love, the same trend which Teilhard had found in the noosphere, the most progressive shoot of organic evolution. And third, this rising shoot is meaningful only if it finds itself in actual relationship with a spiritual and transcendent pole of universal convergence. Thus, the Christian phenomenon provides a cross-check for the concept of the Omega point at the summit of the world.

THE BIOLOGICAL MACROCOSM
AND THE OMEGA POINT

It is important to point out here that the biological macrocosm and the Omega point are not the same thing. The latter is the supreme personal principle of the universe, which it transcends; the former is the hyperpersonal extrapolation of human personalities. As we have seen, personality is convergent; personal centers organize in relation to each other and mutually converge. Omega is the center toward which all other centers converge, "a distinct center radiating at the core of a system of centers" (p. 262).

Therein is the great superiority of Teilhard's synthesis over that which I planned many years ago. As mentioned in the preface, I recognized that the proposal of the biological macrocosm amounted to a redefinition of God and that it was essentially a pantheistic definition, with all of the logical, theological, and moral contradictions which that involves. I also recognized its incompatibility with Christian revelation, which I accepted. Nonetheless, I felt that I had had a glimpse of genuine truth and hence that there must be a way to separate that grain of truth from the chaff of error. It seemed self-evident that all truth must form a unified, self-consistent system. I did not follow this up at the time because the publication of J. S. Haldane's book of 1935 seemed to make my contribution unnecessary, at least for the time.

Teilhard solved this complex of problems with beautiful simplicity by the clear distinction which he made between the biological collective and the Omega point toward which the former converges. Here, it is the Omega point which is God, and the biological collective or macrocosm is part of his creation, even if the quintessential part. Unlike the god of all pantheistic systems, this transcendent Omega avoids the contradictions which plague any system in which creator and created are one. It also avoids the common pitfall of those theologies which place a transcendent God so remote from His creation that He seems to have no relevance. As Omega is "a distinct center radiating at the core of a system of centers" (p. 262), it is clear that this transcendent deity is also very much in contact and in sympathy with his creation, and most especially with that part of his creation which has passed the threshold of thought and which may pass the threshold of the biological collective.

THE REALITY OF OMEGA

One must finally ask two very critical questions about the concept of Omega. First, is it consistent with the facts of evolution, which have been reviewed above and from which Teilhard derived the concept? And second, a similar but significantly different question, is it required by those facts? In answer to the first question, I think that a review of the preceding chapters justifies an unequivocal "yes!" To be consistent with the facts, however, is not the same thing at all as to be required by them. There would appear to be no possibility of an experimental check of the validity or invalidity of this concept, and this would appear to take it out of the realm of the scientific (which is not to say that it is invalid). Julian Huxley, in his introduction to the English edition of *The Phenomenon of Man*, expressed his agreement with most of Teilhard's ideas, but he stopped short of Omega.

Thus, the decision on the reality of Omega depends on philosophical or theological reasoning rather than upon scientific reasoning. Scientific readers will be inclined to accept or reject it according to their religious or philosophical orientation. Actually, although Teilhard tried to write a strictly scientific work, he must have been aware of this departure, for he wrote of Christian teaching that "so exactly, so perfectly does this coincide with the Omega Point that doubtless I should never have ventured to envisage the latter or formulate the hypothesis rationally if, in my consciousness as a believer, I had not found not only its speculative model but also its living reality" (p. 294). For Teilhard, then, Omega was not only a living reality: Omega is the cosmic Christ, invested with all of the majesty of his creation. For a Christian who has adopted the modern, evolutionary viewpoint (and here I include myself) and who has been able to follow the Teilhardian argument up to this point, his conclusion seems logical and harmonious. If I were a Jew, however, I would have to think of Omega in terms of the Messiah to come, although in some way effective in the world today. Finally, even to those outside the Judaeo-Christian tradition, it may be apparent that Teilhard has found true harmony where previously there had been discord, and thus he has strengthened all notes of the harmonious chord.

OMEGA AND FAITH

One of the persistent criticisms of *The Phenomenon of Man* is that in it Teilhard tried to achieve a scientific demonstration of the truth of the Christian faith. This criticism was effectively stated by G. G. Simpson in a very thoughtful review in which he described Teilhard's book as "mystical Christianity ostensibly derived from evolutionary principles." While many have no doubt shared that opinion, and while it is undoubtedly true that Teilhard was a great mystic, nonetheless I believe that the criticism is based upon a real misunderstanding of Teilhard's purpose. Dobzhansky was right when he wrote: "The idea that Christianity can be derived from evolutionary principles, or from any other scientific findings, would have seemed monstrous to Teilhard. What he tried to do was something entirely different, namely to create a coherent *Weltanschauung*, including his mystical Christianity as well as his scientific knowledge" (1967:115). He certainly thought that evolutionary science and Christianity mutually enriched each other, but that is a far cry from the belief that either one can be derived from the other. Teilhard was a profound student of St. Paul, and he certainly would not contradict the Apostle to the Gentiles when he wrote that "Faith is the substance of things hoped for, the evidence of things unseen" (Hebrews 11:1). In a somewhat different connection, Teilhard wrote that "there are rational invitations to an act of faith" (p. 232). In the modern, scientific culture, the Teilhardian synthesis is one of the best and most cogent of these invitations.

CHAPTER FIFTEEN

Teilhard
and His Critics

WAS TEILHARD A SCIENTIST, a philosopher, or a theologian? He himself declared that *The Phenomenon of Man* must be read "purely and simply as a scientific treatise" (p. 29), yet his was a very widely ranging mind, and his work cannot be confined to neatly circumscribed categories. Bertrand Russell has published a definition of philosophy which is apropos here: "Between theology and science there is a No Man's Land, exposed to attacks from both sides; this No Man's Land is philosophy" (Dobzhansky 1967:10). Whatever Teilhard may have been by other definitions, he was certainly a philosopher by this one, for he has been very heavily attacked by philosophers and theologians on one side and by scientists on the other.

With the first group, I shall be concerned but little, both because their work is clearly outside of my competence and because they have been adequately answered by men who are eminently competent in those fields. I cite among Catholic writers H. de Lubac* (1965, 1966, 1971), C. Tresmontant (1959), and N. M. Wildiers (1960), and among Protestants, G. Crespy (1961a, 1961b), M. H. Murray (1966), and C. E. Raven (1962). I would, however, like to add a few lines to one much debated issue. It is often charged that Teilhard gave inadequate attention to the problem of evil and that he was a naive optimist. The facts of his life should

*Since 1983, Henri Cardinal de Lubac.

be adequate warrant against "naive optimism." Aside from that, evil simply was not his problem. In the mid-twentieth century, when existentialism is a dominant philosophy and prophets of doom speak from every editorial page, it is not necessary to add one more voice to the chorus. The existence of evil is so obvious that many people do not seem to realize that there is anything else. In this situation, it is urgently important that someone declare unequivocally that God's creation is basically good; that man's capacity for evil is matched by his capacity for good; that it is possible to realize that good even (and perhaps especially) in the modern world; and that if enough people set about resolutely to achieve the good of which they are capable, then this can be a richly rewarding world and a successful solution of the world is possible. This is the task which Teilhard set for himself, and I think that all men of goodwill are indebted to him for it.

SCIENTIFIC CRITICS

Not a few scientists have defended Teilhard, beginning with Julian Huxley, who introduced the English edition with a long and laudatory essay. In it, he stated his agreement with Teilhard on most of the major points, including the biological collective, but he stopped short of the Omega point. Dobzhansky has commented favorably upon Teilhard in his books of 1962 and 1967. While he regrets Teilhard's use of Lamarckism and orthogenesis, he believes that Teilhard was not really committed to the latter, and of his synthesis as a whole he wrote enthusiastically that "to modern man, so forlorn and spiritually embattled in this vast and ostensibly meaningless universe, Teilhard de Chardin's evolutionary idea comes as a ray of hope. It fits the requirements of our time" (1962:348).

G. B. Barbour (1965) and H. de Terra (1964) have each

written memoirs of their expeditions in the field with Teilhard, and both expressed their profound respect for him as a scientist, as a thinker, and as a man. Finally, J. Needham (1959) and C. H. Waddington (1961) published highly favorable reviews of *The Phenomenon of Man*.

Perhaps the first major attack upon Teilhard from the scientific side was that of his friend George G. Simpson, whose review of *The Phenomenon of Man* dwelt upon Lamarckism and orthogenesis. Simpson believed that these scientific errors were derived deductively from Teilhard's synthesis rather than the other way around, as would be required by sound scientific procedure. In this he may have been partly right, but I hope that I have shown above that neither Lamarckism nor orthogenesis is necessary for the Teilhardian synthesis, and J. N. Deely (1969) has made the same point on a philosophical basis. Simpson summed up Teilhard as "primarily a Christian mystic and only secondarily, although importantly, a scientist" (1960:202). That he was a major Christian mystic is unquestionably true, but it is perhaps unfair to stigmatize him as "only secondarily . . . a scientist," for he was one of the leading geologists and paleontologists of his time, a fact which was universally recognized by his colleagues, including Simpson.

P. B. Medawar's review (1961) is in a class by itself, not only because of its total and intransigent opposition, but also because of the virulence of the invective with which it is expressed. Medawar regarded biology as simply physics, chemistry, and mathematics as applied to organisms, and he was outraged that Teilhard saw those qualities which he ascribed to the within. One cannot help but feel that in this review Medawar may have done more damage to himself than to Teilhard.

R. W. Balek, a chemist, contributed a paper to a volume entitled *The World of Teilhard de Chardin* (1961). His paper begins by praising Teilhard with faint damns, but these become louder and firmer as the paper progresses. He says that, while Teilhard claimed to be writing a scientific tract, he was actually presenting a personal and highly poetic view of the universe, a view which actually had only a tenuous connection with the facts of natural science. He concludes by quoting Simpson's verdict, with which he is in full accord. I must agree that *The Phenomenon of Man* is not a scientific tract in the ordinary sense. As stated in the preface to the present work, my dissatisfaction on this score is among the reasons for the present study. Teilhard did not present enough of the data ("minor details") upon which his generalizations were based; some of his facts outside of mammalian paleontology were insecure; his reasoning was sometimes deductive when it should have been inductive; and his style of writing, which is highly poetic, is often difficult and misleading for those who read it just as they would a technical paper. One need only read a few of Teilhard's technical papers, however, to know that he was fully capable of writing with admirable scientific rigor, strictly factually and inductively. I hope that I have shown in the present work that much of Teilhard's synthesis can be supported in the same way. There is a residue which cannot be so supported, principally the within, the biological collective, and the Omega point. As the first was extensively discussed in chapter 3 of this volume, I will not repeat that discussion here except to mention that, while an experimental test of the within at levels below life seems very remote, nonetheless Teilhard's argument from symmetry is suggestive, and it would be difficult to preclude its correctness. It is unlikely that all of truth is amenable to experimental attack (see Gödel's theorem). As to the latter two, although Teilhard developed them through an elaborate argument, I believe that the intuitive approach which I developed in the preface is perhaps still the most appropriate. Again, for reasons stated just above, I do not believe that their truth is precluded simply because they are not amenable to experimental attack. They are not scientific for this reason, yet they are concepts which could only be formed against a scientific background.

P. F. Forsthoefel also published a paper in *The World of Teilhard de Chardin* (1961). While it is rather more sympathetic than Balek's, he does make some trenchant criticisms. First, he believes that the concept of Omega is beyond science and clearly within the realm of philosophy or even theology. One might agree and still add that science does have some significance for philosophy and theology and that it may be appropriate for a scientist to explore such areas of shared interest. The only mistake on Teilhard's part was to do it in a book which he declared to be purely scientific. This is a result of the complete unity of Teilhard's personality, as discussed in the preface. Further, Forsthoefel says that Teilhard stands almost alone in ascribing elementary consciousness to inert matter. Every pioneer stands alone at some point, and that has no bearing on whether he is right or wrong. Nonetheless, many distinguished scientists have expressed similar ideas. I mention in passing Julian Huxley, J. S. Haldane, J. B. S. Haldane, C. G. Waddington, and Wendell Stanley—a goodly company for any scientist. Finally, Forsthoefel objects to the Lamarckian-orthogenetic bias. As these subjects have been extensively discussed above, I will not repeat but will only remark that I hope that I have shown in the present volume that the Teilhardian synthesis does not need these scientific errors and is if anything stronger on a Darwinian-Mendelian basis.

J. Rostand's discussion (1966) of Teilhard has something in common with Balek's, but he has stated it with much more charm and finesse. He says that, while he admires Teilhard the thinker, the moralist, the writer, the poet, the paleontologist, and the geologist, Teilhard was not a biologist, and evolution is a biological problem, or, more specifically, a problem of cellular biochemistry. All of this may be true, but it is overplayed. There is another side which Rostand has neglected: one of the major achievements of evolutionary science was the establishment in the 1930s and 1940s of evolution as a synthesis of all biological sciences, geology, paleontology, biochemistry, and parts of a good many other sciences as well. Thus, evolution is necessarily a science for research teams, and Teilhard worked as part of such a team long before this was fashionable. In such a synthetic science, it is absurd to ask that theorizing be done only by the biochemists of the team or by those who are masters of all of the fields concerned: such a man may never exist. Teilhard was a master of two of the fields (geology and paleontology), and he had significant knowledge of several of the others. Rostand thought that Simpson was a little too severe in describing *The Phenomenon of Man* as just a pious book, yet I find no clear statement of what more Rostand found in it.

One of the most severe critics of Teilhard is J. Monod, who wrote,

> The biological philosophy of Teilhard de Chardin would not even merit a pause, were it not for the surprising success which it has met even in scientific quarters. . . . His philosophy, like that of Bergson, is entirely founded on an initial evolutionist postulate, but, contrary to Bergson, he admits that the evolutionary force operates in the whole universe, from elementary particles to galaxies: there is no "inert" matter, and therefore no essential distinction between matter and life. The desire to present that conception as "scientific" leads Teilhard to found it on a new definition of energy. The latter would be in some way distributed on two vectors, of which one would be "ordinary" energy (I suppose), while the other would correspond to the force of evolutionary ascent. The biosphere and man are the present products of that ascent along the vector of spiritual energy. That evolution ought to continue until all of the energy is concentrated on that vector: that is the Omega point.
> Although Teilhard's logic may be uncertain and his style laborious, even certain people who do not entirely accept his ideology recognize a certain poetic grandeur in it. I am for my own part shocked by the lack of rigor and intellectual austerity in that philosophy. I see in it above all a systematic effort to conciliate, to make concessions at any price. (1970:44–45)

It is tempting to reply to this indictment point by point. Certainly, Monod's presentation of Teilhard's synthesis is a caricature, and aside from the unavoidable condensation, it appears to represent real misunderstanding. Nonetheless, a detailed reply would be marginal to the real problem because Monod's judgment would be essentially the same even if he had understood Teilhard perfectly and had admired his style and applauded its rigor. The reason for this is contained in Monod's own thesis, to which we now turn.

Reviewing the facts of evolution from the viewpoint of a molecular geneticist, Monod finds two essential properties in which organisms differ radically from all inanimate systems: reproductive invariance and teleonomy. Invariance is primarily a property of the DNA molecule, and it derives from the rule of complementarity. Recall that a DNA molecule consists of two parallel strands of nucleotides, with the base sequence of one being complementary to that of its sister strand. At time of replication, the two strands separate, and each serves as a template on which its complement is synthesized. As the hereditary information is encoded in the sequence of bases in the DNA, this molecular invariance gives stability to the living system.

Teleonomy comprises the ensemble of characteristics of organisms which appear to be goal-directed, like an adaptive behavior pattern, the eye for sight, or a specific enzyme for the digestion of the normal food of the organism. Such minor "projects" make sense only as parts of a general project, and Monod defined the general teleonomic project as the transmission from one generation to the next of the invariance characteristic of the species. As mentioned already, invariance is a property of the DNA, but teleonomy is a property of the proteins which are formed by translation of the genetic message in the DNA.

Of these two properties, invariance is the more fundamental. It existed as soon as an autocatalytic molecule was formed. However, invariance is never perfect: chance

perturbations, biochemical accidents, occur at low but fi-
nite frequencies, with the result that modified (mutant)
DNA is formed, and this is translated as modified protein,
with different teleonomic properties. Now necessity enters
the picture. When two or more similar teleonomic systems
(related organisms) compete, the one with the greater
teleonomic value should survive and leave progeny more
often than the other. This is simply a redefinition of natural
selection. Thus, the great variety of chance events (mutations) at the molecular level has produced a prodigious variety from which selection (necessity) has culled the less
teleonomic and so left the enormous variety of mychotans,
plants, and animals as sketched in chapter 7. In brief, then,
chance and necessity are adequate to explain the entire
world of life, including man. From this it might be concluded that no higher principle need be invoked, but
Monod went further than this.

Teleonomy suggests that the organism not only has its
project but is part of a greater project. Traditionally, man
has conceived the grand project in terms of religions or
philosophies which prescribe laws of nature or of history
within which man finds his place as a necessary part of a
cosmos to which he is allied by bonds to a common Creator
or thanks to all-pervasive laws of which man and the cosmos are fellow products. All such systems which envision
a plan in nature Monod classifies as animism (a term which
is usually reserved for those primitive religions which see
a spirit, potentially benevolent or malevolent, in every rock,
rill, and other inanimate object), and he refers to the animist philosophies and religions as "the ancient alliance,"
his bête noire.

Primitive man could only survive within his group, and
the cohesion of the group depended upon acceptance of the
mythology upon which its laws and rites were based. Thus
the need for animist explanations was almost certainly favored by natural selection and was incorporated into the
genotype. "The invention of myths and religions, the con-

struction of vast philosophic systems are the price which man has had to pay to survive as a social animal without pure automatism" (1970:183), as in insect societies. The efficiency of such mythologies in promoting the welfare of the group is not related to their truth but only to their ability to modify behavior in a way favorable to the group.

Monod is resolutely opposed to all forms of animism, including Teilhard's synthesis, because he feels that they are all in direct conflict with the principle of objectivity. The principle of objectivity requires that the facts of nature be interpreted on the basis of the scientific data and their logical relations, without appeal to higher principles which can be neither verified nor disproven experimentally. In terms of Aristotelian logic, science must deal with efficient causes, not final causes, and any program in nature would be a final cause. Monod believes that the great development of modern science during the past three hundred years has been a direct result of the principle of objectivity. It has been the source of the great riches and power of modern man, and while modern societies have welcomed the benefits of science, "they have not accepted . . . the most profound message of science: the definition of a new and *unique* source of truth, the requirement of a total revision of the foundations of ethics, a radical rupture of the animist tradition, the definitive abandonment of the 'ancient alliance' " (1970:186). The conflict between the animist tradition (which seems to include everyone who disagrees with Monod) and the principle of objectivity is *the* source of the modern anxiety.

Can objective truth have no relation at all to values? Monod thinks that it can for two reasons: values and knowledge are unavoidably associated in action; and more especially because *"the very definition of 'true' knowledge rests in the last analysis on a postulate of an ethical order"* (1970:188). He feels that a true ethics must be *authentic,* and he redefines this to mean that it distinguishes sharply between knowledge and value. He gives no hint as to the contents of such an ethics, and he acknowledges that it is cold and austere, nonetheless he hopes that it may be capable of assuaging the human anguish which arises from the need for a comprehensive explanation, because he believes that scientific knowledge based upon the principle of objectivity and ethics based upon a radical distinction between knowledge and value provide the only acceptable basis for life in the modern world.

This brief abstract of Monod's book is necessarily inadequate, but I hope that it is more fair to Monod than his sketch of *The Phenomenon of Man* is to Teilhard. His treatment of molecular genetics is the brilliant and lucid exposition which one would expect from a Nobel laureate in that field. His lapses in some other areas of evolutionary biology are very real, but they are unimportant for the present discussion, except that they contrast to the scorn with which he treated Teilhard's shortcomings.

The major defect in Monod's argument is that it places upon the principle of objectivity a greater burden than it can carry. The principle only requires that scientific conclusions be based solely upon the data and not upon final causes, which are beyond experimental test. It can neither affirm nor deny the existence of final causes nor of anything else outside the physicochemical realm. This should be an obvious limitation of the principle for, as J. S. Haldane, and excellent biochemist, said many years ago, when only physicochemical data go into a study, one cannot expect any other than physicochemical conclusions to come out of it. Monod in effect concedes this when he describes the principle of objectivity as "pure postulate" (1970:33), yet he goes on to argue that it is the sole source of knowledge, that it requires the abandonment of final cause in any form whatever (all forms being, to him, animism) and he enjoins us in almost religious language to respect and to serve science!

Monod also places too great a burden on the principle of objectivity when he describes it as the sole source of knowledge, even if one makes knowledge coextensive with scientific knowledge, as he seems to do (an attitude which our colleagues in other disciplines might justifiably regard as intellectual arrogance). He suggests that science owes a little to the Judaeo-Christian culture because the long tradition of distinction between the sacred and the profane assisted in the establishment of science. Perhaps so, but the debt of science to the Judaeo-Christian culture goes rather further than that for, as McMullen has shown, science depends upon a complex attitude toward nature which was developed within the Judaeo-Christian culture over a period of nearly two millenia. It began with the conviction of the early Greek philosophers that nature must be understandable, but this was coupled with their belief that work was for slaves, while theorizing and politics were for free men. This did not encourage the development of an experimental approach to nature, and Greek science withered, leaving only one outstanding success: geometry. Meanwhile, the Jewish culture was rising, and with it the idea of *creation*, that nature was the work of a personal and benevolent God. One might hope to learn something about God by studying his handiwork, nature, and therefore this was work worthy of a man. Further, as man himself had been created in the image of God, one might hope that the intelligence of man might be able to understand in some measure the creation of an intelligent God. In early Christian times, this line of thought was strengthened by the idea of the Incarnation, that God considered this material world worthy of identification with Himself. Surely, then, man ought not consider matter as inherently evil. All of this is in sharp contrast to Oriental religions, which have generally deprecated the entire physical order.

Further, the Jews took a radically different attitude toward work: they valued the work which a free man might do, and they believed that in some way a man's work enhanced his value in the sight of God. The cross-fertilization of Greek and Jewish cultures in early Christendom strengthened these traditions. Because of this combination, the early Benedictine monks, who not only kept alive the traditions of a classical culture but also worked their farms, have been called the first intellectuals with dirt under their fingernails. All of this gave great importance to the temporal order, for it was here that man must work out his salvation.

St. Augustine's nature was a transparency, or semi-transparency, through which one could see the wonderful majesty of God, and it was Augustinian nature which was studied in the universities of twelfth century Europe. But then Aristotle was rediscovered, and he took the universities by storm with his vistas of science studied purely rationally (i.e., by logic without experiment, although Aristotle had done experiments, and so had Albertus Magnus), in much the fashion of geometry. In Aristotelian science, nature was opaque, its laws were eternal and necessary, without apparent contingency upon a Creator. Part of the task of Thomas Aquinas was to try to show that the world of Aristotle could be a created world, consistent with the Christian concept of a free Creator. But Augustinian theologians continued to argue that, as the Creator was free to follow different modalities of creation, Aristotelian reason alone was not enough to demonstrate the facts of nature. If you wanted to know what nature really was, you had to go out and observe it. Aristotelians described this as antirationalism, but it prepared the way for experimentation.

This brings us almost up to modern times. By the time Galileo and Descartes began their work, a series of beliefs fundamental to all science had been built up. Every scientist affirms, usually unconsciously, that nature is orderly and that it is possible to discover the order of nature; that sensory evidence is at least potentially reliable; that nature is adequately describable in terms of space-time-energy-mass, the only terms available to science; and that the human mind, working according to the laws of logic, is a trustworthy instrument. None of these propositions has ever been proven, and perhaps they are unprovable. Some or all are rejected by various philosophical schools. Their development within the Judaeo-Christian culture is probably why modern science arose within that culture rather than elsewhere.

Third, in stating the two principles upon which he justifies a new ethics (association of knowledge and value in action, and that the concept of "true" knowledge is based upon an ethical postulate), Monod simply restates things that have long been a part of the "animist" tradition, at least in its Judaeo-Christian form. He thus, perhaps unwittingly, aligns himself with the "ancient alliance."

Fourth, Monod uses a wholly new definition of the word *authentic*. Whether this new definition is itself acceptable (I am tempted to say "authentic"), should be examined by someone with greater philosophical competence than either Monod or myself can claim. Meanwhile, I am doubtful.

Finally, while Monod has proclaimed the absolute necessity of a new basis for ethics, he has not even attempted to show that a satisfactory ethical system can be developed on that basis. Until this is done to the satisfaction of competent ethical philosophers, it may be premature to abandon the Judaeo-Christian tradition, which has perhaps contributed as much to science as has the principle of objectivity.

CHANCE, NECESSITY, AND PROVIDENCE

The present book has much in common with Monod's. In chapter 4, the origin of invariance (a self-replicating system) was described, with the origin of teleonomy resulting secondarily because of selection. In chapter 6, the mechanism of evolution was described in terms of chance (mutation) and necessity (natural selection). The application of these principles resulted in the enormous variety of life described in chapter 7. In all of this, I not only found it unnecessary to appeal to undemonstrated Lamarckian and orthogenetic processes, but in fact I showed in chapter 10 that the Teilhardian synthesis is all the stronger on a Darwinian-Mendelian basis. All of this held true up to and including the appearance of man, but then a new kind of evolution was added to genetic evolution, and that new kind is sociocultural evolution. From this point on, my argument has diverged sharply from Monod's. At this level, processes which could (but need not) be called Lamarckian and orthogenetic are effective, for acquired traits are transmitted culturally, and man does work toward predetermined goals. In chapter 12, we saw that the convergent properties of personality suggest the approach to a critical threshold on the other side of which is the formation of a biological macrocosm and union with Omega, which in chapter 14 I equated with Christ.

If this argument is correct, then man has an especial relationship to God which would seem to suggest planning. Yet man seems to have appeared on this earth by chance and necessity in Monod's sense. Is this contradiction unavoidable, or can it be resolved? I think that it can be resolved. We use chance processes for specific ends in many ways, for example the many applications of the gas laws, chemical syntheses which depend upon selection of a desired compound from among a series of potential products, and even some aspects of computer technology. Is it not, then, conceivable that the infinite intelligence of God might use chance processes for specific ends? that the "blind fantasy of large numbers" and selection might produce foreseen ends even though they are not directed in detail? Monod states that the origin of life, before the fact, had a probability of practically zero. On the other hand, M. Calvin, another Nobel laureate, whose competence in relation to the problem of the origin of life may be even greater than Monod's, has stated that, given the conditions of the primitive earth, the origin of life was almost inevitable. Whichever is right, and Calvin's viewpoint is the more coherent in the present context, life did appear, and selection, acting upon the wealth of variation provided by mutation, necessarily provided the major adaptive types, occupying as many ecological niches as possible. We have seen that one of the adaptive trends so favored is increasing complexity and refinement of nervous organization, providing for ever better rapport with and adjustment to the conditions of life. Monod regards the probability of the evolution of man, before the fact, as practically zero, but perhaps his estimate, failing to take account of the pressure of natural selection favoring better organization of the central nervous system, may have no stronger assurance than did his estimate for the origin of life. Might not an omniscient God have created the forces of chance and necessity, knowing that, without specific direction, their interaction over billions of years must result in an extraordinarily complex adaptive radiation which must eventually result in the appearance of a thinking animal? This does not seem to me to be too remote a possibility. Certainly, its probability would seem to be at least as great as Monod's estimate for the a priori probability of either the origin of life or the origin of man. Only after the appearance of man need the special relationship of man and God-Omega arise.

SUMMING UP

I undertook the present book because I myself had serious reservations about *The Phenomenon of Man*. Now that I have taken a fresh approach to it, using much new material and some new ideas, where do these criticisms stand?

Most of my criticisms can be disposed of rather quickly. I had regretted that Teilhard's poetic style sometimes lacked clarity and precision. The present book is certainly prosaic, and I believe that it is sufficiently precise. I leave it to the judgment of the reader to decide whether I have achieved the clarity sought.

I was also critical of the sparing use of factual data ("minor details") and the consequent reliance upon deductive reasoning, whereas sound scientific practice depends primarily upon inductive reasoning, with deductive reasoning being generally restricted to situations in which the appropriate generalization has already been established inductively from adequate data. In the present book, I have shown by a selected sample that a wealth of data can be marshalled in support of most aspects of the Teilhardian synthesis. Inductive reasoning has been used for the most part, but there are several important exceptions which will be discussed below.

Teilhard's specific data were drawn almost entirely from the mammals. I have tried to achieve a better balance, and I hope that I have taken adequate care for accuracy with respect to all groups discussed.

Like many of Teilhard's critics, I found his use of Lamarckism and orthogenesis disturbing. As these subjects were discussed at length in chapter 10, I will not repeat here, except to say that I believe that I have shown that the Teilhardian synthesis does not require these concepts; indeed, it is stronger without them. In psychosocial evolution, however, factors enter into evolution which could (but need not) be called Lamarckian and orthogenetic. It was this, in part, which caused Teilhard to look for these phenomena at the level of genetic evolution, where they are not valid.

Finally, there is the fact that every scientific conclusion should be subject to experimental test, yet Teilhard drew many conclusions for which he made no attempt to suggest an experimental attack and some for which an experimental study would seem to be impossible. In many instances, I have been able to treat these subjects inductively on the

basis of available data, but some highly important Teilhardian ideas remain outside the realm of science on this
basis. These include the concept of the within, the two
kinds of energy, the concept of critical thresholds as applied to biology, the law of complexity-consciousness, the
biological macrocosm, and the Omega point.

THE WITHIN

The within of matter is discussed principally in chapters 3 and 11. As explained in chapter 3, Teilhard derived
the concept from his principle of scientific symmetry, or
coherence, that every evolutionary movement has its roots
in the past and its extension in the future. Thus, the acute
consciousness of man was traced through the diminishing
degrees of animal consciousness and the much lesser re-
sponsiveness in bacteria to an inchoate basis for consciousness in every material particle, the within. The principle of
coherence is probably valid, yet that does not detract from
the need for an experimental check upon inferences from
it, for such inferences may not be valid. Teilhard did not
attempt an experimental test of the within of matter, and it
is difficult to see how this could be done. Nonetheless, an
impressive array of scientists have thought along similar
lines. Teilhard quotes J. B. S. Haldane for the opinion that,
if the scientific point of view is correct, then ultimately the
properties of life and mind should be found in all matter.
This infers a belief that an experimental demonstration of
such properties may someday become possible. Until that
time, the best that can be said is that the concept of the
within is reasonable and that it may be correct. It was ten-
tatively accepted on this basis in the preceding chapters.
Nonetheless, it is an untested inference from a generalization which might be satisfied in some other way.

One must ask, therefore, whether the Teilhardian synthesis would be possible without the concept of the within
as part of every material particle. It seems to me that all

that is really necessary is that the carbon atom, which is central to the compounds of life, should be capable of forming autocatalytic structures which can encode the teleonomic properties of mind. Granted this much, it is conceivable that the properties of mind might develop in response to selection for higher degrees of teleonomy. Until some experimental evidence can be brought to bear upon these alternatives, it seems to me that this may be one of those undecidable questions which are predicted by Gödel's theorem. Please note that I have not said that Teilhard erred in postulating the within. I have only said that this proposition has not been established scientifically and that, until and unless this is accomplished, other alternatives should be sought and considered.

TANGENTIAL AND RADIAL ENERGY

The problem of the two kinds of energy is very closely related to that of the within of matter, for radial and tangential energy characterize the within and without, respectively. Also it was by application of the principle of coherence to problems of energy that the distinction between tangential and radial energy was derived. Thus, in mechanical devices or in physiological units such as muscle, the laws of conservation of energy and entropy apply rigorously, but in thought, while it is clear that the activity of the brain depends upon energy intake (i.e., food), nonetheless the quantitative relationships are not clear, and the effects appear to be disproportionate to the material cause. Applying the principle of coherence, then, Teilhard saw the two sorts of energy in every material particle. Teilhard believed that the two kinds of energy were interconvertible but that they had different properties and effects, with tangential energy being completely subject to the thermodynamic laws and radial energy being at least potentially capable of separation from its material envelope, in which case it would not be subject to entropy.

Again, experimental demonstration of the two kinds of

energy was not attempted. The investigation of transmission of nerve impulses has not required the use of concepts different from those used in other branches of electrophysiology, as, for example, muscle physiology, although extremely refined techniques of measurement have been necessary. If we ask with respect to the two kinds of energy the same two questions which we asked with respect to the within, the answers again must be: yes, the hypothesis of the two kinds of energy is consistent with the data; and no, the hypothesis is not required by the data. Teilhard himself said that there is, basically, only one kind of energy, which he chose to call psychic energy. As stated in chapter 3, the logical content of the statements that all energy is physical and all energy is psychic is the same. In either case, its properties must still be determined by logical analysis of experimental data. This single type of energy has been exhaustively investigated in its applications to physicochemical reactions, and there is no doubt that it obeys the thermodynamic laws. Its relationship to thought and other phenomena of personality has been investigated both less extensively and less intensively. If it should prove that in this area of personal phenomena energy is potentially separable from its material substrate, then this would be all that is needed for the Teilhardian synthesis. Although a great deal is known about energy exchanges, no one knows as yet what energy itself is, and it can be neither affirmed nor denied that it can exist independently of a material basis. If the reality of the within should be clearly established, then it may also be possible to establish different sorts of energy associated with the without and the within. Meanwhile, it seems to me to be best to suspend judgment and keep the options open.

THE CONCEPT OF CRITICAL THRESHOLDS

Teilhard made extensive use of the concept of critical thresholds and change of state. There is no doubt that significant changes of state may occur when a critical threshold is crossed, as, for example, the changes of state of H_2O at 0° and 100° C. Teilhard used this concept especially in connection with two very important events in the history of life: the origin of life from nonliving polymers and the origin of man from prehuman ancestors. Several additional examples were discussed in chapter 11 of the present book. It seems to me quite probable that Teilhard was right in attributing major biological advances to such threshold effects, nonetheless it should be pointed out that the biological examples differ significantly from the physical examples in that only the latter have been verified by experimental manipulation. For example, one can vary the freezing and boiling points of water by changing the amount of dissolved material. No comparable experiments have been possible with regard to evolutionary thresholds, which rest upon purely observational evidence. Much of classical biology was observational rather than experimental, but it is generally agreed that the great advances of biology in recent years have resulted from the extension to biology of the experimental method. Thus, although it seems probable that the concept of critical thresholds as used by Teilhard is valid, it would be much more satisfying if it could be placed upon an experimental basis. As Teilhard's law of complexity-consciousness is his most important application of the principle of critical thresholds, perhaps no separate discussion of the former is necessary. It seems to me that it is probably valid, but I would like to see it investigated experimentally.

THE BIOLOGICAL MACROCOSM AND THE OMEGA POINT

I think it can be said with assurance that there is no possibility of an experimental approach to the biological macrocosm or the Omega point. They are, as C. Cuenot has put it, metabiological rather than biological in the scientific sense. Teilhard supported them with an elaborate argument, which was reviewed in chapter 12, and to which much of the book may be regarded as preparatory. As described in the preface, I had many years ago approached this problem on an intuitive basis. That is, the progression of the physical world from atoms through molecules to the solar system, the galaxy and systems of galaxies, and finally the universe, might be paralleled in the psychobiological sphere by the progression from the unconscious beginnings of life through the various stages of dimly conscious invertebrates and lower vertebrates to acutely conscious man, and then on beyond to a biological macrocosm which might have a life and a consciousness as far beyond ours as ours is beyond that of our component cells.

As there seems to be no possibility of an experimental test, I am inclined to prefer the intuitive approach to that of detailed argument, the specific steps of which can be neither verified nor disproved. For the same reason, it is misleading to speak of these concepts as scientific. Extending Cuenot's terminology, they could be called metascientific. The British Teilhardians like to call this subject hyperphysics (in contrast to metaphysics as well as to physics).

Whatever the terminology, it is essential to assert that science and truth are not coextensive. Sound science is truth, and there can be no truth which is inconsistent with sound science, but truth goes beyond the limits of natural science. The Teilhardian synthesis begins with science, but it ends with metascience. It comprises a *Weltanschauung* which embraces both science and the Christian faith. As such, I believe that there is a very good possibility that it may facilitate an understanding of man's role in a world in evolution to an extent that neither alone could do. In closing, I can do no better than reaffirm Dobzhansky's judgment of *The Phenomenon of Man*, that "it fits the requirements of our time."

References

Andrews, R. C. 1939. What we'll look like tomorrow. *Collier's* (8 July 1939) 104:12–13, 55–57.

Ayala, F. and J. Kiger. 1980. *Modern Genetics.* Menlo Park, Calif: Benjamin-Cummings.

Balek, R. W. 1961. The birth of life and consciousness. In Robert T. Francoeur, ed., *The World of Teilhard de Chardin,* pp. 92–97. Baltimore: Helicon Press.

Barbour, George B. 1965. *In the Field with Teilhard de Chardin.* New York: Herder and Herder.

Barnes, R. D. 1980. *Invertebrate Zoology.* 4th ed. Philadelphia: Saunders.

Beadle, G. W. and Muriel Beadle. 1966. *The Language of Life.* Garden City, N.Y.: Doubleday.

Bergson, Henri. 1907. *L'evolution créatrice.* Paris: F. Alcan.

——— 1911. *Creative Evolution.* Translated by Arthur Mitchell. New York: Holt.

Calvin, Melvin. 1956. Chemical evolution and the origin of life. *American Scientist* 44:248–263.

——— 1969. *Chemical Evolution: Evolution Toward the Origin of Living Systems on the Earth and Elsewhere.* New York: Oxford University Press.

Chagnon, N. A. and W. Irons, eds. 1979. *Evolutionary Biology and Human Behavior: An Anthropological Perspective.* North Scituate, Mass.: Duxbury Press.

Clark, W. E. Le Gros. 1964. *The Fossil Evidence for Human Evolution.* Chicago: University of Chicago Press.

Cohen, S. S. 1970. Are/were mitochondria and chloroplasts microorganisms? *American Scientist* 58:281–289.

Crespy, Georges. 1961a. *La pensée théologique de Teilhard de Chardin.* Paris: Editions Universitaires.

——— 1961b. *Teilhard de Chardin.* Paris: Au Club de Livre Chrétien.

Darwin, Charles R. 1859. *On the Origin of Species by Means of Natural Selection, or the Preservation of Favoured Races in the Struggle for Life.* London: John Murray. Reprinted 1936. New York: Modern Library.

De Beer, G., ed. 1974. *Charles Darwin. Thomas Henry Huxley. Autobiographies.* London: Oxford University Press.

Deely, John N. 1969. *The Philosophical Dimensions of the Origin of Species.* Chicago: Institute for Philosophical Research. Reprinted from *The Thomist* (1969), vol. 33, nos 1 and 2.

Dobzhansky, Th. 1962. *Mankind Evolving.* New Haven: Yale University Press.

—— 1967. *The Biology of Ultimate Concern.* New York: New American Library.

—— 1970. *Genetics of the Evolutionary Process.* New York: Columbia University Press.

Dodson, E. O. 1971. The kingdoms of organisms. *Systematic Zoology* 20:265–281.

—— 1979. Crossing the procaryote-eucaryote border: Endosymbiosis or continuous development? *Canadian Journal of Microbiology* 25:651–674.

—— and Peter J. Dodson. 1984. *Evolution: Process and Product.* 3d ed. Boston: Willard Grant Press.

Dubos, René. 1968. *So Human an Animal.* New York: Scribners.

—— 1980. *Man Adapting.* Rev. ed. New Haven: Yale University Press.

Forsthoefel, P. F., S. J. 1961. Beneath the microscope. In Robert T. Francoeur, ed., *The World of Teilhard de Chardin,* pp. 98–114. Baltimore: Helicon Press.

Francoeur, Robert T., ed. 1961. *The World of Teilhard de Chardin.* Baltimore: Helicon Press.

Gamov, George. 1952. *The Creation of the Universe.* New York: Viking. An effective presentation of Lemaître's theory.

Gardner, E. J. and D. P. Snustad. 1980. *Principles of Genetics.* 6th ed. New York: Wilcy.

Gillispie, C. C. 1960. *The Edge of Objectivity.* Princeton: Princeton University Press.

Gödel, K. 1931. Über formal unentscheidbare Sätze der Principia Mathematica und verwandter Systema I. *Monatshefte für Mathematik und Physik* 38:173–198.

Greene, J. C. 1959. *The Death of Adam.* Ames: Iowa State College Press.

Haldane, John Scott. 1935. *The Philosophy of a Biologist.* London: Oxford University Press.

Hoyer, B. H., B. J. McCarthy, and E. T. Bolton. 1964. A molecular approach in the systematics of higher organisms. *Science* 144:959–967.

Hoyle, Frederick. 1950. *The Nature of the Universe.* Oxford: Blackwell.

Hrdlicka, A. 1929. Man's future in the light of his past and present. *Proceedings of the American Philosophical Society* 68:1–11.

Huxley, J. 1963. The future of man—evolutionary aspects. In G. Wolstenholme, ed., *Man and His Future.* Boston: Little, Brown.

Hyman, Libbie H. 1940 ff. *The Invertebrates,* vols. 1–6. New York: McGraw-Hill.

Johanson, D. C. and M. Edey. 1981. *Lucy: The Beginnings of Humankind.* New York: Simon & Schuster.

Krutch, Joseph Wood. 1957. *The Great Chain of Life.* Boston: Houghton Miflin.

Linnaeus, Carolus. 1758. *Systema Naturae.* 10th ed. Stockholm: Laurentius Silvius.

Lubac, Henri de. 1965. *The Faith of Teilhard de Chardin.* London: Burns & Oates. (Translation of *La prière de Teilhard de Chardin.* Paris: Arthème Fayard, 1964).

—— 1966. *Teilhard, missionaire et apologiste.* Toulouse: Editions Prière et Vie.

—— 1971. *Teilhard et notre temps.* Paris: Aubiers.

McMullen, Ernan. 1968. Religion and the natural sciences. *Religion: Bulletin of Religion at the University of Kansas* (April 1968), vol. 5, no. 3. Reprinted in *Bulletin of the Albertus Magnus Guild* (December 1970) 18(4):1, 7–8, and (January 1971) 18(5):1–7.

Margulis, Lynn. 1967. On the origin of mitosing cells. *Journal of Theoretical Biology* 14:225–274.

—— 1971. The origin of plant and animal cells. *American Scientist* 69:230–235.

—— 1981. *Symbiosis in Cell Evolution.* San Francisco: Freeman.

Medawar, P. B. 1960. The future of man. *Saturday Evening Post* (1 October 1960) 233:32–33, 91–93.

—— 1961. Critical notice: *The Phenomenon of Man. Mind* 70:99–106.

—— 1964. Preface to *Human Biology*, by G. A. Harrison, J. S. Weiner, J. M. Tanner, and N. A. Barnicot. London: Oxford University Press.

Miller, S. L. and H. C. Urey. 1959. Organic compound synthesis on the primitive earth. *Science* 130:245–251.

Monod, Jacques. 1970. *Le Hasard et la nécessité.* Paris: Editions du Seuil.

Montagu, Ashley M. F. 1969. *Man, His First Two Million Years: A Brief Introduction to Anthropology.* New York: Dell.

Morgan, C. Lloyd. 1923. *Emergent Evolution.* London: Williams and Norgate.

Murray, Michael H. 1966. *The Thought of Teilhard de Chardin. An Introduction.* New York: Seabury Press.

Needham, Joseph. 1959. Review of *The Phenomenon of Man. New Statesman,* 7 November 1959, p. 209.

Oparin, A. I. 1968. *Genesis and Evolutionary Development of Life.* New York: Academic Press. The current version of a classic first published in 1938.

Orr, R. T. 1971. *Vertebrate Biology.* 3d ed. Philadelphia: Saunders.

Osborn, H. F. 1894. *From the Greeks to Darwin.* New York: Columbia University Press.

Pilbeam, D. R. 1970. *Human Origins.* London: Thames and Hudson.

Raven, Charles E. 1962. *Teilhard de Chardin: Scientist and Seer*. London: Collins.

Romer, A. S. and T. S. Parsons. 1977. *The Vertebrate Body*. 5th ed. Philadelphia: Saunders.

Rostand, Jean. 1966. *Hommes d'autrefois et d'aujourd'hui*. Paris: Gallimard.

Russell, Bertrand. 1945. *A History of Western Philosophy*. New York: Simon & Schuster.

Simons, E. L. 1972. *Primate Evolution: An Introduction to Man's Place in Nature*. New York: Macmillan.

Simpson, George G. 1960. Review of *The Phenomenon of Man*. *Scientific American* (April 1960) 202:201–207.

Smulders, Pierre, S. J. 1964. *La vision de Teilhard de Chardin*. Paris: Desclée de Brouwer.

Smuts, Jan Christiaan. 1926. *Holism and Evolution*. London and New York: Macmillan.

Spencer, Herbert. 1862. *A System of Synthetic Philosophy:* vol. 1, *First Principles*. London: Williams and Norgate.

Tamarin, Robert H. 1982. *Principles of Genetics*. Boston: Willard Grant Press.

Teilhard de Chardin, Pierre. 1955. *Le phénomène humain*. Paris: Editions du Seuil.

—— 1959. *The Phenomenon of Man*. Translated by Bernard Wall. London: Collins; New York: Harper & Row.

—— 1965. *Building the Earth*. Translated by Noël Lindsay. Wilkes-Barre, Penn.: Dimension Books.

Terra, Helmut de. 1964. *Memories of Teilhard de Chardin*. New York: Harper & Row. (Translated from the German, *Mein Weg mit Teilhard de Chardin*. Munich: C. H. Beck'sche Verlagsbuchhandlungen, 1962.)

Tresmontant, Claude. 1959. *Pierre Teilhard de Chardin: His Thought*. Baltimore: Helicon Press. (Translation of *Introduction à la pensée de Teilhard de Chardin*. Paris: Editions du Seuil, 1956.)

Waddington, C. H. 1961. *The Nature of Life*. London: Allen and Unwin.

Whittaker, R. H. 1970. New concepts of the kingdoms of organisms. *Science* 163:150–159.

Wildiers, N. M. 1960. *Teilhard de Chardin*. Paris: Editions Universitaires.

Wolstenholme, G., ed. 1963. *Man and His Future*. Boston: Little Brown.

Index

Illustrations are indicated by page numbers in italics.